THE RIGHTEOUS REMNANT

Benjamin and Mary Purnell, founders of the House of David.

The Righteous Remnant
THE HOUSE OF DAVID

Robert S. Fogarty

THE KENT STATE UNIVERSITY PRESS

Library of Congress Cataloging in Publication Data

Fogarty, Robert S.
  The righteous remnant.

  Bibliography: p.
  Includes index.
  1. House of David. I. Title.
BX7990.H75F63   289.9   80–84666
  ISBN 0–87338–251–X   AACR2

To
G. F.
both of them

Contents

Preface
Sex in Michigan, Beards in Baseball, The New Jerusalem
in the New World   *ix*

Chapter One
The Prophetic Tradition   *1*

Chapter Two
The American Prophets   *28*

Chapter Three
The Shiloh at Benton Harbor   *42*

Chapter Four
Chased Like a Fox   *88*

Chapter Five
The Social Compact   *129*

Appendix A
Sixty Propositions   *147*

Appendix B
Colony Membership List   *153*

Appendix C
Biographical Information   *164*

Notes   *172*

Bibliography   *184*

Index   *193*

Illustrations

Benjamin and Mary Purnell ii

Benjamin Purnell 44

Mary Purnell 45

The Purnells as itinerant preachers 46

Arrival of the Wroeites 59

Miniature train at Eden Springs 67

Purnell as shepherd 69

House of David archway 74

Eden Springs depot 77

Colony orchestra 79

Administration buildings 86

House of David draftees 101

Wanted poster 112

Purnell in 1927 114

Baseball park at the colony 122

House of David baseball players 123

House of David basketball player 124

Mary Purnell at the City of David 126

Sex in Michigan, Beards in Baseball, The New Jerusalem in the New World

> The Babe won't be required to wear whiskers, either.
> *Ray Doan, manager of the House of David*
> *barnstorming baseball team, 1936.*

In 1936, the House of David offered Babe Ruth $35,000 a year to play for its barnstorming baseball team. The Babe declined, in spite of the waiver in his case of the rule that all players wear beards.

This sort of information contributed to my perplexity about the House of David. The impressionistic notions of this religious colony I had formed over several years seemed contradictory. On the one hand, there was a description of the group in William Hinds's *American Communities and Cooperative Societies* (1908) which emphasized the messianic pretensions of its leaders, Mary and Benjamin Purnell, and sketched its adventist theology. According to Hinds, the colony was filled with dedicated believers who thought themselves part of the elect 144,000 children of Israel forming the ingathering at Benton Harbor, Michigan, in anticipation of the millennium. They were characterized as being "not only sane, but intelligent, and are assuredly, so far as the observer can judge, morally sound."

Yet there were two other notions—certainly less well defined, though equally compelling—that I had about the House of David. The first revolved around a childhood memory of going to see the Harlem Globetrotters play and seeing a bearded basketball team take the floor for the preliminary game. All I can remember is that they wore beards, and in Brooklyn in the late 1950s the only people with beards were Hassidic Jews. I assumed that it was the local synagogue fielding a team—some local color prior to the arrival of the real exotics. My confusion was compounded years later when I read a pulp article about a scandalous free-love community in Michigan where the leader had a harem and lived like a king. That colony was also called the House of David and bore no resemblance to the basketball team I saw nor did I recognize it again when, as a graduate student, I read William Hinds's account of the colony.

That all three could be the same colony was too preposterous. Who had ever heard of a bearded, possibly Jewish, adventist colony in Michigan that played basketball in Brooklyn and, off court, practiced free love? In 1972 I began, under a grant from the Michigan Historical Commission, to try to make some sense out of my contradictory impressions. What I found, of course, was that the preposterous was not only true, but even more preposterous when one began to probe the history of the House of David. First, and most astounding, was my realization that so little had been written about it and that a rich set of resources existed in the form of court records and investigative reports compiled by federal, state, and local officials because of that scandal-ridden history I had read about in the pulp magazine. Because the records were so voluminous no researcher had sorted through the material located at the State Historical Commission and in the records of the State Attorney General's Office, both in Lansing. With the aid of some Antioch College students, I read those records and analyzed them with an eye toward constructing a colony history from its inception through to its legal dissolution.

This history of the House of David is necessarily incomplete because colony records remain closed, and efforts to gain access to manuscript and diary records have proved fruitless. I have chosen to publish now in the hope that the appearance of this study will elicit further materials. That the House of David was the target for prosecution is incontrovertible, and we will see that the fear of persecution was a part of the tradition from which the House of David grew. The continuing mania for secrecy is not mere paranoia on the part of the remaining remnants of the colony, but rather a natural suspicion of the motives of the outside world, so often hostile, so seldom objective in its dealing with millennialists. The colonies—there are now two—remain closed to any attempt to write a full history. The colony must therefore be seen largely through the eyes of its official prosecutors who, despite the scope of their investigations, remained outsiders.

To begin to understand the House of David, one must realize that it was not an isolated or local phenomenon. The Israelite kingdom that existed near Lake Michigan from 1903 to 1927 was the direct outgrowth of a tradition of Anglo-American millennialism with roots in the seventeenth century. Six months of reading at the British Museum in 1975 established the Anglo-American connection, proving that the road to Zion ran from London through Benton Harbor and that the way had been shown by a series of prophetic leaders who both inspired and directed the sects that gathered about them in England, Australia, and America.

What we have then—for the first time—is an account of the colony, its prophets, and its tensions with the world. There is much that could be added to this narrative, but I have chosen to focus on the development of the Anglo-Israelite tradition and the social compact forged by a series of prophets with their followers. For over a century this compact shaped the boundaries of the New Jerusalem and dictated the roles played by prophet and disciples alike.

The emergence of millennialist and adventist sects is part of a complex social and religious phenomenon that is shaped by the personal eccentricities of religious leaders, and the history of such groups is often a confused welter of pamphlets, schisms, prophetic utterances, and obscure scrapes with the authorities. But the line of continuity which the House of David espoused was by no means either fictive or farfetched. Benjamin Purnell of the House of David identified himself as the seventh prophet in a line of prophets that ran from Richard Brothers, the "Prince of the Hebrews," whose prophetical career began sometime after he encountered the mystical "Avignon Society" in the 1780s, through Joanna Southcott, domestic from the Cotswolds, John "Zion" Ward, an Irish-born prophet, William Shaw, whose works were circulated only within a small circle of believers, John Wroe, a hunchbacked prophet of dubious morals, and finally the American-born James Jershom Jezreel.

Benjamin Purnell was the legitimate, albeit self-proclaimed heir to a long and continually sustained prophetic tradition. This astonishing manifestation of religious ferment and social experiment of which the House of David is a part not only thrived over generations but also produced a body of theology in prophetic books, proselytizing pamphlets, sectarian newspapers, chiliastic tracts, and even grandiose architectural undertakings. Fierce energies were generated, and when the prophets ran afoul of duly constituted authority, their persecution tended only to increase the ardor of the zealots.

In telling the history of the House of David, I have emphasized specific conflicts during the first twenty-five years. These conflicts mirrored changes in the colony's theology, social practices, and internal structure, changes brought about by the erratic behavior of Benjamin Purnell. His actions forced the social compact to be redrawn because of external and internal pressures, culminating in a legal ordeal that put the strongest faithful to a fearful test. What emerges from this account is a view of a community constantly drawn to the edge of destruction by the actions of its leader yet somehow sustaining itself and retaining its balance.

This, then, is a limited case study of community survival and the dynamics of a prophet's interplay with his disciples. The ultimate tool for that survival was forged when an individual joined the House of David community at Benton Harbor with the knowledge that he was entering into a compact with God and the Purnells. In order to do so he had to deny the existence of sin, death, and the devil, and then to acknowledge the rule of Mary and Benjamin Purnell. These members lived in a utopian colony rooted in several centuries of millennialist history. Some of the less fortunate came to know the prophet for what he actually was and seemingly learned to live with his human, if not devilish ways. A few repudiated the religious and social compact, became "scorpions" (the community's term for turncoats), and told their story to outsiders and shaped the destruction of the House of David. All were party to the socio-religious agreement that was part entertainment, part pulp drama, and part religion called "The New Eve, the Israelite House of David."

Acknowledgments

Support for this volume came from several sources. The Munson Fund provided me with a grant to examine the records of the Michigan Historical Commission. Harry Kelsey, then director of the Commission, Donald Chaput, and Dennis Bodem guided me through their collections. During my initial survey of the material on the House of David in Lansing several Antioch College students acted as research assistants. They were Patricia Black, Steve Benowitz, Jerrold Hirsch, and Laurie Marshall. Initial drafts of this manuscript were read by Dwight Hoover and Ken Lawless, both of whom improved its organization and style.

John F. C. Harrison read an early chapter on the Anglo-Israelite history and provided insights and encouragement. I am indebted to another English historian, W. H. G. Armytage, for his friendship and advice during a sabbatical year in London. My colleagues in the History Department at Antioch—Hannah Goldberg, Michael Kraus, and Frank Wong—were always helpful. Joseph Cali and Bruce Thomas, Olive Kettering Library, Antioch College; Richard Hathaway, History Unit, Michigan State Library; Bruce Harding, Federal Records Center, Chicago; John Aubrey, Newbery Library; Robert Lindenfeld, *Benton Harbor Herald-Palladium*, and Don Hollister all helped find sources for this work.

Robert Gregg, City of David, graciously consented to an interview about the House of David and shared his unswerving faith with me.

CHAPTER ONE

The Prophetic Tradition

The righteous remnant . . . will be assembled once more in Palestine and Yahweh will dwell among them as ruler and judge. He will reign from a rebuilt Jerusalem, a Zion which has become the spiritual capitol of the world and to which all nations flow.

Norman Cohn, The Pursuit of the Millennium

Scholars have made repeated attempts to chart the history of communal enthusiasm in both the Christian and non-Christian worlds, yet the specific origins of a particular group are often difficult to trace precisely. The chiliastic mind and the apocalyptic mind infected early Christian settlements, drawing on a rich Judaic tradition that foretold of a new Palestine, a new Eden, in which the chosen people would gather together in a New Jerusalem under the just and benevolent rule of Yahweh. "Promises of future compensation for present affliction," to quote Norman Cohn, were part of the early Judaic heritage and current in the belief system of the early church.[1] Whether imminent or remote, the notion of a coming kingdom on earth was a strong and enduring part of the Judeo-Christian world view. Despite Church disapproval, chiliastic schemes and the apocalyptic mentality nevertheless persisted in the "obscure world of popular religion."[2] The Essenes and the early Gnostics were both part of this tradition, and others sustained it throughout early Church history and into the medieval period. Heresy trials were launched against individuals connected with such groups as the Brethren of the Free Spirit, the Adamites, and the elusive

1

Luciferians.[3] Such groups rose and fell with their own peculiar interpretation of the failings of the Church and with their own promises of a new dispensation and a new order. Persecuted minorities found analogies between their own condition and that of the early Israelites, and while "each fresh translation of the Bible and the authorized version was being prepared in the early seventeenth century they gave fresh texts to sustain the hopes that the Lord could gather in the elect to himself in Jerusalem."[4]

Belief in the special role that the Israelites were destined to play in the ingathering of the elect can be traced far back into history, but my concern is with that portion of the history specifically relevant to the House of David, located at Benton Harbor, Michigan, from 1903 until the present. The best place to begin a study of their history is, however, in seventeenth- and eighteenth-century England. At that time there was a significant rebirth of millennialist fervor which resulted, some three centuries later, in the formation of a colony in western Michigan. For it is in seventeenth-century England that the first movement of modern millenarianism became a potent social and religious force.[5] Keith Thomas suggests that it was a combination of prayer and prophecy that produced a "notable shift from passive to active millenarianism" after 1640. For Thomas, the shift was a dramatic one:

> Probably more important than the effects of high prices and other economic hardships of the late 1640's was the apocalyptic sense generated by an awareness of living in a time of unprecedented political change. The realization that the Civil War and the execution of the King had no parallel in earlier English history exerted a decisive influence. . . . It also accounts for the conviction held by so many of the Civil War sects that the period in which they lived was somehow the climax of human history, the era for which all previous events had been a mere preparation. For the Fifth Monarchy men it was above all the execution of King Charles which left the way open for King Jesus.[6]

After the execution of Charles I in 1649, the Fifth Monarchy men began to exert a strong social and political force; they hoped to hasten the New Jerusalem by their own political power. With the return of Charles II to the throne in 1660, their influence waned, leaving England little to fear from these Christian zealots, who had once been able, some argue, to overturn the government by the weight of their swords and the strength of their vision.[7] Yet the interregnum was a remarkable period, a time when many believed that the Kingdom of God was at hand and that the old basis for political legitimacy had been swept away. The 1649 publication of Gerard Winnstanley's *The New Law of Righteousness* led to the formation of the Diggers, a radical religious sect who seized and dug up the common land at St. George's Hill, Wheybridge, in defiance of the local landlords. Winnstanley preached that he was "of the race of the Jews" and that since the time of William the Conqueror the Godly people of England had lived under tyranny and oppression. Winnstanley's followers promised to make barren land fruitful and to distribute the benefits to the poor and needy: "When the Lord doth show me the place and manner, he will have us that are called the common people, to manure and work the common land."[8]

Although the Diggers had a short history they were one of a number of groups that sought an outlet for social and religious grievances. It is essential to remember that such groups mirrored more than political and social discontent. Prophetic leadership and sect formation reflected the belief that England was a nation favored by God; that Biblical exegesis led to a perfected life; and that divine inspiration could come to any man. This notion, identifiable in the Bible but subject to modern interpretation and geographic modifications, of a new chosen people—chosen but open to be led by any man or woman from any station in life—was fundamental to communal religious experiments throughout the next century and a half, as we can see with the Shakers, the Mormons, and the House of David.[9]

Numerous prophetic figures came to the fore in this period. John Robins was proclaimed "King of Israel, Melchisdec [*sic*] and Adam restored" in 1650, declaring that within twenty days before Christmas he would divide the seas and bring home the true Jews to the land of Judea. Josuah Garment, a Ranter and disciple of Robins, John Robins, and Thomas Tany all hinted at the close connection between Israel and the English people. Tany had a revelation in 1649 that he was a Jew of the tribe of Reuben, and he then assumed the name "Thearan John, High

Priest of the Jews" and "Thean Ram Taniah, Leader of the
People."[10] He later claimed to be the Earl of Essex and heir to the
throne of Charles I with a claim on the French throne as well.
Finally, he pitched a tent on Eltham Common, near London,
where the Israelites were to gather before their departure to
Jerusalem. Influenced by the German mystic Boehme and fired
by his own imagination, he was last heard from in Amsterdam in
1668 pursuing his Israelite crusade.[11] The practice of taking on a
new name is not uncommon with individuals who are "twice
born." Among the Israelite prophets the usurping of regal titles
served the same psychological function as the magical name
change. One later prophet would change his name to Jezreel,
and another would fix on Milton as the new core for his religious
identity.

Particularly affected by this upsurge in religious prophecy
and enthusiasm—and subject to scrutiny as potential witches—
were the Quakers.[12] A good example of Quaker enthusiasm
during the period is the career of James Nayler, the so-called
"Quaker Jesus," who within months of his conversion by George
Fox in 1651 had a vision announcing he was the messiah. As was
often the case with such Ranters, he was jailed for blasphemy, yet
followers flocked to him. In 1656 he began his famous ride from
London to Bristol, surrounded by a band of his followers chant-
ing "Holy, Holy." They believed they were bringing Jesus to his
native city, but they only attracted the attention of the authorities, and Nayler was brought before a special Parliamentary
committee to answer charges of blasphemy. Although he was a
meek Christ, his prosecutors thought him dangerous enough to
pronounce a cruel punishment. With Cromwell's blessing,
Parliament found Nayler guilty of "horrid blasphemy." Rather
than serve the death penalty they mercifully had his tongue
bored through with a hot iron and branded him on the forehead
with the letter *B*. Afterward he was sent to Bristol and paraded
through the city sitting backwards on a horse before being jailed.
Throughout all this Nayler remained steadfast in his belief that
he had a Christ-like mission.[13]

Women were prominent among the many self-proclaimed
prophets of seventeenth-century England. The conventional
outlets for religious expression, the pulpit and the pamphlet,

were denied women. But some women found a certain acceptance in the unconventional role of prophetess. Keith Thomas recounts that between 1647 and 1651 "the deliberations of Oliver Cromwell and his colleagues were interrupted, so that some obscure prophet, often a woman, could be admitted to deliver her message."[14] The belief that God was on the prophet's side enabled women to gain an audience heretofore denied them. The social and political implications of such prophetic messages have not been explored fully, though some recent studies have shown the way. Both men and women flourished in this prophetic role during the interregnum, but the restoration of Charles II was a fatal blow to all the dissenting groups, though chiliastic figures did continue to appear in the late seventeenth and early eighteenth century.[15]

Prophets did continue to produce new visions and new charters for the commonwealth, but their pronouncements were more moderate in tone and their actions more restrained than during the heady days of the 1640s and 1650s. For example, Jane Lead, a disciple of Jacob Boehme, published *The Heavenly Crowd Now Breaking* in 1681 and eventually gathered about her a set of disciples into the "Philadelphian Society." The Philadelphians believed in "the real advent of Christ, the resurrection and transformation of all believers, and the establishment of the glorified church on earth."[16] These followers of Jacob Boehme did have a precursor in Richard Baxter's group of Behminists who believed in the perfectability of man in this world.[17] Boehme's works had been introduced into England in 1644 and were translated into English between 1647 and 1662. His writings were read for their mystical and occult qualities. The Behminists, like the Quakers, were ultimately persecuted for their beliefs, but under Jane Lead's direction they took on the characteristics of a sect and greatly influenced the course of English mysticism. At one point they came in contact with the Camisards in France, who were to play an influential role in Shaker development. Although such groups as the Philadelphians were organized in London, their influence was often felt on the Continent, as there developed an international brotherhood that fed on prophetical writings and messianic beliefs and that actually constituted a movement toward new forms of religious inspiration and worship.[18] The eighteenth-century Avignon Society is a good example of this trend. Thus, though the restoration had temporarily succeeded in placing the lid on much dynamic religious activity, the events of 1640–60 had set in motion a current that would find an outlet during the next three centuries in religious prophecy, social radicalism, and utopian community organizations.

During the early eighteenth century new forms, new voices, and new communities did appear in England to challenge ortho-dox patterns at every turn. The French Cevenoles found in England a refuge from French Catholic persecution in 1707; Count Frederich Zinzendorf introduced the Moravian religious groups in 1743; Ann Lees organized her shaking Quakers at Bolton in 1774 and by 1800 had even established a series of communities on America's eastern frontier.[19] Swedenborgian-ism began to inform the mystical tradition after 1757 and, of course, influenced Blake and Coleridge in their varied enter-prises.[20] With the end of the eighteenth century, England had a substantial, rich history of religious enthusiasm and communal and prophetic sects.

It was the Behminist influence that served as the catalyst for the first "true" prophet in the line of seven that leads directly to Benjamin Purnell, founder of the House of David. Richard Brothers, "Prince of the Hebrews," first came in contact—probably in 1784—with a strange mystical society at Avignon, France, known to outsiders as the "Avignon Society," but to its members as the "New Israel." Its creed has been described as a "crazy blend of Catholicism, Swedenborgianism and occultism," and it had an immediate political program in mind: to make the Polish count Tadeusz Grabianka first King of Poland and even-tually ruler of the world. "As God's new messiah," Grabianka "would conquer Palestine at the head of the Polish armies, trans-fer his capital to Jerusalem, and extend his sway, till every King surrendered his crown to him. But first since the old Israel was apostate he must gather a new tribe, whom he grouped into twelve tribes with old Biblical names."[21]

When Grabianka arrived in England in 1782, he attended the salon of the mystical Jacob Duche, former chaplain to the First Continental Congress, and then a Loyalist outcast in London. While living in London during the 1780s Duche threw open his house to students interested in Boehme and Swedenborg, many of whom became involved in the religious enthusiasms of the next forty years. Although Richard Brothers did not attend these salons, we know that he agreed with Grabianka that a king should rule the world and there is a possibility that Brothers visited at Avignon.[22] However, certainly one of his supporters had visited the society and after a prolonged stay in 1789 came away with the following impressions: "Nothing could exceed the brotherly kindness shown us by these men, who told us we were welcome to the house provided by the Lord for those children whom he might be pleased to send to the reunion from all parts of the earth. They said that whatever was there was ours as much as theirs, that they had not anything they called their own, the Lord had done away with a distinction of mine and thine in their minds."[23] During their seven months' stay William Bryan and another supporter of Brothers, John Wright, read and copied extracts from the mystical journals of the Society, "by which we were informed of the many changes taking place and to take place, in the nations of the world, to prepare the way of the Lord's coming, and the restoration of his people, the whole house of Israel, according to the prophecies of the scriptures."[24]

Richard Brothers was born at Placentia, Newfoundland, in 1757, appropriately enough on December 25. His father was a gunner in the English forces stationed there during the Seven Years' War, and young Brothers was sent to England to enter the naval school at Woolwich. In 1771 he went to sea as a midshipman, advancing through the ranks and taking part in the "Victory of the Saints" against the French in the West Indies in 1782. In January, 1783, he was promoted to lieutenant, but six months later was retired on half pay when the Peace of Versailles forced a reduction in the fleet. From 1783 to 1786 Brothers traveled to various European countries and for a period of time served in the merchant marine. He married Elizabeth Hassall in 1786 and settled at Bristol. When he found shortly afterward that his wife had been unfaithful to him, a separation soon followed.[25]

Brothers lived in London on his retirement salary at first, but toward the end of 1789 he began to entertain doubts about

his past military life, which was now "totally repugnant" to him.
He doubted whether he ought to hold his commission or to take
the oath of loyalty required of him every six months when he
drew his pension, which he now saw as "the wages of plunder,
bloodshed and murder."[26] Whether influenced by the Quakers
or simply by the belief that he could not serve allegiance to a false
sovereign is unclear, but his letters to the admiralty began to
question the oath-taking procedure. First, he argued that swear-
ing was wrong and second, that such a declaration, though
supposedly a "voluntarily made oath," was in fact compulsory.
The authorities were impressed by his second argument and
changed the oath; however, on the first requirement, the oath-
taking itself, they stood firm. Since Brothers would not take the
oath, the pension was withheld and the stage set for a legal and
political battle.

During this period it appears that Brothers began an intensive reading of the Bible, Jane Lead's Philadelphian tract *A
Fountain of Gardens*, and the English mystic John Lacy's *Prophetical Writings* (1707), which had been inspired by the newly arrived
French Cevenole migration to England. Drawing inspiration
from the political, mystical, and religious traditions of the earlier
century, Brothers began to have visions.[27] Some dwelt on the
millennium, which Brothers calculated was near; others emphasized his own role in saving the city of London from Satan's
destruction. The promulgation of these visions was interrupted
by a demand from his landlord that he pay some £33 in back rent.
Although Brothers was due his service pay, he still refused to
take the oath and the debt went unpaid. As a result, he was placed
in the workhouse and remained there for six months, dwelling
on his visions and sorting out the spiritual role he should play. He
now became convinced that his hour had come: he was to lead the
Jews in regaining the Holy Land, where he would rule as God's
vice-regent in Palestine. He wrote: "I am the prophet that will be
revealed to the Jews to order their departure."[28]

Who were these Jews? Of the original twelve tribes, two were
to be found scattered over Europe, he said, while the other ten
were "merged in the population of Great Britain."[29] Thousands
of British families who had forgotten their Hebrew origins
would discover, when the call came, that they were the children

of Abraham. This spiritual fifth column was assumedly awaiting Brothers's announcement of his mission to lead the twelve tribes to Palestine. On May 12, 1792, he wrote to the king, the prime minister, and the Speaker of the House of Commons, informing them of his divine instructions to come to the House of Parliament and reveal his vision. That vision was about an impending war between France, on the one side, and Austria and Prussia on the other. This war, he said, would usher in the messianic age, yet England should stay out of this destructive and God-sent conflict. He wrote, furthermore, that the revolution in France was a judgment from God and that efforts to save the toppled monarchy would be in opposition to God's plan. His message was ignored, and when he presented himself at the House of Commons, he was refused admission.

On returning home from this rebuff, Brothers had another vision, this one about the destruction of Whitehall. He was sent to debtors prison shortly after for failure to pay his rent, but after eight weeks in jail Brothers signed letters of attorney allowing others to draw his pay. Like Thoreau he let his fine be paid. On his release from prison he intended to "leave England for ever and have nothing to do with prophesizing."[30] However, after walking some fifteen miles from London he found himself forcibly turned around by some mystical power and commanded to return. His prophetic mission was too strong and God's will too clear. On his return to London, he remembered an earlier vision which had carried him to the private royal apartments at St. James Palace. In it the king, seeing Brothers approach, rose from the throne and "sent him a magnificent star, at the same time breathing on it and kissing it as though a last farewell." Brothers sent off this vision to the king and, in 1794, issued a public proclamation of his own kingship under the title *A Revealed Knowledge of the Prophecies and Times, Wrote Under the Direction of God By the Man Who Will Be Revealed To The Hebrews As Their Prince.* He then issued in the form of a pamphlet a second command, one that no king could take lightly: "The Lord commands me to say to you, George III King of England, that immediately upon my being revealed to the Hebrews as their Prince, and to all nations as their Governor, your crown must be delivered up to me, that your power and authority may cease."[31]

Even though George III had given over the star in the earlier vision, this was no time to demand crowns from kings since revolutionaries were in ascendancy in England, joining popular democratic societies inspired by the French Jacobin clubs, and revolutionary ferment existed throughout the European empires.[32] Suddenly this harmless, half-mad prophet seemed a threat.

By this time it was also possible to see certain strains in his thinking which suggested a rough creed, one that future prophets (including Benjamin Purnell) would modify, elaborate on, and freely borrow from for their own messianic uses. First, there was the notion of the millennium and the imminent restoration of the Jews to Palestine; second, that the returning Hebrews were, in the main, "invisible Jews" (descendants of the original Israelites or Jews who had converted to Christianity); third, that Richard Brothers was a prophet with special powers of healing and salvation, since his prayers had saved England from destruction on several occasions; fourth, that all war is wrong, particularly war with France; fifth, if the Continential wars were to continue, dreadful calamities would follow, most particularly the loss of crowns.[33] "God's Almighty Nephew," as he called himself, even had a timetable for his migration to Palestine. In July, 1795, he expected to be in Constantinople on his way to Jerusalem; by August the English government would fall; by November he would be revealed as the Prince of the Hebrews and George III would give up his throne. Then the exodus to the Holy Land would begin, using French, Spanish, and English ships placed at Brothers's disposal by the various governments. Finally, in 1798, the rebuilding of Jerusalem would begin.

Insane, of course, but many gathered about him. His followers were not all poor and credulous, as E. P. Thompson suggests, but often were individuals of substance, standing, and a mystical turn of mind.[34] There was Nathaniel B. Halhead, M.P., from Lymington, for example. Halhead was a distinguished linguist and scholar, a boyhood friend of Richard Sheridan, and the author of *The Grammar of the Bengal Language*, who became Brothers's chief defender in Parliament.[35] There was William Sharp, an engraver with an international reputation, a member of the Imperial Academy of Vienna and the Royal Academy of

Munich, and a sometime radical who did engravings of Brothers, Thomas Paine, and later Joanna Southcott.[36] In addition, there was an eccentric group of clergymen who accepted Brothers's claims. Thomas Philip Foley was a wealthy fellow of Jesus College, Cambridge, who, after learning about Brothers, had a conversion and commenced an intensive study of prophetic texts. Another cleric, Thomas Webster, was a lecturer at two London churches who had published several volumes of evangelical sermons before coming under Brothers's influence. According to one source Webster "began to see visions himself and once fell into a trance, while taking a funeral to the cemetery and then published a description of what he saw accompanied by colored illustrations."[37]

Considerably more distinguished than the clerics was Brothers's publisher, George Ribeau, the friend of many intellectuals and an unlikely source for Ranter tracts. Yet Ribeau advertised himself as "Bookseller to the Hebrews" and issued fourteen books and pamphlets under that imprint.[38] One book, *Revealed Knowledge*, was enormously successful, going through several editions and attracting followers to Brothers, particularly in the north of England. Some of these figures remained with Brothers throughout his career while others drifted off into Southcott's movement when she made her bid for leadership among the millennarians, particularly after Brothers's confinement in jail after 1800. For example, George Turner, a merchant from Leeds, was an early follower of both prophets and later made his own bid for the mantle, only to fail. However, he is listed in the House of David chronicle as the third prophet leading to Benjamin Purnell. Brothers's appeal was considerably wider than Thompson suggests, as Ronald Matthews indicates:

The North answered too, and in Leeds, in Hull, skilled craftsmen and wealthy merchants came forward with their tributes to this retired lieutenant turned officer of God's judgment. For those prepared to be credulous, Brothers' warning of impending doom and his claims that he had already saved London from destruction were overwhelming complementary reasons for believing in him. In such a troublesome future, to whom could one better trust than a man with the Almighty was so great.[39]

John F. C. Harrison makes the same point in his analysis of
Brothers's followers in his brilliant *The Second Coming*.[40]

Brothers's most steadfast disciple was John Finlayson, a
Scottish lawyer who sold his practice for £25,000 and went to
London to serve his master. After Brothers's decline as an influential prophet and even after his death, Finlayson continued to
support his cause by issuing pamphlets and manifestoes, some
profusely illustrated and giving considerable detail concerning
the plan for the Christian kingdom. The Brothers-Finlayson
kingdom was to be monarchical and had an elaborate constitu-
tional and legislative system which outlined, in minute detail, the
forms and regulations of the new society. These plans were a
combination of meticulous sense and nonsense, of commonplace
wisdom and prophetic megalomania. Although not published
until 1830 (six years after Brothers's death), *The New Covenant*
suggested certain areas which were of particular interest to
Brothers. For example, an elaborate court system flourished in
which justice was speedy; individuals could not be arrested for
debt, though provision was made to repay monies owed; lands
laying waste and homes left empty had to be sold to relieve the
homeless; and the "disorder termed lunacy is erroneous,"[41] yet
provision was made for lunatic behavior.

It was a precise program which arose, in part, out of
Brothers's persecution mania and reflected his own turmoil. He
wrote, "No man must be deemed insane who is inoffensive in his
actions, and is civil in his actions, and is civil in his language, who
is able to work at any kind of employment for a livelihood, to
receive or give instructions, or to take proper care of himself. All
men are not born with the same faculties for learning, teaching,
inventing or executing; and wisely has God ordered it so, to make
the diversity of properties in the mind appear, by the greater
variety of ways and improvements for the general good of all."[42]
That self-description shows Brothers's plight in clear relief and,
by reflection, the plight of his followers, who were seen as equally
insane for following the "Prince of the Hebrews."

Prior to 1794 Brothers had been incarcerated in the workhouse on one occasion and on another jailed at Newgate for bad
debts. In 1795, he became embroiled with the law once again, this
time with officials who suspected political intrigue behind his

popularity. For a brief period in 1794–95 there was great notice taken of Brothers's prophecies; visitors came to his flat in Paddington for inspiration and guidance in those troubled times. Caricatures appeared of him in the press; one by James Gillray depicted him as a Jacobin carrying a bundle of the elect with him. Brothers and his followers were shown trampling on kings and devils alike. The government suspected that something else might be lurking behind this maniacal and grandiose facade since his supporters came from "that dangerous class of merchants, small tradesmen and superior artisans that had been the backbone of the revolution in France."[43] Indeed, a *London Times* article asserted that individuals came to hear him inveigh against the king and the current administration.

In March, 1795, Brothers was arrested under an Elizabethan act that charged him with "unlawfully, maliciously, and wickedly writing, printing and publishing fanatical prophecies, with the intent to cause dissension, and other disturbances in the realm." He was brought before the Privy Council, or a committee of the Council, and questioned. They found him eccentric and harmless; yet the king, whose hold on the real world was always tenuous, seems to have feared Brothers and wanted him put away. A panel of physicians found him conveniently and properly insane, and he was committed to a private hospital in Islington. Halhead, his devoted Parliamentary follower, tried to have the Commons consider the case by moving that a copy of Brothers's writings be laid on the table of the House. But there was no interest in the motion, and Brothers began an eleven years' stay at the asylum, despite the constant efforts of his followers, particularly Finlayson, to secure his release. The debate over the legitimacy of Brothers's prophecies continued in certain circles with, for example, David Levy and Moses Gomez Pereria challenging his views about the "external Jews."[44] While Brothers languished in prison attention was turning toward a new prophetess, Joanna Southcott, who was issuing her own revelations and capturing Brothers's followers.

The Southcottian movement grew to considerable proportions, well beyond Brothers's crusade. Its support was based on her followers' personal fealty to Southcott as a prophet rather than on any particular themes in her prophecies. Born at

Tarford near the village of Gettisham, Devonshire, on April 4, 1750, Joanna Southcott was the fourth daughter of William and Hannah Southcott. She had been a trusted though somewhat melancholy domestic servant to an Exeter family, the Taylors, since 1784. In the late 1780s she began to show the first signs of her divine calling, and in 1792 she began to proclaim publicly her prophetic mission on earth. She indicated to her employers that she was a "prophetess" and began to write what has been called a "mixture of rambling prose and aboral rhyme" under inspiration.[45] In was a mixture of prophecy and personal history that Harrison describes as the "story of a labouring woman in the later part of the eighteenth century. In simple language and with artless honesty she portrays her daily experiences, secret hopes and bizarre fantasies."[46] Like Brothers, she had visions and received messages—particularly about war and destruction—as higher powers used her and worked through her for divine purposes. From 1793 onward she began to prophesy regularly and demand, first from the dissenting clergy and then from the bishops of England, that they examine her prophecies. Bundles of manuscripts were sent to clergymen and bishops who, in turn, ignored Southcott and her messages; however, one cleric, James Pomeroy, agreed to read the writings and for a time fell under her influence.[47]

Pomeroy, a vicar of St. Kew in Cornwall, was a successful preacher who visited her in 1796. She gave Pomeroy some of her predictions, including one prophesying the death of the Bishop of Exeter. When that and other prophecies subsequently came true, Pomeroy began to act as her conduit to the outside world. During the next four years, she bombarded Pomeroy with prophecies and requests that he get her work examined by a clerical committee. Yet no followers came forward and no clerics, aside from Pomeroy, would read her work, so she decided to publish some of her communications. In February, 1801, the first part of *The Strange Effects of Faith* appeared, followed by five additional parts within the year. On the first page of the tract, she issued a challenge that she and her followers repeated in various forms over the next hundred years: "If any five ministers who are worthy and good men, will prove that these writings come from the Devil I will refrain from further printing. If they cannot I will go on."[48]

Although five ministers failed to respond, she did draw a mixed bag of seven prophetical jurors (including three ministers) to Exeter to examine her prophecies. In the group were former followers of Brothers: the Reverend Thomas Foley; William Sharp, the engraver; George Turner, the merchant from Leeds; and several others. After the seven had spent a week at Exeter examining Southcott's current prophecies, they departed for London, taking with them all the other prophecies made since 1794. Since that year she had "sealed" her writings with her own unique seal: the initials *I.C.* with two stars. Her "great box," as it was later called, of sealed writings began to take on great significance for her since they represented the touchstone of her legitimacy as a prophet. Through the welter of her writings and inspirational messages it is possible to see the rough outlines of a theology that was remarkably similar to her contemporary, Ann Lee of the Shakers, even though the Southcottian creed did not urge sexual abstinence for the members:

> Perhaps the simplest way of summarizing Joanna's doctrine is to say that she was a theological feminist. The core of her teaching is built around her interpretation of one sentence in the third chapter of Genesis, when Jehovah is addressing the serpent before the fallen human parents. "I will put enmity between thy seed and her seed; it shall bruise thy head and thou shalt bruise her heel" . . . For that to be achieved, the seed of Eve—and in this connection 'her seed' must mean not merely a descendant but a female descendant—must challenge the devil to mortal combat. By so doing, she would cast back upon him the guilt which women had originally occurred by transmitting his temptation to man in Eden.[49]

Joanna Southcott was to be the instrument, the "Lamb's Bride," who would destroy Satan and thereby usher in the new kingdom. As heretical as her teachings were, there is no indication that she wished to found a sect or, like Richard Brothers, to lead the Israelites to Jerusalem; rather, her services and practices were "conducted with rigorous adherence to the Church of England ritual."[50]

She entered into another phase of her work during 1802 by moving to London and beginning the process whereby she "sealed" her believers. It is in Revelation 7 that the ideas of sealing, election, and a specific number of the elect are all brought together:

> And I saw another angel ascending from the east, having the seal of the living God: and he cried with a loud voice to the four angels, to whom it was given to hurt the earth and the sea, Saying, Hurt not the earth, neither the sea, nor the trees, till we have sealed the servants of our God in their foreheads, And I heard the number of them which were sealed: an hundred and forty and four thousand of all the tribes of the children of Israel . . .

> Therefore are they before the throne of God, and serve him all day and night in his temple: and he that sitteth on the throne shall dwell among them. They shall hunger no more, neither thirst any more; neither shall the sun light on them, nor any heat. For the Lamb which is in the midst of the throne shall feed them, and shall lead them unto living fountains of water; and God shall wipe away the tears from their eyes.

When one of Southcott's wealthy supporters, Elias Carpenter, brought her a gift of a ream of paper from his mill, she cut it into squares, put a circle on each page, and wrote inside the circle: "The sealed of the Lord, the elect and precious, man's redemption to inherit the tree of life, to be made heirs of God and joint heirs with Jesus Christ." Unlike some other prophets she never sold the seals for profit as was later charged, but with her move to London and growing interest in her writings, these bits of paper became tangible proof of her growing mission. By 1807 she had sealed 14,000 out of the possible 144,000 elect.

In 1803 "the Lamb" embarked on a missionary trip to seal believers throughout England. Fresh tracts were printed, such as *Communications of Joanna Southcott the Prophetess of Exeter*. She continued to issue challenges to the clergy to examine her prophecies, although by now she thought it necessary to have twelve bishops, instead of the simple clergy, examine her works. The bishops stayed away, but her sealing campaign brought converts to her; other prophets began to hear voices, however, and thus threatened to splinter the growing Southcottian movement. In addition, the release of Richard Brothers seemed momentarily to threaten her supremacy, but because his old followers had been sealed by her there was no substantial defection. The movement was more vulnerable to the antics of someone like Mary Bateman, a professional abortionist and thief who "secured a seal and posed as a preacher of the new revelation" and produced some eggs, which she said her hens were laying, inscribed with the legend "Crist [*sic*] is Coming." She has been described as a "Yorkshire witch."[51] Such later prophets as Benjamin Purnell would find that in the public eye there was a fine line between prophecy and witchcraft; stories about the diabolical qualities of Purnell's leadership were current during the early 1900s. Bateman was hanged for poisoning in 1809; her arrest and trial did damage to the Southcottian movement, and as a result Southcott abandoned the practice of sealing the believers.[52]

During this period she lived in a cottage in the Cotswolds, supported and cared for by wealthy followers, and though outwardly serene about her predictions, she was secretly troubled about the source of her visions. Were they from God or the Devil? Such doubts made her an unhappy woman for much of her career even though the movement grew and she had little to worry about concerning financial matters since her followers were generous in their support. In 1814 came the final revelation and test that was both to sustain and to destroy her mission. In that year a voice, by now a familiar one, spoke to her: "This year in the sixty-fifth year of thy age thou shalt bear a son by the power of the most high." Earlier the voice had instructed her to marry and although the command had, at first, confused her, she had tried to comply as best she could, by marrying at a later date. In March, 1814, at age sixty-five, she publicly announced that she was pregnant for the first time and that she was going to give birth to the Shiloh. In addition, it would be a virgin birth because all men had been excluded from her room since October, 1813.

Newspaper attacks on this prophecy and the blasphemy of this "deluded, elderly virgin" began at once, but her supporters reacted with great enthusiasm. They presented her with a crib, said to have cost £200, made of satin wood and gold and "hung on swivels by a cord of gold attached to a pedal, so that it need not be necessary to leave over and perhaps incommode the supernatural babe."⁵³ The press, noting this and other extravagant gifts, ridiculed the approaching event. Visitors flocked to her residence, some to ridicule, others to ask for advice. But when over twenty physicians, including the distinguished surgeon Richard Reece, confirmed her pregnancy, new converts poured into the Southcottian chapels and a new hymn, to the tune of "Rule Britannia," was sung:

> Rule King Shiloh! King Shiloh, Rule Alone
> With Glory Crowned on David's Throne.

In order to fulfill an earlier prophecy, she now took a husband. She had hoped that the Reverend Pomeroy would accept the honor, but he declined and thus she married John Smith, steward to the Earl of Darnley, described as "a very respectable friend about her own age."⁵⁴ A whole host of suitors had presented themselves as marriage partners, including George Turner, who had received a supernatural revelation that he was to be her husband ("Thou art the man," he was told), only to find that Joanna rejected it as a false message. When her hysterical pregnancy came to an end in December, 1814, she was forced to call her disciples to her bedside to confess that "it all appears delusion." Her followers found it difficult to accept that she was not going to give birth to the Shiloh. Indeed, for a while rumors spread that she was the "woman of the sun" identified in the Book of Revelation, whose divine child was snatched up into heaven to escape the dragon.

In the end, however, nothing could save her from the shocking realization that her long career as a prophetess had been misguided from the beginning. On the morning of December 27, 1814 a brief announcement was published stating that "to all appearances" she had died. Her lingering death made her followers hopeful to the end that a further revelation might save her life's work. Four days after her death fifteen doctors met for a postmortem examination under Dr. Reece's direction. When they found everything normal for a woman her age except a few gallstones, they issued the following statement: "We the undersigned, present at the dissection of Mrs. Joanna Southcott, do certify that no unnatural appearances were visible, and no part exhibited any appearance of disease sufficient to have occasioned her death, nor was there any appearance of her ever having been pregnant."[55] Her funeral was a quiet one with only a few mourners in attendance. She had left a large body of disaffected believers without a leader, without a Shiloh, without a millennium, and without an ingathering.

But Brothers and Southcott, in their separate ways, had created both a tradition and a body of believers. It was a prophetic tradition based on inner sight, apocalyptic Biblical exegesis, millennial expectations, and sectarian politics. Their followers had moved along a path toward religious ultraism and with the death of their leaders wandered in search of new security. Brothers and Southcott represent two strands in the prophetic tradition: one social, with an emphasis on an earthly kingdom; the other personal, with an emphasis on mystical fealty and devotion to a sacred person; one male, one female. The two forces were never far apart, and if Brothers and Southcott had ever joined forces they might have led a major sect. For what characterized Brothers was his forceful demand for an audience, his audacious manner, and the authority of his commands. Southcott was a calmer figure, equally perseverant, but without audacious claims—until the end—to a special leadership role. He was a king, she a queen, both intending to rule and have followers. Some of the prophetic leaders who followed them combined the two regal roles while others instituted a dual sexual system of governance. Under either system there was a recognition that sexual and symbolic functions had to be represented in any theological and social system that drew its inspiration from the religious ferment surrounding these two figures. Later the House of David would capitalize on the dual strands in the prophetic tradition, with Benjamin Purnell acting as King David and his wife, Mary, as queen.

There were numerous contenders for Joanna Southcott's prophetic mantle and her momentarily disaffiliated followers. It is estimated that at least thirty prophets attempted to revive the remnants of the Southcottian movement after her death.[56] In addition, three distinct interpretive traditions about the meaning of her death developed: one believing that Joanna Southcott would soon reappear; a second that the Shiloh had been born but had been snatched into heaven and would return in good time; third, that the Shiloh was a spiritual son and a convert to the Southcottian creed who would carry on her work. With such a range of interpretations there were bound to be contradictory voices speaking to different aspects of the Southcottian movement.[57] For example, one group ritually killed a black pig because there was a reference in the literature to the Devil adopting that disguise. Another group, called the "Household of Faith," was led by a watchman, Samuel Sibley, who took them through the streets of London: "They marched in procession through the Temple Bar, each decorated with a white cockade and a star of yellow ribbon. Sibley led, bearing a brazen trumpet adorned with light blue ribbons, and two boys carried flags of light blue silk. . . . Sibley sounded the trumpet and proclaimed the coming of the Shiloh. His wife cried: 'Woe to the inhabitants of the earth, because of the coming of the Shiloh.' "[58]

Such a creed was, of course, open to numerous visionary interpretations. Out of this confused condition came the steadiest candidate, George Turner, whose claim to the prophetic role was based on sound historical logic. He had been a follower of Brothers, had been one of the "seven sisters" who affirmed the Southcottian predictions in 1803, and had had a vision that he should be Joanna Southcott's husband. In February, 1815 his "voice" told him that the Shiloh had been taken from Joanna's womb and that he would reappear after a period of trial and faith-testing for the followers. Naturally the voice also told Turner to prepare the way for the Shiloh. With that message in hand, Turner journeyed to London to gather support for his spiritual stewardship and to issue further revelations.

Like Brothers, Turner was afflicted with the sort of religious megalomania that made his predictions, plans, and projects grandiose and, at the same time, catastrophic; yet, when compared with Turner, Brothers's pronouncements stand as models of restraint and good sense. There is a certain dignity and symmetry in Brothers's plans for the Israelite kingdom that is lacking in Turner's apocalyptic style. Beyond that Turner added a worldly element to the design by insisting that the Shiloh have a palace to live in—a variant on the luxurious crib that Southcott's supporters had prepared for the heavenly babe in 1814. "The

walls must be of pure gold," Turner wrote, and they must be
"adorned with precious stones. There must be in attendance
70,000 men with musical instruments and 70,000 singing
women. He must have 550,000 servants and his carriage must be
pure gold."[59] Turner also prepared a place for himself in the
palace since he was preparing the way for the Shiloh: "And thou,
George Turner, must have 300,000 servants. Thy house gardens
and walks must be similar to the Shiloh's."[60] These last pronouncements were written while Turner was confined to the
"Retreat," a Quaker asylum where he had been placed in 1817.
He had predicted an earthquake and an attack on the king,
leading to his arrest and a charge of treason. He was found not
guilty, but was sent to the asylum. After three years there, he was
calmed sufficiently so that on his release he was able to resume his
prophetic role in a more subdued manner.

    In his own way, Turner organized the Southcottians into a
coherent church with rules and regulations, becoming to them
what Joseph Meachem was to the later Shakers, a rule giver and
organizer. He disciplined the sect's preachers, laid down rules
for church attendance, and strengthened ties with the established churches by insisting that women must be churched,
babies and children baptized in their parish churches, marriages
celebrated there, and every believer a regular communicant. On
his release from the "Retreat" in 1820, he instituted a marriage
rite for all those who wished to be brides of the Lord. Turner
sealed the faithful with a kiss just as Joanna Southcott had used
her pieces of paper. In his own way he simply elaborated on the
formula she used with so much success. Like her, Turner
married in anticipation of the coming of the Shiloh, whose
appearance he predicted at a banquet in London before seven
hundred followers. At this feast he stated that the Shiloh would
appear as a young boy in that city on October 15, 1820. When the
young Shiloh failed to appear the Turnerians redoubled their
efforts to prepare the way by purchasing a house, hiring
servants, and bringing gifts for the overdue Shiloh. After the
Shiloh failed to appear on yet another appointed day, Turner
wasted away—like Southcott—and died in despair on September
21, 1821.

    While Turner was organizing the Southcottian followers,

infusing them with Israelite history and highlighting the secular comforts needed for the Shiloh, another prophet had been at work. He was John "Zion" Ward, an Irish shoemaker who had read Southcott's *Fifth Book of Wonders* in 1814 and on her death had offered himself as the next messenger. His offer was refused, and he turned to work for Mary Boon in order to promote her prophetic cause among the dispersed Southcottians. Boon has been described as a "peasant woman of frightful aspect, with only one eye and a hare lip which extended so far up her face as completely to divide her nose in two parts."[61] One of her beliefs was that every law of the Bible had to be followed and therefore she observed the Mosaic law, a practice that Ward and other prophets would adopt. After leaving Boon's service, Ward fell under the influence of the freethinker Richard Carlile, who persuaded him to reject a literal interpretation of the Bible for an allegorical one that foretold future events.[62] While serving a term in the workhouse for neglecting his family Ward had a vision in which Joanna Southcott came to tell him that he was the Shiloh. This encouraged Ward to believe he was also Jesus Christ, Satan, and Adam—in fact, the perfect type prefigured in both the Old and New Testaments. In 1829 he published his *The Vision of Judgment, or The Return of Joanna From Her Trance* and launched an evangelical tour from which he gained little except the taunts of crowds and the scorn of newspapers. He was attacked wherever he went and won over his audiences only when he dropped his Biblical pronouncements and launched instead into an attack on the clergy, the government, the landlords, and others with power. By 1831 he had established a following, with two chapels in London, scattered settlements throughout the North, and a newspaper, *The Judgment Seat of Christ*.[63] As his attacks on the clergy became more heated, however, he was charged with and convicted of blasphemy. But when his two years' sentence ended in February, 1834 he renewed his evangelizing, attracting to his group this time such figures as James Pierrepont Greaves, an educational and social reformer.[64] Ward even had a scheme for a land colony "where those who are willing to leave the world can live together as one family," but the plan failed to materialize. He continued to preach his message until 1837, when he died on a missionary tour.[65] John Ward was a curious combination of messiah, sceptic, and deluded man, but bore also the important role of the third "true" messenger in the Anglo-American line of continuity leading to the House of David.

Little is known about the fourth messenger, William Shaw, whose revelations between 1819 and 1822 were never printed and whose message was essentially a jeremiad against the city of London that it repent.

The fifth prophet, John Wroe, has a fully documented history, one that in many ways prefigures the career of Benjamin Purnell. According to one source, "as a lad [Wroe] was neither robust in mind or in body" and as a result of a life of hard labor was severely hunchbacked.[66] For some, his physical condition was an analog for his distorted and evil mind, but his followers seem to have overlooked his deformities and to have seen only his Shiloh-like characteristics. He joined a Southcottian group at Leeds in 1820 after having had visions and a heavenly visitation a year earlier. On one occasion he presented himself to a synagogue in Liverpool asking to be accepted as a Jew. Like other prophets, he made predictions, some of which came true.[67]

After George Turner's death Wroe made a bid for the Southcottian leadership, but at first only a single group—those at Ashton-under-Lyne—accepted him as a leader. When the other congregations rejected him, Wroe set out on a missionary voyage which took him to numerous European cities. It was during his missionary journey that he let his beard grow and afterward required his followers to do the same—thus the custom of wearing beards among the House of David's men can be traced to the Wroeite practice, which had Biblical roots in the Nazirites, an eighth-century B.C. sect mentioned in Numbers and Samuel. They refused to cut their hair, to drink wine or alcohol, or to come in contact with a corpse. The Nazirites were a special class of sacred persons like the prophets; Samson was probably a follower. Wroe's believers were generally prosperous and were drawn from the towns and villages in the North. These "Christian Israelites" also distinguished themselves by their dress; Wroe required them to wear dark, broad-rimmed hats, and claret-colored Quaker coats. They followed the Mosaic law, eating only kosher meat and avoiding spirits, snuff, and tobacco. Wroe himself had been publicly circumcised in April, 1824, and shortly thereafter instituted the rite as part of the Israelite system. He demanded and received complete obedience from his followers, and he established a disciplinary system which was closely paralleled by the regimen at the House of David some seventy years later. Physical punishment was inflicted through a committee, and an elaborate spy network existed in the society to identify transgressors of church rules.

One historian describes Wroe as "half saint, half satyr" and that characterization is close to the mark. In 1827 Wroe was acquitted of a charge of having criminal intercourse with his twelve-year-old apprentice, and three years later three young women confessed to having practiced "idiotic indecencies" with him, though the nature of the charges remains unknown. A committee of the church found him innocent of the charges, but his reputation for sexual excesses caused members to drift away in the 1830s. While very little is known about Wroe's career, we do know that around 1840 he began a vigorous missionary campaign that took him four times to America and four times to Australia. It was in Australia that he left his greatest legacy to the Israelite tradition that ends with the House of David. During a visit in 1850 he stated that the "Australian colonies will occupy a distinguished position in opening up the way for the gathering of the elect on the advent millennium and in the great work the colony of Victoria will be beyond all others pre-eminently conspicuous."[68] Israelite sanctuaries were built in Sydney, Adelaide, and other cities. By 1853 there were also fifty societies in England, thirteen in Ireland, a few in Wales, and several in the United States, including societies in Massachusetts, Rhode Island, and New York. Controversy and scandal followed him to Australia and Allan Stewart's account published in 1851, *The Abominations of the Wroeites*, provides a link between the older traditions and the practices of the House of David under Purnell that led first to notoriety and then to ruinous decay.

Stewart, for six years a member of the Wroeite community at Hobart Town, Australia, wrote of his introduction into the society, described certain of its rites, and detailed his disillusionment with the society. When he wrote *Abominations*, he was an apostate from the church, yet his testimony contains many elements that were central to the Wroeite faith and his evidence

seems believable, given Wroe's previous history. Stewart's first
contact with the sect was an ennobling one: "Rambling about on
Sundays I now met some of Wroe's preachers, listened to their
sermons and read their tracts, which gradually worked upon my
mind, till I had really thought I had met with the best and purest
people on earth, who could most assuredly show me the way to
heaven. I joined their society, was circumcised and devoted
myself to their cause."[69] He was an enthusiastic convert, one
eager to do what the faith demanded even if he suffered ridicule
and persecution in the process. After six months, Stewart was still
a probationary member even though he attended chapel, had
taken a binding oath, had been given a seal—a piece of green silk
with Hebrew letters on it—and had put on the "sacred gar-
ments," consisting of a linen tunic with linen pants, to be specially
worn at services. Full membership into the society came when he
underwent the "cleansing process," or the "law of Christ," as he
called it.

The cleansing rite began one day when he was approached
by a female member of the church and asked if he felt himself
"under transgression"; if he did, he should present himself to
her. Believing that he had somehow transgressed the Wroeite
law he went to the woman's house next to the chapel. She began
the ceremony by opening the Wroeite songbook and asking him
to read the following passage:

A Holy sight it is to see
Brother, sister uniting be
And for each other to set free
To inherit immortality.

What followed was a sexual initiation rite. Stewart was instructed to strip and was given a piece of paper and pin. The
ceremony, as told by Stewart, then proceeded: "She dipped her
hand in a basin of water, which action she repeated twice during
the process. In her left hand she held my private parts, while she
manipulated my posteriors, pausing at intervals, at each of which
I thrust the pin into the paper and repeated the following words
after her: 'In the name of the man Jesus Christ have I received
this cleansing for my sins.' "[70] Later Stewart underwent the cleaning process a second time, but then brass buttons were sub-

stituted for the pin and paper as he dropped a button after each pause.

Again, his account is the testimony of an apostate, but it outlines such characteristics of the faith as circumcision, special clothing, the wearing of beards, and cleansing rites. One central facet of the faith was the unswerving belief in Wroe's divine mission. His Australian followers, for example, financed a mansion for him at Wakefield, and the building, called Melbourne House, kept the prophet in comfort and style until his death in 1863.[71]

Clearly certain elements of the Wroeite tradition reasserted themselves under Benjamin Purnell's leadership of the Israelite House of David. The notion of the elect 144,000 certainly did not begin with Wroe, but it was a major part of his creed, and the House of David's emphasis on sexual abstinence was clearly derived from an 1853 pamphlet *A Guide To The People Surnamed Israelites*, even though the Wroeites were not known to practice celibacy.

The shaping of the Israelite "theology" was long in the making, and it passed through many hands and texts before reaching western Michigan. The prophetic tradition from Joanna Southcott to John Wroe developed fitfully and there was little direct lineage among them all. The Southcottians disavowed Wroe and his alleged excesses; Brothers and Southcott were different; yet all the early prophets were nurtured and developed within an enthusiastic tradition. "The false prophets were keen to wear Joanna's mantle, but they had to give new interpretations to her message,"[72] according to John F. C. Harrison. The Israelite movement took on an Anglo-American connection after Wroe's visits and the establishment of churches in the United States. Here a membership grew and a pattern similar to the English experience took shape. Israelite churches, a sectarian literature, squabbles over leadership, and other features of the English experience gradually emerged. What is more important for this study is the awareness that when one looks at the eccentricities and contradictions of the House of David, one is looking at the accretions of a century of social and religious practices defined by the prophets and practiced by a large body of followers from different social classes on the Continent. The shaping of the colony and its peculiar organization began well before 1903 and had a limiting form when it reached America. To be sure, there were new elements added, old practices dropped or modified, but there is more continuity and constancy in the bonds that link the messengers than has been suspected. Benjamin Purnell was the seventh and final messenger, and the House of David colony was shaped by his personality. However, it was also shaped by a century-long process that offered him a prophetic future if he paid attention to the messianic past.

CHAPTER TWO

The American Prophets

We never saw England . . . .
*Excerpt from a letter to Leeds Times
from American Israelites, June, 1857.*

John Wroe's missionary journey to the United States in 1840 resulted in the formation of a group in New York, large enough for the *New York Sun* to take notice of in 1841: "We have obtained some information of the peculiar dogma of their sect [Christian Israelite] and the history of their rise and progress till this time, they seem a harmless and inoffensive people; and their doctrines if strange are still of the evangelical school of morality, holding all the dogmas of the gospel and adding the stern code of the Mosaic dispensation."[1] This brief notice is the only reference to their existence in the 1840s. If we look at the career of an early convert, and later prophet, we can see what forces were at work in shaping the Israelites in America.

Daniel Milton, born Daniel Trickey, was converted to the Christian Israelite Church in the spring of 1844 by two traveling Wroeite preachers, John and Margaret Bishop, who had visited the Second Adventists (Millerites) at Portsmouth, New Hampshire, with Wroe's Mosaic message. Portsmouth had been a center of Millerite controversy ever since Miller's visit in 1840 had produced a six-weeks revival and many converts.[2] In 1843 Bishop published his *A Brief History of a Church Surnamed Israel*, in which he makes clear his connection with the Southcottian tradition: "So that the writer of this (with many thousands besides) believed that the world has been warned by a visitation from Heaven in Prophecy, to prepare for Christ's second coming, ever since 1792."[3] The time was almost near for the elect 144,000 to come together because Satan was drawing the world's attention to two "astonishing theories—one, a new moral world is to be created independent of Divine Revelation [the Owenite prophecy]—the other, that the Earth is to be burnt up in 1843 [the Millerite prediction]." Miller had predicted that sometime between March 21, 1843, and March 21, 1844, the Second Advent would occur and when that date passed "many walked no more with us." The town was therefore ripe in the spring of 1844 for a reinterpretation of the millennial message. There were high expectations that something was going to happen in the spring, and although Wroe's message was rejected by the Portsmouth congregation, Trickey readily accepted it. He wrote: "After hearing him preach, and having some controversy with him on the ministry of the society, I joined as a believer in the Christian Israelite Church."[4] Shortly after, Trickey moved to New York City and on the Bishops' advice took a "believing Wroeite wife," Margaret Bishop's daughter. His marriage to Barbara Wilkinson was solemnized by John Bishop and a newspaper notice announced their sacred union:

As male and female in fair Eden stood
As male and female were saved from the flood
So male and female do in union join we
For Satan's fall; and Jesus kingdom come.[5]

The Israelite kingdom in New York in 1844 consisted of about twenty members with a traveling ministry. It was not until 1850 that the congregation was incorporated with "Daniel Milton" as president and one of the trustees. According to Milton he legally changed his name from Trickey to Milton in 1854, though no record of such a change exists in the New York City courts, and it can be assumed that the change was more symbolic than legal and affirmed the Anglo-Israelite connection. Between

1844 and 1854 Milton worked in New York as a carpenter, had six children, and may have engaged in some Wroeite missionary work. According to a letter sent to the *Leeds Times* in June, 1857 the American Wroeites were native to the United States and "never saw England." They were all coworkers in the ship-building industry in New York. In 1857 a controversy developed between Milton and his father-in-law, with John Bishop charging that his converted son-in-law had neglected his family and was insane (like Ward, who had been in the workhouse for neglecting his family). Apparently the suspicions about Milton's sanity began with his proclamation in 1857 of a prophetic role. Milton announced that: "The true prophet, who is the branch, the spirit of the truth, has now come, and all those that are waiting for the adoption, to wit—the redemption of their bodies (labor and are heavy laden). . . . As they will put on immortality without tasting death. Therefore let it be known that Daniel Milton has been called of God, the God of the living, to preach this eternal gospel for the ingathering of his Israel."[6] The dispute between the two men may have been purely religious, with Milton asserting his divine authority over his father-in-law, but it wound up in a Brooklyn court in October, 1858, after Milton was arrested. The court committed him to an asylum-jail, and in true prophetic fashion the experience strengthened his resolve. Upon his release from the asylum in 1860 he took up the controversy with Bishop once again, but this time as an "expelled member" of the Christian Israelite Church.[7] He issued pamphlets in his own defense and made two trips to Wroe's stronghold, Melbourne House, to plead his case and offer himself as the Shiloh. On Wroe's sudden death in 1863 Milton presented himself once again, posting advertisements for his cause and preaching in a field near Wroe's palace. He was fined and sent to jail for fourteen days for trespassing on Israelite property.

Milton was the first bona fide albeit unsuccessful American prophet of the Israelite tradition. His career was similar to those of the English pretenders: it began during a period of intense religious awakening; it developed within the Israelite tradition; it led him to proclaim his messianic role and pursue it. In fact, he maintained his claim for another forty years with very scant success, never gathering a substantial body of followers. Milton seems to have stayed in England, specifically at Wrenthorpe, near Wakefield in Yorkshire, after his visit in 1863 and lived into the early years of the twentieth century. In the scale of things he was more eccentric than the other prophets, but that perspective detracts from our understanding of his mission. His failure as a prophet cannot be blamed entirely on his eccentric behavior, because the pattern of prophetic annunciation, persecution, and proselytizing had worked for other leaders.

Between 1863 and 1876 there was no clear-cut successor to Wroe, though one couple, the Heads, exerted considerable influence on a Southcottian sect in Kent that had split away from the Wroeite faith in 1830. Throughout the Victorian period there were two strains of belief: one that manifested itself in charismatic eccentrics like Wroe and Ward, and another that manifested itself in the continuing belief of the Southcottian followers, who attended chapel, who petitioned to have Joanna's messages read by the clergy, and who "maintained their numbers by handing on their passionate hopes to their children and grandchildren."[8]

One such example of this continuing, varying tradition was at Chatham, Kent, where a body of believers reflected both trends. Chatham had been one of the first towns to form a Southcottian group and had continued to meet after the prophetess's death. The group eventually became followers of Wroe, whom they considered divinely inspired, but they rejected him in 1830 because of the scandals surrounding his missionary work. In that year they renamed themselves the "New House of Israel" to distinguish themselves from the "Old House" that continued to accept Wroe. During the 1870s there still existed a group at Chatham, and it was from that group that the next messenger emerged. Groups like the Southcottian-Wroeites at Chatham were, in their own way, settled churches and provided future prophets with a membership base.[9] Since the Shiloh had been promised by Joanna Southcott, there was always room for more speculation about her spiritual son. Beyond that there was the tradition that the movement would be led by a woman, and prophetesses continued to appear throughout the century. Like their male counterparts, they issued apocalyptic warnings, circulated petitions urging the destruction of Satan, promised an ingathering of the elect, and produced a large pamphlet literature. One such figure, Elizabeth H. Vaughan, received her prophetic call at the age of sixty-six and before her death succeeded in collecting some 450,000 signatures on a petition against the devil.[10]

Out of this confused situation a prophet did appear who brought together the Anglo-American Christian-Israelite tradition. James Jershom Jezreel, born James White, rose to prominence in the 1870s and 1880s, and became the sixth messenger in the House of David chronology. Born in the United States, his early life is a mystery, and his known life story begins with his enlistment in the British Army in 1872 and his stationing at Chatham where he became acquainted with the "New House of Israel." He attended meetings of the Southcottian group and within months of his acceptance into the society had a vision and published extracts from it under the title *The Flying Roll.* As part of these prophecies White changed his name—like Tany and Trickey before him—to James Jershom Jezreel, with the initials J. J. J. representing *J*oanna Southcott, *J*ohn Wroe and *J*ames White. According to *The Flying Roll,* Jezreel was directing his message toward the ten lost tribes of Israel, who were scattered over the earth's surface unaware of their true identity. For Jezreel, there were three churches: the first Christian, the second Jewish, and the third a remnant of the scattered tribes. This last group was going to be gathered together into a third church, "The New and Latter House of Israel," headed by Jezreel and consisting of 144,000 believers, or 12,000 from each of the twelve tribes of Israel. Once gathered together, this remnant would redeem its body, soul, and spirit to gain immmortality. In short, Jezreel, like Ward and Wroe before him, was promising his followers that they would not die.

In 1876 Jezreel emphasized that the time was growing near for the ingathering. Promising that the English remnant would be saved first, the work of bringing the English Israelites together was therefore his first priority. According to P. G. Rogers: "Most of his followers were won over from the established Southcottian sects, like the Christian-Israelites of John Wroe, so that they really only changed one version of the basic faith for another when they joined Jezreel."[11] But his mission had to be deferred for some five years since Private White was required to serve that period with his regiment in India, though he kept in close contact with his followers in England. Between 1879 and 1881 three volumes of *Extracts From the Flying Roll* were published, including one edition at Grand Rapids, Michigan in 1879. These volumes spread his message in both countries, and Benjamin Purnell later wrote that he was converted after reading Jezreel's *Extracts*. The theology of the House of David was clearly "Jezreelite," though the notions of immortality, sealing, and the cleansing of the blood had their origins with other groups.

When mustered out of the Army in 1881, Jezreel married one of his early converts, Clarissa Rogers, and began at the age of forty-one a full, though brief, career as prophet. Just prior to Jezreel's release from the Army, Clarissa Rogers had embarked on a missionary tour of the United States in the hope of converting some of the Christian Israelite groups. Since *Extracts From the Flying Roll* had just been published, there was good potential for recruitment in the Middle West, particularly in Michigan.[12] Of the fifteen "headquarter" churches of the "New and Latter House of Israel," three were in America and two of them in Michigan, at Fowlerville and Detroit. During her stay in the United States, Clarissa Rogers converted one Noah Drew, a Michigan farmer who became their most ardent American disciple. After Jezreel's release from the Army in 1882, he was rejected by the Wroeites at Ashton-on-Lyne and decided to carry his message to the new land. The Jezreels wrote to Drew and invited him to take part in a grand evangelical America tour; he accepted their invitation, and his farm at Fowlerville became their camp. They preached at Howell, Brighton, and Detroit and although they attracted curious crowds they gathered-in few followers. But the prophet and Noah Drew had a falling out, and Drew was "cut off" from the group. Writing from Boston in August, 1882 Jezreel described the situation:

The Western expedition got up by Noah Drew and his family is disbanded and scattered and Noah Drew, Emily Drew, Job Drew are all cut off. Noah is in the state of New York. Emily, his wife, is in Ohio hundreds of miles apart. Job and his wife have returned to her father's farm. Jenny, the youngest daughter, is in Fowlerville, Michigan and Esther and myself with Marshall and Bill Drew are with me in Boston and so is Amelia Maxwell. The Cause of all this complete scattering is because I was compelled to draw the rod and it come down with the power of the Shiloh and in less than six days hundreds of days lay between us as before mentioned.[13]

All the members in America and England were warned not to "receive, communicate or converse" with Drew, and two of his children remained with Jezreel in Boston to spread the gospel. There were, according to Jezreel, some 150 members of the group living in Boston, and a few were making preparations to come to Acton with him. It would be up to Benjamin Purnell to gather up the fragments of the Jezreel gospel and plant the Southcottian and Wroeite message firmly in America. But the ground had been tested, and a thin line of faith established once again between England and America. Jezreel returned to England late in 1882 to continue work among the Wroeite and Southcottian remnant. In May, 1883 they journeyed to Australia to pursue the Leeward Wroeites who had settled in considerable numbers since the 1840s.

Their diligent missionary activities produced results by 1884 with funds and converts entering the house. By March, 1884 they were able to open "Israel's International College" for fifty students, who studied a combination of the Jezreel gospel, musical training in the harp, and "general practical knowledge."[14] According to his biographer, Jezreel had a distinctive flair for showmanship, and his open-air services at Woodlands Lane, Gillingham, Kent, were part religion, part show.

This combination of religion and showmanship was copied by the House of David as it sought to entertain as well as instruct visitors about the ingathering. Dwight Moody and Ira Sankey had livened their revivals in the 1870s in London with song and dramatic ceremony, reviving in "English evangelism the deeply felt national love of sound and color, extending back to medieval England with its constant emphasis on ritual and ceremony."[15] Moody and Sankey were revival showmen, and by the 1880s their evangelic techniques were widely copied. The Israelite pavilion meetings on Sunday afternoons were announced with attractive notices: "The meadow will be thrown open to the public at 6 P.M. Band Playing. The preaching will commence at 6:30. The public are cordially invited. All seats free." The entertainment consisted of hymn singing, religious exhortations, and musical selections by a band consisting of a harp, piano, piccolo, and violin. The service was calculated to win over some old South-cottians in the audience since the young women wore straw hats with the sealing initials *I. C.* on them and plain brown smocks. William Sharp's famous engraving of Joanna had her in such a homely outfit and the scene was calculated to stir up old memories for the believers. The Wroeite service had consisted of considerable pomp and included "much singing, and a band of thirty or forty musicians provided the accompaniment. A hierarchy of high priest, priest and levites, wearing distinctive robes, conducted the services."[16]

As new recruits arrived from other parts of England and Australia, they placed their funds in a central treasury which the Jezreels used to expand their business operations. Shops were opened in the village under Israelite supervision, and all stressed the purity of the goods sold. The ingathering went forward under both the Jezreelites and later the House of David on sound, expansive business principles. By the end of 1884, Jezreel was ready to take a major step for the ingathering by having a sanctuary for his work. After receiving a revelation about the building, he purchased a six-and-a-quarter acre site near the top of Chatham Hill, Kent, and began the construction. Originally the building was to have the dimensions of a perfect cube with 144 feet on each side, but he tempered his Biblical vision to a structure that approximated the perfect cube.

"Jezreel's Tower," as it was called, was to accommodate 50,000 people in its amphitheater, would have a rotating platform for the choir, and was to be illuminated by both gas and electric light, an innovation for its time. Total cost was estimated at £25,000, with labor and monies donated by the faithful. In a letter to his followers, Jezreel stated that the building had to be completed by January 1, 1885, and that he "needed ten thousand pounds to accomplish all the Lord requires me to do." But when the date arrived only the foundations and the basement of the enormous tower had been constructed. To make matters worse,

James Jershom Jezreel died in March, 1885. What had escaped Richard Brothers and George Turner had also eluded Jezreel: he had died without a monument.

There was only one real contender for the prophetic crown, though there was a small flurry of activity on behalf of other pretenders. Clarissa Rogers Jezreel became "Queen Esther" of the "New and Latter House of Israel." She had traveled widely, was an accomplished speaker, and carried herself with prophetic assurance. According to Wroeite practice Esther was a figure of Jesus, the woman's seed in Mosaic times who contended with the sinful world. She established herself at Gillingham in regal fashion and was soon known for her stylish clothes and elegant carriages. She also undertook the job of completing the tower and continuing the missionary work. Regular meetings continued at Chatham Hill, where the public was entertained by "Israel's Band" and Esther's evangelical preaching. Publications went out all over the world. The church had seemingly weathered the transition and was blessed with a young, intelligent, and gifted prophetess. The sect was shocked to learn that neither king nor queen was immortal when Esther Rogers died during the summer of 1888 at the age of twenty-eight.

Shortly after her death a series of articles appeared in the local paper, the *Chatham and Rochester Observer*, which purported to tell the darker side of the sect's history. Although Jezreel's biographer discounts the stories, they should not be lightly dismissed given the earlier histories surrounding the Wroeites and Southcottians. What makes the charges interesting is that they parallel the charges brought against Benjamin Purnell some forty years later. First, it was reported that James Jezreel had flogged young women in the society, had kept a "black hole" for the punishment of disobedient members, and had used personal confessions taken from new members as a whip over their heads. In addition, he supposedly had quarreled with Esther Jezreel on several occasions and had "cut off" (expelled) members when they questioned his divine authority. Jezreel was depicted as a Svengali-like figure—a man with an obscure past, a charismatic presence, and a dubious character. There were hints in the press that Esther's reputation was tarnished, but such rumors failed to dim her image among her followers. Regardless of the truth of the stories, they remain fascinating simply because of the manner in which they became fact under the rule of the seventh messenger, Benjamin Purnell. Whether Purnell heard about these practices, learned them from his prophetic mentor, Michael Mills, or simply reenacted an accepted prophetic role is open to conjecture, but it is certain that he did not invent them.

With the death of Esther, a large number of claimants came forward: Edward Rogers, Esther's father; her nephew, young David Rogers, who was actually considered but rejected; and Daniel Milton, who came forward again from the "Sixth Church of Divine Revelation" at Ashton-under-Lyne, but was rejected once more. Another unnamed American formed a "House of Israel and Jacob" and began to circulate a penny publication, *Messenger of Wisdom*, in a bid for support. The most contentious challenge came from the Canadian-born American, Michael Keyfor Mills, whose colony in Detroit was prospering and whose claim to the throne was as legitimate as the others.

Born in Canada in 1857 Mills spent his early life with his grandfather, Thomas Mills, a Baptist minister, and worked as a mechanic before starting his own successful manufacturing company.[17] In 1888 he read Jezreel's *Extracts From the Flying Roll*, let his hair and beard grow, and embarked on a missionary tour with one Eliza Court, a Jezreelite preacher. In 1891 he had a vision that he was "Prince Michael" come to do battle with Satan. He took up Richard Brothers's old regal title and from then on was referred to as "Prince Michael." He gathered about him 150 followers in a "God House" in Detroit where at least part of the Christian Israelite congregation occupied a common lodging. Elias Carpenter, one of Joanna Southcott's most devoted followers, had opened a chapel in London called the "House of God" where he sealed believers and held meetings to study her works. Mills was establishing a similar sanctuary where individuals could be "cleansed" and "justified" as foretold in Daniel 8:14. The colony became both a house of worship and a home for the sealed believers.[18] How Mills attained leadership of the group is unclear, but he was confident enough of his mission to journey to Gillingham, Kent, and to offer himself to the Jezreelite congregation. According to a Detroit newspaper, Mills had gone to England "to make himself known to the following of the Flying

Roll. The English Israelites, however, gave Michael and his band a mighty cool reception and they returned to Detroit about the 21st of February last."[19]

On his return to Detroit, Mills and the Israelites were plunged into controversy. It began when Charles Richardson petitioned the courts to obtain custody of his daughter from her mother, who had taken up residence with the group.[20] Newspaper accounts charged that Mrs. Richardson was actually living as the spiritual wife of a community member, and the ensuing publicity highlighted the colony's existence in Detroit. When the Israelites accompanied Mrs. Richardson to court, they were set upon by a crowd that "hooted at them, [while] others pulled their hair [and] many suggested lynching them."[21] It was reported that thousands of hostile people gathered in front of the colony house on Woodward Avenue to protest and demand a mass meeting of area residents. A committee was formed and met "to mark out a line of conduct and action. . . . That we may hereby check, eradicate and destroy the existing evil in our community and forever cleanse and purify our neighborhood from the foul and disgraceful stain with which it is now afflicted."[22] The main thrust of the protest came from real estate interests and merchants intent on maintaining North Woodward Avenue as a respectable community. "No cranks need apply" was their rallying cry. The committee's chairman pointed out that the area had once been known for its million dollar real estate deal, but now a "certain class of citizens had gone into the business of raising crops of hair." A rallying resolution against the Israelites was passed:

> Whereas certain revolting facts regarding the Prince Michael gang have come to light showing conclusively that the whole establishment is founded upon immorality, and that of the lowest and most loathsome die; and whereas, the permanent existence of the Prince Michael colony on the North Side is the ruination of all property interests therein, a menace to society, therefore be it resolved, that it is the duty of every citizen to discourage in every way possible the settlement in our midst of this lazy, thriftless, sensual class of people, whose whole time is spent in absolute idleness and be it resolved, that any person renting, leasing or selling property on the North Side to any member or agent of the Prince Michael gang shall be looked

upon by the citizens as an enemy to the good name and future prosperity of this most beautiful section of our city.[23]

During the height of the Richardson controversy, Mrs. Mills admitted that she had witnessed her husband in adultery with the Jezreelite preacher, Eliza Court. She was then persuaded to go before a police justice and make two complaints: one charging him with adultery and the other with lewd and lascivious cohabitation. On her complaint, Mills was arrested and jailed; five colony women were also arrested as material witnesses. The subsequent divorce and criminal proceedings produced sensational accounts about the colony in Detroit papers. Because most of the Israelites were British subjects, fifty of them asked the protection of the British consul. They complained they were being "persecuted, mobbed, stoned and thrown into prison." Local police protection was minimal and one petitioner to the consul complained that "while walking out with my brethren Benjamin Purnell and William Owen," he was set upon and beaten. They received threats on their life and a box belonging to Mills containing confidential statements made by his followers ("in accordance with the rules of their church") was stolen from the "God House." In short, like the Israelites before them, they felt they were being persecuted for their religious beliefs, and there was ample evidence to support their claim.[24]

The most damning testimony in the criminal trial against Mills was delivered by three women colonists who charged him with perpetrating immoralities of every kind on female members of the colony. The prosecuting attorney charged that Mills "told [Bernice Bickle, a witness] that he was the son of Man whose special business it was to sow good seed for the purpose of purification. . . . He told her that if she would submit she would never suffer death and would be cleansed from evil."[25] When fourteen-year-old Bernice Bickle took the stand she added sufficient details to the prosecutor's allegations to secure Mills a five-year sentence at the Jackson State Prison on charges of adultery and statutory rape. Years later, similar testimony would be repeated in courtrooms in Grand Rapids and Lansing by women seduced by Benjamin Purnell, but in 1894 it was his prophetic tutor, Michael Mills, who was on the stand.

Bernice Bickle outlined her initiation into the Israelite faith: "Mr. M. K. Mills came to Sarnia with some of his followers, that being my home, and proclaimed to all the Israelites who gathered at my uncle's house that he was Michael, the prince mentioned in Daniel 12:2, they all accepted him. He said he had been cleansed from all evil, and the Lord spoke to him and told him that all Israel must wear their hair down. My mother came home and told me all this. I thought it was a fraud but said nothing."[26] She was sent to Detroit and on her third evening at the New House of Israel she had a visit from the Prince: "I felt tired and went to bed early the next night and after a little while Michael came in and talked what I thought was improper. I was still more surprised when he undressed and got into bed. He told me that Satan sowed the tares, but the Son of Man sows the good seed and that he was the Son of Man and to get evil separated in our bodies through connection which was not carnal in our eyes."[27]

While Mills was serving his sentence, the colony was kept together under Eliza Court's direction. On his release from prison Mills married her, and moved to Windsor, Ontario, and then to England in 1905. From 1905 until his death in 1923, Mills contested for the leadership of the Jezreelites and ownership of the tower. Considered by locals as a crank and crackpot, he died alone and unhonored as a prophet.[28] Like Richard Brothers, he had lost influence and power during his stay in jail, and it was during that period that another "pretender" came forward to claim the prophet's place. Benjamin Purnell, a member since 1892 and one of the four "pillars" of the sect, proclaimed in 1895 that he was "the true seventh messenger and Prince Michael an imposter;" however, he was rejected and expelled from the sect after a power struggle with Eliza Court. Such a rejection had not deterred Zion Ward, George Turner, or Daniel Milton, for that matter, and seven years later Purnell emerged once again as the "true" seventh messenger and head—with Mary Purnell—of the Israelite House of David at Benton Harbor, Michigan.

By the end of the century, the Christian Israelite movement was an Anglo-American movement, with prophets, churches, and publications in contact with both shores. Daniel Milton and James Jezreel were American-born; Milton and Mills ended their prophetic careers in England close to the Wroeite center in Yorkshire. Beyond that, the connections with Australia that John Wroe had forged were destined to play a significant part in the House of David history. The prophetic tradition begun by Brothers and Southcott a century earlier had taken an eccentric path at times and had moved into areas that neither would have recognized as their own; nevertheless they were claimed as both inspiration and source. Each prophet and each sect promised a new key, a new set of revelations, a new dawn. The battle lines between sects and prophets were drawn and redrawn within a common core of history that was open to all new prophets. For example, a prophet now had worldly aspirations and expected to be kept in a style befitting his station; yet the essential character of that role remained unchanged: to lead the elect into the New Jerusalem in anticipation of the millennium. There they would all be saved from the destructive forces of Satan and live purified, immortal lives. They were a community of the elect sustained by a common belief and held together by the force of that belief and the strength of the leader. That bond was further intensified when reinforced by daily contact with other believers, and common residence, and some separation from the world. Such a community developed on the shores of Lake Michigan one hundred years after Joanna Southcott published her *Mystical Sentences* and fifty years after Daniel Milton announced he was the Shiloh. Under the prophetic leadership of Benjamin and Mary Purnell the tradition found new inspiration, new energy. A new compact was once again forged, based on a millennial tradition deeply rooted in Judeo-Christian history, a century of Anglo-Israelite sectarianism, and an American promise that community experimentation was a viable alternative. Between 1903 and 1930, one thousand believers signed the House of David compact in the hope that the prophecies in the Book of Revelation would unfold in their lifetime and that their community in Berrien County, Michigan, was the true site for the ingathering of the elect. Benjamin Purnell's spiritual empire was about to create and sustain its earthly dimension with a skillful blend of evangelism, entertainment, hard work, prayer, and maybe just some sex now and then.

CHAPTER THREE

The Shiloh at Benton Harbor

The trumpet is blowing and we go to the ingathering of
Israel for Benjamin, our leader in Michigan, has spoken.
We believe in the immortality of the body and those that live
with us shall remain unchanged when the end comes, and
the earth is restored to its Eden state.

*Israelite converts departing for Benton Harbor
from England in 1905.*

Photographs taken of Benjamin Purnell at the height of his power
and influence in 1916 show a large—5'9", 200 pounds—man with
flowing hair and a full beard, dressed in white, wearing a broad-
rimmed hat, and sporting a large gold medallion round his neck.
These photographs convey a sense of power, assurance, and
worldliness that marks the man as both prophet and king. A
similar impression radiates from photographs of Purnell's wife,
Mary, whose dress and bearing gave credence to her title, "Queen
of the House of David." There are other photographs of the pair
as well: some taken during the police raid on Purnell's hideout at
the Diamond House in 1927, and others taken during his trial
while he was wasting away with tuberculosis. But during the flower
of his prophecy he was, as the trial judge Louis Fead stated, "a
striking and picturesque figure."[1] An earlier view—dated
sometime around 1900—shows a homelier side of the Purnells,
standing beside their traveling wagon, which had taken them
throughout the lower midwest as itinerant ministers after their
expulsion from a Detroit religious colony.[2] It was this image of the
prophet and his bride that the House of David literature emphasized, with the accent on his lowly origins and preaching career.

Little is known about Benjamin Purnell's early years except that they were far from regal. Born of a poor farm family in Greenup City, Kentucky, on March 27, 1861, he had little schooling. He married young to a local girl, Angeline Brown, on August 22, 1877. After their marriage, she continued to live at home while he began "traveling around," probably preaching. In 1879 a daughter was born to the Purnells, yet he continued to travel and preach, settling for awhile in Richmond, Indiana, where he worked as a broommaker and where he "embraced the faith that was brought about by my reading the *Flying Roll* by Jezreel."[3] He must have been one of the earliest American converts to the Jezreelite creed, though there is no specific indication that he joined any group at this time. He did alter his circumstances a year later when he met Mary Stollard and, as one critic put it, "presently appeared before the justice of the peace in Aberdeen, Ohio, and underwent the odd procedure of formally acknowledging themselves as man and wife."[4] In short, Purnell was a bigamist, though he eventually filed for a divorce from Adaline in Greenup City in 1883. Mary Stollard remained his life-long companion, and her intelligence, sense, and cunning promoted his prophetic career considerably. Two children were born to the Purnell-Stollard union, and both children had tragic deaths that were closely related to their parents' prophetic careers.

Little is known about the Purnell-Stollard pair between 1880 and 1892. It can be reasonably assumed that they led an itinerant existence in the midwest, possibly acting as ministers for the Jezreel gospel because it is during that period that Clarissa Rogers and James Jershom Jezreel visited Michigan and established a number of churches in the area.[5] In January, 1892 the Purnells joined the colony of "Prince" Michael Mills at Detroit, and Benjamin Purnell eventually gained a leadership position within the "New House of Israel." According to the Purnells' own account, spreading the faith in Detroit was both exciting religious work and a time of trial:

During this time there was a great work of preparation going on by crucifixion and suffering. I went through long and hard fastings before traveling; often I went without food for several days. In 1894 I worked and preached hard from one to three times a day in the

Benjamin Purnell as he was often seen at the House of David.

open street, and in the churches and halls, and then never knew where to lay my head at night. . . . We had better success when we simply blew in and went to entertaining them, and they almost always got interested and kept us, and cried when we left.[6]

Purnell's memories of his residence in the Mills colony may, in part, help explain his later flights from the law, since the public outcry surrounding the Mills trial and the vigilante tactics taken against the Israelites could only instill fear and a self-protective attitude in the mind of someone like Purnell, who was to repeat the same pattern that led to the conviction of Prince Michael in 1894. The police, the courts, and the press were all to be distrusted, and Purnell quickly observed that the only safe refuge was in flight.

Yet more important than this signal lesson for the future was the revelation that came to him while in Detroit, as he said, "at the cockcrowing of the morning of the 12th of March, 1895."[7] It was

Mary Purnell as "queen" Mary.

the revelation that he was the seventh messenger, the Shiloh, who had come to supplant the false prophet Mills and lead the Israelites. But he was rejected by the Mills colony, and the prophet took to the road again with Mary and one Carrie Moore who reportedly bore him a child. How long this trio, or quartet, traveled

The Purnells as itinerant preachers before the establishment of the colony in
1903.

together is unclear except that the years between 1895 and 1901
were characterized by his "wanderings" throughout the midwest
as a rejected prophet in search of a mission and congregation.

During the winter of 1899 Benjamin and Mary Purnell
settled in Fostoria, Ohio, and used the homes of two believers,
Silas Mooney and John Pelton, as the bases for their preaching
and proselytizing. According to Pelton, "they [the Purnells] had a
team and wagon and traveled around giving out tracts, taking
freewill offerings for same." While in Fostoria, Purnell completed writing *The Star of Bethlehem*, made up of "old histories and
six messages that had been written by six messengers before him,
of which John Roe [*sic*] was one and Judge Real [*sic*] was
another."[8] The Peltons supplied the $400 needed to have the
tract printed, and were, according to one source, the first full
converts to turn over all their possessions to the seventh messenger. Yet the Purnells' stay in Fostoria was marred by a number
of incidents that turned the townspeople against the preacher.
His relationship with Mrs. Mooney became a public scandal when

they were "caught having sexual intercourse in the berry patch on Mooney's place."[9]

However, it was the accidental death of the Purnells' daughter, Heather, in 1902 which caused greater conflict and resulted in their forced departure from this Ohio town. When Heather was killed in an explosion at a fireworks factory where she worked, the Purnells refused to have anything to do with her body. They claimed that they "would be defiled if they went near her as she had gone to hell and that the dead must bury the dead."[10] This Wroeite practice precluded any expression of sympathy for the dead and was implicit in the Jezreelite belief in man's immortality, for to acknowledge a death was to acknowledge the existence of sin's corrupting influence. This Perfectionist belief was constant in the Southcottian tradition and explicit in the writings of both John Ward and John Wroe. But of course the townspeople of Fostoria failed to support this tradition, and they became so enraged over the Purnells' conduct toward their own daughter that it became impossible for the Purnells to go into the street for fear of being mobbed and they made plans to leave.

Fortunately for them, there was a group of Flying Rollers located near Grand Rapids, Michigan, and when an invitation came in 1902 to join with them the Purnells and the Mooneys decided to move northwest to Michigan. Purnell was now forty-one, and his prophetic career was a distinct failure, since he had repeatedly and unsuccessfully tried to gain a body of followers. Charges of immorality, the hostility of crowds, and constant reversals had not deterred the earlier prophets, and Purnell continued to believe that his chiliastic message would win converts at any moment. Hindsight now tells us that he had, in 1902, the potential to be an erotic messenger in the tradition of John Wroe and James Jezreel. Like them, he had proclaimed his inspiration, published a prophetic book, had an eye for pretty women, and was willing to go wherever and whenever the Spirit called.

The move from Ohio to Michigan proved fortuitous because it provided two important factors necessary for a successful prophetic career: a potential body of believers and some wealthy sponsors. How long the Jezreelites had been in Grand Rapids or how many disciples existed is unknown, although Jezreel's *Extracts* were published in that city in 1879. We do know that two parcels of land were ceded to the new community by local residents during the early years and that the Jezreel-Rogers influence was evident from that period.[11]

Purnell had moved his millennial ingathering to that section of Michigan distinguished for its fruit culture. Johnny Appleseed is credited with the profusion of apple trees there, which grew in a coastal zone tempered by Lake Michigan. Early pioneers had found dewberries, huckleberries, cranberries, and wild grapes and by 1900 that fertile soil was producing bumper crops of berries and peaches for the midwestern market. Although Father Marquette had sailed up the St. Joseph River in 1669 and René Cavelier had established a fort at the mouth of the river in 1700, it was not until 1783 that a trader planted the first domestic cherry and apple trees in the region.[12]

St. Joseph was incorporated as a village in 1836, but some settlers, finding land prices too high, settled east of the river where the town of Bronson Harbor was developing. In 1869 that settlement was incorporated as Benton Harbor. It grew rapidly like many towns of the period and by 1878 had a small business section, which included a general store, hardware store, livery stable, gristmill, and a combined blacksmith and wagon-works shop. The blacksmith and wagon-works shop of Theo J. Baushke figured prominently in the colony history, for his brother and partner, Albert Baushke, provided, according to one source, $100,000 to help sustain the House of David in its early years. Benton Harbor was connected to Chicago by a freight and passenger steamer that made daily runs and by the Chicago and Lake Shore Railroads.[13]

As with all booming towns Benton Harbor had its complement of churches. By 1870 the Baptists, the Congregationalists, Methodists, and Universalists had outposts in Benton Harbor. And before the turn of the century the Catholics and Espiscopalians had built churches. Benton Harbor began to outstrip the population of its neighbor St. Joseph, and by 1904 it had 6,702 residents versus the 5,322 across the river. Berrien County, which at that time was still predominantly rural and agricultural, had a total population of 49,362.[14] Although there was considerable competition between the two cities, there was a mutual need for increased commercial activity in the area, so the towns boosted one another rather than forcefully competing for trade. Fruit had been shipped from the area as early as 1840, but not until after 1880 did fruit-growing dominate the economy. Improved rail and lake transportation and the establishment of canneries made it possible to emphasize fruit cultivation.

By the time the Purnells arrived in Benton Harbor three million crates of fruit were being shipped out of the area annually. There were several summer resorts and hotels with extensive grounds which attracted visitors from Chicago and Milwaukee. Up until the arrival of the Israelites in 1903 the most distinguished local figure was Ben King, a poet and musician, noted for his humorous verses. The town built a public library in 1903, a public hospital in 1905, and Benton Harbor was well on the way toward creating a substantial history of its own. The Israelites moved into a booming town that had by virtue of its location, climate, and entrepreneurship established itself as "the center of lake commerce on the eastern shore of Lake Michigan."[15]

Michigan had never been known for its communal societies though it has had several. The Alphadelphian Association was founded as a Fourierist phalanx in July, 1844 by a group of Universalist ministers and editors. Through the pages of a Universalist paper, *The Primitive Expounder*, edited at Ann Arbor, the group promoted a socialistic colony in Kalamazoo County. In December, 1843 fifty-six interested parties met at Clark's Lake in Jackson County after they had read a call for the meeting in *The Primitive Expounder*. They drew up some preliminary plans, adopted a constitution, and chose a committee to examine some sites. The committee chose a 2,814-acre site, near Galesburg on the Kalamazoo River, in Comstock Township. Fifty-one heads of families signed the constitution of the Alphadelphia, or First Brother, Industrial Association. This joint stock venture lasted from July 23, 1844 to May 2, 1848. The group published a paper, *The Alphadelphian Tocsin*, farmed, and quarreled a good deal. At one point they contemplated a merger with the Integral Phalanx in Sangamon County, Illinois, but nothing came of it. The lead-

ing figure at Alphadelphia, Dr. Henry B. Schetterly, left in 1846
and subsequently joined the LaGrange Phalanx in Indiana, then
moved on to the Wisconsin Phalanx at Ripon, Wisconsin.[16]

The Hiawatha Valley Association was founded in 1893 on a
site eighteen miles north of Manistique. Inspired by the writings
of Walter Thomas Mills, a group of socialists tried to emulate his
plan for a cooperative colony outlined in his book, *The Product
Sharing Village*. Walter Byers, a local farmer, wrote to Mills and
offered to deed his farm for the experiment. Mills responded
enthusiastically to the idea, and, in fact, his mother, three
brothers, and two sisters came to the colony from Iowa. Like
other colonists before them, they issued a newspaper, *The Industrial Christian*, to propagate their philosophy: "Let us inaugurate
a system that will make it more honorable for the jockey to trade
off his ideas for a better one, instead of trading off his old horses
for better ones. Let every man, woman, and child use his or her
strongest energy in defending, in spreading, and in perpetuating
the ideas and workings of product sharing already begun here."[17]

The group had a sawmill, a dairy, a shoe shop, and a printing
establishment. But they were too remote from their markets and
by the end of 1895 the colony broke up. During the winter of
1895–96 there were still some fifteen families at the site, but the
Mills family had moved away and the group had abandoned their
time-credit labor scheme. The ones who remained had donated
land to the venture.

In 1897 a holiness religious colony was founded at Grosse
Pointe by the Reverend B. Middlekauf. The *Detroit Evening News*
carried conflicting reports about the group. One news story cited
a member who believed he was Jesus Christ while another story
indicated the group was running a training school for missionaries.[18] Little else is known about the colony. Another possible
group with an equally obscure history is the Gibsonville Altruistic
Community at Grand Blanc. Gibson was a graduate of the University of Michigan and was elected to the State Senate in 1894.
There are isolated references to Gibson's 1897 planned community of homes, but little else.[19] These groups predate the
House of David, and there may have been others. The Sunrise
Community at Alicia was started after the fall of the House of
David, and several cooperative societies were started in the
1920s.[20] The Israelites at Benton Harbor were, however, the

largest and certainly the most flamboyant communal and co-operative group in Michigan history.

The House of David promised more to its followers and demanded more of them in faith and commitment. Purnell's message was essentially the same as that of his predecessors: he was preparing a place for the "executive rulers of the earth, called the elect 144,000. . . ; and the mysterious mysteries must be unsealed and revealed to them; and they must gather for the work and fulfill the scriptures."[21] He saw himself as the Ishi-husband (the Christ or creator husband), the seventh messenger who had come to open the seventh seal and prepare the ingathering place for the Israelites. He was the Shiloh, a term drawn from Genesis 49:10: "The sceptre shall not depart from Judah nor a lawgiver from between his feet, until Shiloh come, and unto him shall the gathering of the people be." There were conflicting interpretations about the exact meaning of the phrase and the wording of the passage, but it is clear that eighteenth- and nineteenth-century opinion, as reflected in Cruden's *Concordance*, believed that the term Shiloh was "one of the glorious names of the Messiah."[22] The Messiah's coming was central to the Judaic tradition, and his second coming an integral part of Christian eschatology. In England a tradition developed that the Shiloh would come first to that land to gather in the faithful there, but it was Purnell's belief, of course, that "upon closer examination and by the spirit of the word, and by rightly divining that Michigan is highly favored with these blessings and ought to rejoice with all Israel."[23] He thereby transferred the traditional seat of Anglo-Israelite hope from an island with a long history of New Jerusalem expectations to a peninsular state in a nation steeped in Zion's promise.

Drawing on a number of Biblical sources, in particular the prophetic books, Purnell developed his truths into a millennial message that served as a religious magnet for the House of David. He gave the dates of the ingathering, the coming of the Shiloh, and other important events with the great precision and surety central to the prophetic tradition, for no one notices or believes a hesitant messenger. For Purnell, the important dates were 1792 (when Joanna Southcott's prophecy began); 1861 (his birth date); 1902 (the publication of *The Star of Bethlehem*); 1905 (the date for the millennium); 1907 and 1916 (later, revised dates for the millenium). His preferred New Testament sources were the books of James and John, slighting Matthew, Mark, and Luke possibly because their names failed to resound with the prophetic letter *J*. His only source was the writings of Jezreel.

Purnell's writings are a mixture of conventional prophetic exegesis and a rambling numerology wherein diverse sources (usually from *J*) reinforce the central message: that the Shiloh has come in the person of Benjamin Purnell. The following is an example of the compressed and curiously logical style that won him converts in such large numbers; the first John mentioned in the passage is the apostle, the last James is Jezreel:

> John said, from the time the women [*sic*] set her hand to write [1792] within 70 years the spirit of life shall possess the temple, which brings it to the birth of Mary and Benjamin, 1861 and 1862, and thirty years brings 1891, and three makes 1894. And in 1895 the branch was grafted he announced his Shiloh-hood that year and twelve brings 1907. James ends his mission in 1885 and thirty years brings 1915.[24]

This form of writing was clearly aimed at Christians steeped in the prophetic tradition and, more directly, at the large body of Southcottian believers for whom the struggles within the movement had some meaning.[25]

Purnell promised—and this was central to his appeal—that his followers could attain immortality of the body through good works, both physical and spiritual. From Jezreel's stronghold in the south of England in Kent to the north of the United States in Michigan may seem a long journey, but Zion's highway was a short path for all believers because it led to immortality. Immortality was a cornerstone of Jezreel's theology and, if newspaper reports can be trusted, an integral part of both his and Mills's plan for religious and sexual seduction. What these prophets promised their followers was the security of being part of the ingathering and the assurance that they would be helping to usher in the prophecies laid out in earlier periods. They would be fellow travelers on an immortal mission led and directed by a divinely inspired leader. Members and leaders entered into a compact that outsiders saw as bizarre and corrupt, but for the believers it had its own necessary logic.

In Book 2 of *The Star of Bethlehem*, Purnell stated that "the best wine and bread which comes down from heaven is the seed of the immortal women, or the mother through the mortal; it will give him the immortal life and thus raise him from mortal to immortal and set him back where she found him."[26] In short, all men could attain God-like immortality. In another passage there is the specific promise that "they who now enter into and keep the marriage covenant in these 1335 days of Daniel shall receive immortality."[27] Good works alone were insufficient to achieve this state; a believer's blood had to be "purified" of evil traces placed there and inherited through Adam's original sin. This purification could be accomplished by keeping the "virgin law," or total abstinence from sexual activity. The law applied to everyone, even married couples who entered the colony, and, in theory, the Purnells were bound by it. The virgin law was based on the belief that Adam and Eve were, in the beginning, without sin (evil) and that evil was communicated to Eve by sexual intercourse with the devil serpent (called Gadreal, who was, according to the House of David version, black); therefore, through intercourse with Eve, Adam's blood and that of his descendants became tainted.[28] Only abstinence from sexual intercourse could thereafter cleanse the blood and purify it of its evil elements. When that occurred, the body would then live through a thousand-year millennium.[29]

The Israelites, like the Shakers before them, combined elements of premillennial and postmillennial thinking in their social and sexual program. They were premillennialist in their insistence that an event (the destruction of the earth) would occur, but postmillennial in their faith that Purnell was ushering in a new system for salvation. One did not have to wait until after the destructive event; one could begin working toward perfection upon entry into the society. Celibacy was the key to personal immortality: "If you partake of the tree [woman] for the purpose of bringing forth children after being called to the visitation [ingathering] is it not sin, and the child is born in sin because it is brought forth with the tares or seeds of Satan. The enemy who sowed the tares in the field which is in its blood from your body."[30] This was the doctrine of the prophet who was to be accused of having sexual relations with a believer in the berry patch. Not surprisingly, members would eventually find that a double standard existed and was, in fact, implicit in the spiritual hierarchy that existed at the colony.

According to Purnell, the membership at the House of David could achieve the highest state of perfection—immortality —only by first passing through four stages. The first stage, the condition of mankind since the Fall, found man with evil in his blood from Eve, through her encounter with the serpent; the second stage existed when the new members, after entering the society, had their blood slowly cleansed and became "sons of God"; the third, when they were "without blood" and were sustained by an immortal life-giving spirit within them; during the fourth stage they became "God-men" at the beginning of their personal millennium. All new members were at the first stage when they entered the community, while Purnell was already at stage three and was preparing the way for the fourth stage—the ingathering—at Benton Harbor. The work of the ingathering, or the collecting of the elect 144,000, was the colony's primary purpose; all its social, economic, and religious activities were directed toward that end. On joining the colony, new members usually turned over their life savings, then worked long hours without pay, and in complete obedience to the Purnells. For some, the promises of immortal life were so seduc-tive and their faith in the prophet so strong that they perjured themselves in order to protect their leader and law-giver from the ravages of this earthly kingdom.[31]

Who were these obedient followers of the Purnells? Where did the members of the colony come from, and what did they expect to find? Because of elaborate court testimony during the trials in the 1920s and intensive interviewing by prosecuting officials preparing the case against Purnell, there is a large body of material, albeit slanted, about the aspirations and expectations that led many to this strange Biblical community.[32] In fact, the only substantive biographic sources for the colony membership are in George Nichols's Trial Notes (see Appendix C). In prepar-ing for the trial he collected voluminous information about the internal affairs of the colony. Through his informants he was able to piece together a series of family biographies, families who had "been broken and scattered through the faith." Within this history of family disintegration there is valuable information about individual motivations for joining the colony, reasons why members left, and details of the colony's social life. These sketches tell us something about the dark and autocratic nature of Purnell's leadership, the cruel and often demeaning demands he made of his followers, and the agony he caused some believers. What they fail to tell us is the attraction of the ingathering, the religious disquiet in the members' lives that turned them toward the Shiloh and Benton Harbor, and finally, their private hopes when they joined.

We are forced to read between the lines of court records and from biographic sketches which were wrested from various sources by a prosecuting attorney's investigators—investigators who, we may presume, had little understanding of or sympathy with the religious eccentricities of the Israelites. Because of the recent events at Jonestown and the charges made against Synanon and the Children of God communes we strain to understand what motivates and drives individuals to join such a cult, to divorce themselves from society, to journey to a new place and reject the old. Unless we grapple with those questions and come to understand the historical patterns and internal logic of such groups, they will remain ciphers, isolated aberrations that appear and disappear with hardly a ripple, except for the experiences felt by the members themselves.

Those who came to the Israelite House of David can be divided into three groups: a small core of believers who joined in the early days at Benton Harbor; the Wroeite converts who came from Australia in 1905; and those millennialists (most native-born Americans) who came between 1905 and 1917 and who believed in the Shiloh myth and the ingathering.

The first group knew the Purnells personally and, touched by their preaching and tracts, joined with them. An original party consisting of the Purnells, Silas and Cora Mooney, Joseph Fowler, John Snyder, and Charles E. Norris all came to Benton Harbor in April, 1902. This group of believers lived in what was known as the Red House on Superior Street. Several local families—the Baushkes, Schultzes, and Dribsteins—were joined by a large group from California led by Mary McDermott, a Jezreelite minister, to constitute the core membership. McDermott had left her home and family to join the Israelites, and in the early years she acted as the colony press agent and "advance agent of the millennium." M. S. Tyler, Thomas Adkins,

J. D. Tucker, and Edwin Johnson all came to the colony from southern California in 1903. One area resident, George Shoemaker of South Bend, joined in 1903 after hearing Purnell preach: "Struck deeply by his philosophy I became an advocate and attended his meetings every Sunday at Benton Harbor going to and from the latter place by rail. I thoroughly believed in the institution as depicted to me and in the original pact which I signed; but as time past it was seen that Benjamin and his ruling powers were not living in obedience to the written law of the sect."[33] Individuals like Shoemaker constituted the nucleus of "The Israelite House of David, the New Eve, the Body of Christ," which was formally incorporated as a "religious ecclesiastical organization" on May 3, 1903.

Under the "objects and purposes" section of their incorporation, the founders listed only broad religious purposes and made no mention of their peculiar practices or expectations about the millennium.[34] The original legal charter would have to be amended frequently in the future, but the 1903 articles simply registered the colony as another sect and allowed it to "print, publish, and distribute books" as well as "receive gifts and donations." Gifts and donations, particularly from Albert Baushke, a wealthy Benton Harbor carriage maker, enabled Purnell to establish the foundations of the colony.[35]

Upon entering the society, members were required to give up "all they possess," and demonstrate that they had read the divine messages given by "the messengers known as Benjamin and Mary" and that they were prepared to give up any "unnecessary visiting and gossiping among the Gentiles, and those not in the faith."[36] Between 1903 and 1907 over 300 individuals followed these simple requirements and came to Benton Harbor, signing over their property and themselves to the Purnells' vision of the New Jerusalem.

Although the quota of potential members was considerable, the membership was restricted and a careful screening process instituted for prospective joiners. After an initial inquiry was received, various devotional tracts and a copy of the pamphlet, *Shiloh's Messenger*, were sent with the suggestion that interested parties should subscribe to the monthly paper, *Shiloh's Messenger of Wisdom*. Following that, correspondents were advised to obtain *The Seven Books of Wisdom* so they could advance in understanding the faith. When individuals finally made an application they were sent a questionnaire asking about their wealth, personal property, and family relations.[37]

The following reminiscence of an entry into the community in 1914 is typical for native American members:

> In January, 1914, we [the Humphreys family] were all living in Fayetteville, North Carolina and were working for a packing house and butcher. My husband came home one evening and said he had met a minister who preached a new faith and who was going to preach again in the evening on "Where Did Cain Get His Wife" and after he heard him preach he brought this book home and also the *Book of Wisdom* and began talking it over with me. We read the books and then wrote to the House of David and had some correspondence with them and sent us some blanks to fill out which asked our ages and about our property. At that time we owned a thirty-five acre farm located in Bladen County. We were interested in what they wrote about the ingathering and we also believed we were in the wrong business and so we quit the butchering. We had a long letter from the House of David advising us to keep our counsel and not tell anyone what we were planning to do as someone might think we were insane and might even have a guardian appointed for us.[38]

The Humphreys did come and stayed for several years before leaving in disillusionment.

From 1903 to 1907 the community recruited members from Michigan and other areas of the United States and also overseas, particularly England and Australia. Harry Williams arrived in this early period and had his first contacts with itinerant ministers, as his later testimony indicates:

> Q.   How did you come to join the society? Who solicited you?
>
> A.   Charles Norris, Edgar and Charlie Dissen. I came to the colony at one of their afternoon meetings; had heard of the sect; read one of their papers, made me feel as though I wanted to see them, being religiously inclined; I argued with them all afternoon.
>
> Q.   What representations did they make to you?
>
> A.   That they were living as one family on the Apostolic plan. That was the only place to make eternal life; they represented that I would live forever; that this was the only place to get eternal life.[39]

It was during this period that representatives from Benton Harbor journeyed to England and Australia to try to pick up the varied fragments left by the six messengers.[40] In 1905 Mary and Benjamin Purnell made a trip to Australia to win the Australian Wroeites for the Michigan colony. Of the 207 members entering the House of David colony between 1903 and 1907, eighty-five came from the Wroe church at Melbourne, Australia. The Wroeites had received "the works of Benjamin" earlier in 1904, and fourteen members had cabled their acceptance of him as the seventh messenger. According to one account, Purnell dramatically arrived at the congregation during a midnight service and converted a large number on the spot. Several large families—the Bulleys, the McFarlanes, and the Tulks—migrated in the first group from Australia in February, 1905. They brought with them over $100,000, and were steadfast in their allegiance to the prophetic pair. The trip back from Melbourne was not without incident: some later charged that Purnell had debauched several women and had stolen funds on the boat, but the religious band made the passage safely to Lake Michigan without any serious defections.[41] A smaller group followed the first contingent, and by the end of 1905 the Wroeites constituted a full third of the total membership for the period.

Although the Wroeite group from Australia came the greatest distance for the ingathering, they were closest to the "historical" Shiloh, that ever-changing prophet who had taken on so many forms since emerging from the fantasies of Joanna Southcott and Richard Brothers. For them the Shiloh was an idea whose time had come in the form of Benjamin Purnell. Their arrival in Benton Harbor was the logical conclusion of a religious heritage that had been planted in Sydney, Australia in 1843, 1850, 1853, 1859, and 1863 after each one of John Wroe's visits to Australia. In 1850 he had been reported in the *Melbourne Argus* predicting that Australia would "occupy a distinguished position in opening up the way for a gathering of the elect on the advent of the millennium."[42] In 1853 the first "Israelite Sanctuary" was built in Sydney, the work of Wroeite preachers from England who had migrated to New South Wales several years before Wroe's first visit.

When the Wroeites arrived in the United States they were distinguished by their dress. The men wore flat-topped hats and corduroy clothes and the women wore "peculiar shaped" sun bonnets of colored grasses. The Wroeites rejected the mixturing of fabrics in clothing because such combining symbolized the commingling of good and evil that constitutes imperfect man, and they never wore black, the symbol of death. For the perfected 144,000 such clothes were for unregenerate men. As a group the Australians were older than their American counterparts, and despite their age and long association with the Israelite tradition they believed themselves behind the Benton Harbor

Benton Harbor Herald-Palladium

Arrival in Benton Harbor of the Australian Wroeites, 1905.

Israelites in holiness: "We are not so far advanced as the Benton Harbor branch. We obtained a dispensation from the fifth angel or messenger, John Wroe. As soon as Mary and Benjamin came to us we recognized they were possessed of divine power and we left all to follow them."[43]

William Bulley was the leader of the Australians. He was seventy years old and had been an Israelite since 1851. "I went to Australia with nothing but my grip in my hands sixty years ago and have seen the movement grow."[44] For Bulley the Israelites were a growing and living church, and the appearance of Mary and Benjamin Purnell in 1905 only confirmed his faith. He brought to the colony his wife, two sons, four daughters, and their wives, husbands, and children. There were twenty-three Bulleys in all.

The Bulleys and the rest of the group had come to Benton Harbor by way of Suez, England, and New York. When their special train rolled into Benton Harbor from Detroit it was festooned with banners, which announced the "Israelites From Australia, Bound For the Ingathering at Benton Harbor, Michigan." They were met at the railroad station in Benton Harbor by the American Israelites, and these two branches of the Southcottian church paraded through the streets to the House of David. One reporter who covered their arrival wrote: "An amazing feature of the Australian incursion was that they were found to possess all the salient characteristics and beliefs of the American Flying Rollers, or 'Israelites' as they call themselves. Some of these characteristics are long hair, vegetarianism, celibacy, and race suicide."[45]

By race suicide the reporter meant their belief that celibacy was a characteristic of the elect 144,000. According to an Australian Israelite:

> It is easy to see how different is this from the race suicide condemned by your great president. In the first place we hold that after the end of the present order, which event is to take place in 1916, it will be found that it would not have made much difference whether the present inhabitants of the world had practiced race suicide or not, provided the race suicide had been accomplished. For with the inauguration of the millennium, under the glorious rule of Christ, there will be a transformation of the human body that will render it immortal. By the exercise of his divine power at his second coming the Christ will cause the blood in our bodies to become transformed into spirit.[46]

They were premillennialist in their expectations; yet embodied much of the assurance which characterized postmillennial groups. They were waiting for the millennium in 1916, but had found a ready faith and system of belief in the Anglo-

Israelite tradition. Like many other successful communal groups they were intermillennial:

> It is our belief that when Christ inaugurates in 1916 his glorious reign of the millennium he will find here on earth, but especially in Benton Harbor's House of David, the Israelite remnant described in the book of David as the 144,000 that shall constitute the elect. There because they have faithfully awaited his second coming and they shall rule jointly with the Redeemer until the millennium ends with the destruction of the earth. Then they shall ascend with Christ into heaven where, because of their Christ-like and perfect bodies, they shall sit nearest to the heavenly throne and be greater than the angels even as in the Scriptures Christ himself is said to be greater than all the host of angels and seraphs and cherubims.[47]

Such was the faith that they brought to America, and it was little wonder that they unquestioningly accepted Purnell's leadership once in this foreign land. They were initially pleased with what they saw at Benton Harbor. After arriving at the colony they toured the community and then sat down to a vegetarian meal which featured eighteen different kinds of vegetables. Such a bountiful spread had come from colony fields and for some was the last sumptuous meal the Purnells would provide.[48]

Benjamin and Mary Purnell had journeyed back from Australia with them and presided over the festivities welcoming them to the gathering-in site. He wore his white flannel suit with matching white canvas shoes. In his shirt front he sported a topaz stone along with other jewelry that made "a great display." He preached to the new arrivals that: "Like the waters that cover the sea, our faith will cover the world." Mary Purnell told them they were "reincarnated angels." A reporter covering the arrival of the Israelites dwelt at some length on the physical magnetism of the pair and their imposing self-assuredness:

> Benjamin is of medium height, rather slenderly built and has an extremely fine face. His hair is of light reddish brown and hangs down on his shoulders in long silken curls. His beard is silken and curly and his features aquiline and well formed. His complexion is clear, pink and white, and his eyes are blue and clear. His manner is

gentle and well bred. His hands are white. *Every movement is as of a man at peace with himself and the whole world.* He teaches and preaches gentleness and peacefulness and he impressed his personality upon all whom he comes in contact with. He undoubtedly has a wonderful influence over men, for his followers listen to his voice, as though it were the voice of the deity. They eagerly drink in every word he says and believe implicitly that he has been sent to lead the world into the millennial period.[49]

Purnell was depicted in the colony literature as the good shepherd, as Jesus meek and mild. Mary Stollard was no less a leader, but occupied a secondary role in the colony. She was described in the press as "a slender woman, with jet black hair, an aquiline nose, snappy black eyes, and an aggressive wide-awake manner. She is a nervous little woman and bears the weight of her duties easily. She shares with her husband all the honors attached to his position and is his constant helpmate. She wears her hair down the back, never uses a hairpin, and attires herself in calico except on Sunday when she dresses well." The other Benton Harbor Israelites also struck a handsome pose: "There are many other believers in the faith in the house on Superior Street. There is one young woman whose red hair hangs down her back like a curtain of flame and there are several men with hair hanging about their shoulders. Many of the men are both handsome and distinguished in appearance."[50]

What the Wroeites came to was a prosperous and established colony consisting of 281 acres of farmland plus an additional 365 acres they rented. But the Australians had skills in practical trades that contributed to the maintenance of the colony: "All classes of trades were represented among the Australians, including tailors, linotype operators, and a French cook."[51]

Those who came into the House of David were not all wealthy by any means; one community estimate suggested that perhaps as much as 70 percent had "little or no wealth on joining," yet there was a clear emphasis on property holdings and assets in the forms sent out to prospective members.[52] The first conflict surrounding the colony came in 1905 when Mrs. Jane Leith wanted to give her property to the colony and sued her husband for her share. The *Benton Harbor News-Palladium* noted that the "followers of this angel pair are growing in numbers in this section of the state."[53] Mrs. Leith died shortly after her entry into the colony, and when her son wanted her funds returned Purnell did so. Much of the colony's wealth was created by industry, shrewd management, and the dedicated labor of the believers. They had a flair for business enterprise and were—like the Jezreelites before them—convinced of the righteousness of their mission.

But the task at hand in 1905 was to gather-in converts, and after the success of the Australian trip another team set out for England to search for the lost tribe in the homeland. Compared with the Australian expedition this venture had to be considered a failure, returning with only thirteen new converts. Mary Bryson, one of the early English converts, commented on the promises offered by the two Finsbury-based evangelists: "They [James Tucker and Charles Norris] made representations that this was the last messenger sent by God to gather in the elect and if I did not obey the call and come to London when I was called I would not get a chance again; and I could not remain long in London because London was going down in the water in sixty days and if we wanted to save our lives we would have to come over to the Ark; the Ark was in America."[54] The "Ark" was, of course, the colony at Benton Harbor—a sanctuary and a refuge. She came to the Ark and stayed for fifteen years, leaving in 1920 only because she felt overworked, though her faith was still sure. She had paid her own way to Benton Harbor since community agents had encouraged only those who could afford their own passage and were capable of hard work. Assumedly the elect 144,000 were true Puritans.

Another English colonist, Mary Chew, expected the colony to enter into its millennial phase quite soon, in fact, in the year 1906: "In the month of September, 1905," she wrote,

James Tucker and Charles Norris, representatives of Benjamin and Mary went to them [possibly a Southcottian group] at Southport, England, and solicited them to go to Benton Harbor and join the colony. James Tucker told them that the world was coming to an end in 1906 and that they would have to be in Benton Harbor at the time or they would be destroyed, as all that believed in the "Star of Bethlehem" must be at Benton Harbor before June 22, 1906, as the world was coming to an end on that date, and if they were not there and members of the colony they would be destroyed.[55]

When Mary Chew entered the colony she and others were initially granted special privileges and made to feel that the community would provide for them in bountiful fashion. Extra provisions were furnished and special attention directed toward new arrivals, though such attention failed to continue in most cases. Initially, members felt that they had established a haven for themselves from a threatened world; with the colony's prosperity over the years that security was enhanced. Hilda Pritchard Achterberg later remembered her initial contact with the colony: "The band was playing, and Benjamin came walking toward us all dressed in white. I thought I was entering paradise when we went through the archway."[56] The Humphrey family also remembered their first morning at Benton Harbor in heavenly terms: "We were awakened by the singing of birds, and the place was so lovely we felt we had reached a happy home."[57] They eventually left that happy home; yet they had brought with them a high sense of anticipation, both religious and social, and those expectations were sustained over a considerable period.

One member from Australia, Isabella Pritchard, told her story to an interested writer after she left the House of David, and her experiences can be found in her rare autobiography, *Echoes of Life*. She was born at Collingwood, Australia, in 1857 and raised in a pious Baptist family. At eighteen she was apprenticed to a dressmaker and in 1881 married. According to her own story she could not have been happier with her four children, her small cottage, and a loving husband. But then she came in contact with the Israelites:

I first heard of the House of David through a friend who came to my home in Collingwood. She brought a small handbill on which the announcement was printed that the Israelites were to hold a meeting at the Fitzroy Town Hall the following Sunday evening [in 1904]. My friend and I conversed regarding the affair. Our curiosity was aroused and we decided to attend the meeting. The handbill announced "Israelites From America." As you know that which hails from afar has an unexplained appeal.[58]

Her initial impression of the Israelites in that meeting reveals much about their appeal to potential converts:

In front of the Fitzroy Town Hall I first saw the Israelites. They were the members of the band, which was engaged at the moment of our arrival, playing sacred airs. These men were from the John Wroe Church in Australia which is like the House of David. They had been coaxed from their order to join the forces of Benjamin. I noticed their flowing beards and hair. It reminded me of the Christ and caused my mind to be deeply impressed. The religious music, of course, played a part, but it was chiefly that their appearance was similar to that of the Blessed Master.

The hall was crowded, and the meeting could truly be described as wonderful. It was soul-inspiring. Of such a nature that any mortal who possessed the least knowledge of the Divine Love, would be touched. Benjamin and Mary Purnell were there. This happened in the year 1904. One year previous to the date of my husband's death.[59]

This was the first of many great gatherings sponsored by the Purnells. They rented a hall over a music shop and held regular meetings for several months. Isabella was converted to the Israelite faith. She wrote that she had tears in her eyes when the more than eighty Wroeites sailed to America with the Purnells for the ingathering at Benton Harbor. She was mesmerized by the Purnells, by the music, by the meetings, and by the presence of these Christ-like figures, but she remained in Australia with her family. But when she was soon ripped from the secure moorings of her domestic life by her husband's death, she then turned toward Benton Harbor and the Shiloh: "My husband passed away shortly after the departure of the Israelites, and I could not think of a better life for a widow, than that of living as a true Christian. The religious colony represented the spot where it seemed possible to live the ideal life, therefore I obeyed orders, sold my house, and with my children went to reside at the home of Mrs. Andrew Bell of North Fitzroy."[60]

Isabella took part of the proceeds from the sale of her home to conduct Israelite meetings and secure additional recruits for the American colony. For six months she labored for the Australian Israelites before receiving a call from America to join the

House of David. By the time of her departure she was a committed believer. Not only did she, her four daughters, and the Bell family come to the new Eden, but they brought along a kangaroo, a wallaby, and some birds for the House of David Zoological Garden. Pritchard paid all the boat, rail, and freight charges for both women and beasts. When the group did arrive in Benton Harbor it was greeted by a band: "It was during the morning of February 22, 1906 that our party arrived in Benton Harbor. A vanguard of Israelites met us at the station. They had provided what was termed 'preachers wagons' to convey us from the railroad station to the colony headquarters. The House of David band marched ahead of the vehicles in which we rode, and we formed quite a parade through the streets of the city on our way to the Israelite house."[61]

When they reached the colony site she was "entranced by the natural beauty." Jerusalem, a dwelling house, was being constructed, and the only major buildings standing were the Ark and Bethlehem, also dwelling houses. After her long and arduous trip halfway around the world she found the colony a serene and peaceful place. "The members of the cult were extremely friendly and it seemed from the quiet air about the place that it was truly the ideal attained, where religious cults were concerned. During the first evening at the colony we attended meetings, where Benjamin Purnell and his wife, Mary, spoke, and again we were deeply impressed."

She was then asked to make a confession of her life wherein "not one thing is to be withheld." Confessions were taken on entry and were required monthly thereafter. They were deposited in a box in the colony headquarters, and only Benjamin and Mary Purnell were supposed to read them, but the seven female "sweepers," or disciplinarians, had access to them. The standard confession form had a statement at the top: "I confess before the God of the Living and his people that I have sinned in word, thought, and deed." Purnell was known to read confessions about sexual matters to young women and, according to Pritchard, "when brothers who strive to live in the faith admit that they are guilty of certain self-abuse . . . these confessions are read before FAVORITES of the House, including young girls who are ordered to shun the offending member."[62]

Isabella and her daughters lived in peace in Benton Harbor for eight months. Their first inkling that anything was wrong in paradise came when they overheard Coy Purnell, Benjamin's son, making advances to a neighbor's daughter. According to colony rules Pritchard was supposed to report such activity (any personal items kept from the leadership were called "hidden leaven"). She went to Mary Purnell to tell her about Coy's wayward ways. She was cautioned by Mary never to divulge any such information to Benjamin, explaining that "Benjamin had no use for Coy, his son." But her report somehow reached the Shiloh, and the girl and her family were sent to a nearby farm, while Pritchard, for her part in this affair, was moved with her children to another farm where about forty members lived. They remained there until the colony amusement park, called Eden

Benjamin Purnell poses, right, with one of the two miniature trains in Eden Springs, the colony's amusement park.

Springs Park, opened in 1908, to which the entire family was sent to work. The girls played in the orchestra, and Isabella Pritchard worked at a souvenir stand near the bowling alley in the amusement park, where she sold violins, ukuleles, beads, fancy wire work, pennants, picture post cards, and other trinkets.

The centerpiece in the House of David's business enterprises at Benton Harbor was Eden Springs Park. It contained a variety of delights, including a mineral spring, a fish pond, a miniature railroad, a menagerie of birds and animals, and a small

lake. In the Wroeite and Jezreelite tradition it instructed while it
entertained: "refreshment parlors . . . besides clean and whole-
some entertainment consisting of original dialogues and
speeches explaining the faith of Israel, also instrumental and
vocal solos and duets, and band concerts by one or more of the
five bands in the Israelite House of David."[63] The park was also a
lucrative business; during her last season at the souvenir stand,
Isabella Pritchard estimated that the stand took in $3,000, and it
was just one of several on the amusement park grounds. Receipts
were collected daily by colony officers accompanied by special
deputy sheriffs. In its early years the colony banked only a small
portion of their earnings, keeping most in the colony safe, because they did not want the "Gentiles" (the public) to know how
much money had been earned. Benjamin and Mary often
strolled about the grounds and must have been prime tourist
attractions in their own right.

    Although the summers were a busy time for the colonists the
winters were long and sometimes hard. To relieve the boredom
of a Michigan winter pageants were performed in which Mary
and Benjamin took the lead. In one production he played the
"Prince of Peace" and Mary was the "Madonna" who held a small
baby in her lap. He was the celibate Christ and she the virgin
mother. Isabella Pritchard thought the pair "formed beautiful
living pictures." In another theatrical production—one probably
performed for visitors to the park—four characters, a professor,
a Jew, the Israelites, and John Wroe engaged in a dialogue. Part
of the play emphasized Purnell's ascendancy as a true prophet:
"It's true, John was once a bright and burning light, a great
prophet, but his light was as the sun going down and left them as
blind men groping in a dark cellar without light."[64] From the few
members' accounts that we have there emerges a common per-
ception of the Purnells held by the membership. They were seen
as handsome, regal, and gentle. A post card sold by the colonists
catches some of those qualities. It portrays a flock of sheep
grazing peacefully by a stream, being watched over by Benjamin
with a shepherd's staff in his hand. He resembles Jesus, the Good
Shepherd tending his flock. The colonists at Benton Harbor
believed that they were part of a special flock, that their shepherd
and shepherdess were divinely appointed, that they had arrived

Colony postcard depicting Purnell as a shepherd tending his flock.

at the banks of the River Jordan to await the millennium, and that they were drinking the waters of eternal life. At one of these midwinter pageants Purnell worked a water and wine miracle for his followers that had them further convinced of his messianic mission. In this tableaux Purnell was Jesus once again and had his favorite disciples gathered about him: "They were dressed even as the men in the time of the 'Holy One.' Glasses were brought, also a pitcher from which Benjamin began to pour water into the glasses. Many of the members marvelled at what had taken place but my eyes [Mrs. Pritchard's] were partial open. The liquid changed color in the glasses a chemical having been previously placed in them. Still many of the Israelites believed that Benjamin had performed a miracle."[65]

Individuals and families came into what were, in reality, separate communities. First, there was the millennialist organization chartered under the laws of Michigan and founded within a tradition that had roots in England, Australia, and America. Converts from the John Wroe church in Melbourne and native

Americans converted to the faith had clear expectations about
the Biblical commonwealth they entered, and many lived fully
satisfied lives in that expectation. Second, there was the "notor-
ious" House of David, which burst into full view during the
1920s, filling Michigan newspapers with lurid stories about
seduction, abduction, and fraud. Throughout the first twenty
years of the colony's existence, there were hints in the press and
courts about disreputable activities at the settlement. Even more
startling to the outsider was the revelation that many members
actually never knew about King Ben's exploits. These individuals
lived a sober community life, embracing the Israelite faith and
working to bring in the millennium. Therefore, it is important to
keep in mind two communities: one, abstinent, religious, and
simple in habits; the other, luxurious, scented with scandal, and
fascinating in its complexity and success. Where the two societies
crossed over and how they mixed is impossible to tell, and until
additional sources become available certain relationships—both
social and personal—will remain obscure.

There was a formal organizational structure which acted as a
superstructure. Benjamin and Mary were considered the
"anointed heads" of the society and were "to hold office during
the corporate existence of the society." Directly under them were
twelve trustees, who were appointed by the Purnells for four-
year periods and subject to removal with the concurrence of
other appointed trustees. Because they appointed the trustees,
the Purnells ruled as autocrats. There was provision in the constitution for a president, vice-president, secretary, and treasurer,
but the anointed heads had the additional responsibility to
appoint individuals to those offices, which were routinely
handed over to trusted lieutenants. None of the officers received
a salary for serving the colony, "since the title shall be taken and
held in the corporate name of the society [and] one had to trust
the divine mission of Benjamin as his wishes are reflected
through the trustees of the Israelite House of David."[66]

The formal and legal structure was changed over the years,
usually after some crisis or lawsuit indicated the need for some
further legal safeguards. The *Articles of Association and By-Laws*,
adopted in December, 1907, proved too simple for a growing
organization, especially one recently beset by legal claims.[67]

Therefore, a new constitution was drawn up in 1908 which removed the Purnells further away from the membership by introducing another layer of religious officers. Two new groups of community officials were created: the four "pillars" and four "head female officers." In the organizational chart, the pillars served just below the Purnells and above the twelve trustees. They were given wide legal powers to "use funds of this association as they deemed best for any and all charitable purposes."[68]

Just exactly what the functions of the female officers were is unclear, though they were probably synonymous with the community "sweepers." The seven sweepers were the disciplinarians to whom all confessions went and from whom orders concerning colony work came. The origins of the term are lost; however, it is analogous to the term used by the Shakers during their spiritual upheaval in 1842–43. Mother Ann's "sweeping gift" was a part of a general purification rite, which involved both spiritual and temporal cleaning. A day was set aside when the Shaker households, already notoriously clean, were purged of "evil spirits," who hid themselves wherever there was dust or dirt. In the spiritual cleansing process "spirit brooms" were used; these "spirit brooms" served to stir up a religious revival among the members. Though there is no established direct link between the Israelites and the Shakers, they did hold in common four principles: separation from the world, common property, confession of sin, and celibacy. The House of David probably inherited the practice of using women as sweepers from the Wroeites, where the women were the confession takers and purifiers as John Stewart so graphically portrayed in his *The Abominations of the Wroeites*. The elaboration of distinct orders with symbolic and literal functions was not unique to the Shakers and, in fact, may have been simply a gesture toward religious equality, but given the roles played by Joanna Southcott, Esther Rogers, and now Mary Purnell, their special status indicated the special role women had played in the Southcottian tradition.[69]

The revision in 1908 of the *Articles* also strengthened the colony's legal position and placed the Purnells in even stronger control of the business and commercial affairs of the community. In 1911 a further amendment to the community bylaws was made to protect the leaders against lawsuits and legal action,

which was a constant problem in a society in which the membership deeded over their possessions. Communal groups have
always been the subject of litigation by former members and have
had to protect themselves:

> If any person seeking membership in this voluntary association
> known as the Israelite House of David shall have conceived the idea
> that any miraculous cure is to be preferred upon him or her, or that
> the property and possessions of this commonwealth, actual or sup-
> posed, is to yield any special benefits to him or her as an individual,
> other than the benefit all receive in common, or to exempt him from
> the natural consequences of any wrongful or sinful conduct.[70]

Obviously, the community did offer the special benefit of immortality, but legal action on the failure to produce it was unlikely. The amended 1911 articles went on to emphasize that the
society offered no "inducements to join and that their specific
task was to establish an ingathering for the elect."[71] These later
revisions in the formal charter were clearly intended to protect
against previous promises and mistakes, and indeed during the
period from 1903 to 1907 promises were made that could not be
fulfilled.

Having agreed to join the "Israelite House of David, the
New Eve, the Body of Christ," what then did individuals and
families find? Some found exactly what they were looking for
and had been promised (less immortality): a religious organization directed toward religious ends. These individuals stayed
for long periods, content with the simple Gospel message revealed by Purnell. Others, however, were swindled of their funds
and debauched under the guise of a religious belief system. Since
both communities existed side-by-side when the conflict over
Purnell's leadership emerged, families divided over the faith.
During the trials of the 1920s, for instance, mothers and
daughters testified against each other and disputed claims about
the nature of Purnell's activities in the community.

The first substantial indication of dubious practices and
procedures came in 1906 when Helen Kraft sued to get back her
belongings (mostly furniture) and the $138 she brought with
her. In a deposition made to the Berrien County Court in March,
1906, she outlined her grievances and leveled a number of

charges against Purnell which were repeated later on numerous occasions. She stated that she worked long, hard hours at the colony and that her children "as an act of the creed" were taken away from her care and schooled in the "readings and writings of Benjamin, a little arithmetic and some spelling. They had no regular textbooks or regular lessons assigned to them."[72] Mrs. Kraft further complained about inadequate food and clothing for her children:

> This deponent further states that during the time she lived there, their chief and principal diet and in fact all they practically had, was beans and potatoes. That at times they had some milk, this in limited quantities. . . . She nor her children were never furnished with any clothing, except that they brought with them from Missouri, except their shoes, that being a part of the creed that black should not be worn and they were furnished with tan colored shoes.[73]

Yet Mrs. Kraft was subjected to something worse than a gruel diet, separation from her children, and limited footwear; she had to put up with the sexual advances of the seventh messenger. Her statement continued: "The deponent further states that while she was a member of the colony, Benjamin Purnell . . . came up to this deponent and attempted to put his hand in front of her dress." When she resisted she was "removed to what is known as the far eighty or the John Downing place." Throughout the next twenty years, Purnell made numerous advances to women and when they fought back or declined his prophetic love he shipped them to the "far eighty."[74] Those who accepted his call he moved to his bedroom and, in time, all the rooms in the central house where the King lived were occupied by young women. A portrait of Purnell as a lecherous rake who used the colony as his seraglio emerges in reading the testimony of disillusioned female ex-colonists. In many ways his actions were implicit in the prophetic role he took from Wroe and Jezreel, but his activities long remained hidden or, at least, undisturbed by the legal machinery of Michigan.

Helen Kraft ended her deposition against Purnell with a statement that succinctly summarizes all the testimony that apostate believers would deliver against the prophet over the next twenty years. Where they expected to find faith, they found

Archway at the entrance to the grounds of the House of David.

deceit; where they expected to find celibate purification, they found Purnell's aggressive sexual advances; and where they expected community of purpose and interest, they found discord and discrimination. Mrs. Kraft's deposition of 1906 would be echoed by others throughout the colony's history and until Purnell's trial in 1927:

> This deponent further says that at the time she joined the colony and previous thereto, she was taught from the writings of said Benjamin that in his teachings and preachings, he represents he is the Son of Man, by that meaning he is the personal representative of God here on earth; that his body is cleansed, by that meaning he can do no wrong and that his body will never die, but that at a given time he, among the selected few amounting in all to one hundred and forty four thousand (144,000) shall live on forever. That after she had been in the colony and saw the manner in which they lived and Benjamin's actions with this deponent and other women, in this, he would put his arm around them and kiss them, she became disgusted and suspicious of his teachings and finally left the colony because she believes Benjamin is a "fake."[75]

Others would litigate and complain to local officials until the colony toppled under damaging evidence so overwhelming that the state was forced to act.

What, however, was life like for those believers who carried on the work of the ingathering and remained? Members were housed in large residence buildings built over the years as the community grew and prospered. The colony had grown slowly during the 1903–5 period, but with the arrival of the Australians there was a sudden burst of building activity. The first substantial dwelling was the Ark, a frame residence house. In 1905 this three-storied residence was completed and in 1906 Bethlehem, another three-storied residence facility, opened. These nearby buildings were joined by an arch in 1906 that bore the inscription "The House of David" and signified the two branches of the Israelite house that had come together. There were also rooms over the printing office, and when members worked at the outlying farms there were cottages provided for them. The Purnells lived at Jerusalem until Shiloh was built in 1909 to house them and other colony leaders.

One member reported that forty girls and ten men (the girls between the ages of twelve and twenty) lived at Jerusalem. The men were housed on the top floor, the girls on the second floor. Mary and Benjamin lived in separate rooms on the second floor, and Hazel Wade testified that Frances Thorpe, the colony treasurer, had a key to Mary Purnell's room and he was seen leaving late in the evening on several occasions. It was at Jerusalem that Benjamin Purnell began making his advances toward the young women. Shiloh was constructed in 1909 as a residence and administrative office for the leadership. It was a two-storied building made of concrete blocks. The majority of its residents were young girls between the ages of twelve and eighteen.

Sleeping arrangements followed a simple pattern of two individuals of the same sex rooming together, though in certain cases husbands and wives shared a celibate room. Room assignments were constantly changed to serve economic and spiritual needs (e.g., farm labor, missionary trips), and such assignments were made by Mary Purnell. Although the practice of moving individuals around was an accepted fact of community life, the early arrivals from Australia tended to settle in certain rooms on a permanent basis. Families were rarely housed together. Children were separated from their parents at the age of twelve and moved into different quarters.

All the colonists took their vegetarian meals in a common dining room, and like numerous communities before and since, thought their food unique enough to market a community cookbook. Mrs. Kraft's testimony indicated that the members had an inadequate diet, but it seems they received sufficient if plain food. For breakfast they often had toasted bread, oatmeal, coffee or tea. For lunch and dinner they were served vegetables and pies. Butter, milk, and eggs were lacking, with those products sold in Benton Harbor to produce income for the colony. There was a private dining room for the Purnells, in which the food was superior to the common fare in the communal dining room.[76]

The food the Purnells received was not the only item that distinguished them from the rest of the membership. They both dressed handsomely while the membership wore common clothes. Some members later charged that there was an inadequate supply of warm clothes during the winter months and that their underclothes were made from flour sacks. Isabella Pritchard alleged that Mary Purnell changed her gowns five or six times a day and boasted of her fine apparel while the rest of the membership wore rough clothing fashioned out of the sacks. Flour sacks were also used for tablecloths, sheets, and pillowcases. Salespeople and those who traveled as missionaries received a better cut of clothes. The colony had its own tailor shop and dressmaking establishment. Goods were bought in quantities in Chicago and requisitions for clothes and other personal items made through Benjamin Purnell and Ada Ross.

The education of children was minimal and perfunctory. Purnell held it in low esteem: "Education counted as dung. Low estimate. Dung more useful. Dung can be put on the ground and do something."[77] Members were told that schooling within the colony was better for children because they would not be ridiculed because of their long hair. At the height of the community there were 175 children in the school under the supervision of two teachers. Only one child in a twenty-year period went beyond the eighth grade, the state's minimum legal requirement. It was essentially a religious school. Community children became, in effect, Benjamin's, and he saw their educational needs as primarily moral and directed toward furthering the work of the society and the ingathering. Faith training, Biblical lessons, elementary spelling, and mathematics were all that one needed for this Michigan Eden.

Although the Purnells had little interest in education as such, they did have an interest in controlling their own school and maintaining their influence in the school district. On one occasion they deeded a pear orchard to twenty members so that they could vote for the colony candidate in a school election and then had the property deeded back after the election. They even discussed having colony members adopt orphan children so that

Visitors flocked to Eden Springs Park, opened in 1908, to ride the miniature railroads, stroll through the zoo or gardens, or eat at the vegetarian restaurant.

they could vote at election time. The curriculum prescribed by the state was never followed and Purnell's writings were the only textbooks. A box was kept in the corner of the schoolroom in which the children threw their Israelite texts when they thought anyone was approaching, then taking out their state-required books.

A later commentator noted that the colony's members "all seemed happy in their work" since their labor scheme was both flexible and efficient. Several businesses besides farming were

conducted. The communal economy was rooted in practical
needs, and jobs were rotated to serve changing needs. As new
members entered, buildings were erected which served as tangible evidence that the colony was succeeding in its mission. With
the construction of the amusement park in 1908 there came a
steady stream of curious visitors, who, although puzzled by the
colony, still found it an entertaining and pleasant vacation spot.

Missionaries were sent out to recruit new members, and the
Purnells had a "School of Prophets" where preachers learned the
Israelite creed, and how to sell it. While on the road they carried
cards that announced their ministry:

> This is to certify that——had in the judgment of this church been
> called by the Spirit to special work in the vineyard of the Lord; and
> after strict examination and due trial, is set apart and fully ordained
> a minister and apostle of Jesus Christ; and as such, we commend her
> to God and the word of his Grace to all true believers who look for
> the second appearing without sin unto salvation.[78]

Records in the attorney-general's office at Lansing reveal a
harsh and even cruel society which made excessive demands,
spied on its members, and used fraud to sustain itself. The seven
sweepers kept the colony disciplined and Purnell's messianic
vision allowed no shirking in business affairs. Regulations demanded that the grounds could not be left without permission.
There was no room visitation, no "unseemly letter writing," and
no solitary walking. A "Rule Book" for the guidance of members
prescribed every facet of daily life: members were instructed to
"go to bed at 10 p.m. and arise at 5 a.m."; they were prohibited
from playing cards, wearing black, arguing, or mixing with Gentiles. In particular, girls were given specific advice about their
conduct. They were warned against "pleasure seeking, and se-
lecting certain company and becoming thick. The hatching is not
good."[79] Assumedly such rules kept the colony a docile place and
troublemakers, known as "scorpions" to the community, were
watched and eventually expelled. The expulsion process followed two routes: first, by making the scorpions' lives so miser-
able at the colony that they left, or second, by creating an incident
with the undesirable member so as to blackmail him into leaving.

Charges of sexual immorality were often levelled at the scorpions
in an effort to force them from the society.

The young girls who lived at Shiloh worked in various
offices around the colony, or at the printing office or the laun-
dry; they played in one of the two colony orchestras or worked as
domestics around the colony. Edmund Bulley estimated for the
courts that during one summer season over 200,000 visitors
came to the colony to be fed, entertained, and instructed in the
faith. In 1920 he enumerated the colony's industries: a printing
plant, machine shops, planing and sawmills, a dairy, tailorshops,

Michigan State Archives

One of the two colony orchestras.

a factory for cement products, the amusement park known as
Eden Springs, a miniature railroad, a bandstand, a baseball park,
a vegetarian restaurant, and refreshment stands. The House of
David was a defensive community that kept to itself, patrolled its
members, and was wary of the world, though it presented a
confident façade in its enterprises and on the playing field. Such
a life was limiting, of course, but life in such sectarian colonies—
like that of the Hutterites—had always appeared barren to out-

siders. The public record can often reveal what was wrong with
such a society, but it cannot adequately convey to us what was
right, how the group satisfied the social, emotional and religious
needs of the believers.

The Kraft case, for example, tells us much about the colony
and shows that there was good reason for the world to be wary of
the Israelites. The years from 1905 to 1907 were ones in which
the colony grew in a number of ways. Its membership, its finances, its physical and economic base were all established during that period. By weathering the initial years and by testing its
membership's faith during the formative stages of organization
the colony was in excellent position to survive much more tumul-
tuous times over the next fifteen years. The first years are the
most difficult and the most binding years for any communal
group. They are the years when resources are meager, when
local opposition has to be met and won. But they are the years
when the spirit of community, the sense of purpose and dedication, is also high. From 1907 on the society grew more successful
and, paradoxically, more at odds with the world. Its methods of
self-perpetuation became more extreme, and, in the long run,
were self-defeating for Purnell and the colony. At the end of this
period and following quickly on the Kraft dispute there was a
major dispute that threatened to destroy the gathering and it
served as the impetus for the House of David to turn inward and
further secret itself from the world at large that it hoped to
convert.

It all began in 1907 with a letter to the British consulate in
Philadelphia and ended three years later at the state attorney
general's office in Lansing. Wilfred Powell, the British consul,
received a letter from William Cleveland, who had come to the
colony in March, 1905, from Melbourne. After reading some
community literature, Cleveland said, "I fell victim to his [Pur-
nell's] teachings and their instruction was to sell everything and
place the proceeds in one fund and live in common as [a] family
of God as they did in Apostolic days."[80] But by April, 1907
Cleveland's faith had weakened because, as he wrote, "after
being here this long, I have found out the whole thing is wrong
and his [Purnell's] relations with the women there won't stand the
light and his prophecies are not coming true. As the time fixed

has gone by and nothing has occurred as he said in his books it would."[81] When Cleveland tried to regain the $150 he had placed in the common treasury he found he was returned only $55. He then engaged an attorney, wrote to the consulate for aid, and thus set off a chain of investigations. Cleveland contended that he had been misled by the colony, that he had been treated poorly while there, and that he was entitled to his initial contribution plus transportation back to Australia. He also alleged that the Berrien Township supervisor had refused to help him because "he is in good standing with Mary and Benjamin as they vote for him in a body and have about a hundred votes."[82]

After an inquiry from Powell, Deputy Attorney General Chase began an investigation by requesting information about the House of David from the Prosecuting Attorney for Berrien County, Charles E. White. White indicated that it "is very difficult to learn anything about the inner workings of this society," but his general impression was that they were "a somewhat immoral organization and that their influence is not the best."[83] Yet it appears that what particularly concerned White was that individuals expelled from the society might become a burden on the local authorities. According to White, though the colonists were secretive, their conduct toward outsiders was good, but he had heard "little things" about them and believed they were "extremely immoral." Furthermore, any action taken against them would "certainly meet with public approval."[84] Chase now believed that it was "wise" to investigate further and get at the real truth. He followed a lead suggested by White and wrote to a Benton Harbor Presbyterian minister, Elisha Hoffman, asking for general information about the colony. Chase outlined the problem to Hoffman: "Complaint has been made that their morals are not good—that they deceive the people and get their property away from them. In other words, they are a band of fakers working under a religious cloak."[85]

Hoffman made his report to Chase early in June, 1907, concluding that numerous individuals had become disgruntled wih the House of David because "there is discrimination in the treatment of members, some put to suffering for want of things they might justly and reasonably expect." Hoffman characterized the general membership as "honest and sincere people with good moral impulses, averaging, however, very low in intelligence and education," and confirmed the allegations made by Kraft and Cleveland about immoral conduct by Purnell. "He seems," concluded Hoffman, "to be very free, from the statements made to me, taking improper liberties with the women who have faith and comeliness." The report ended with a pledge of support to Chase and a two-part recommendation: "One, this institution should be made morally clean. Two, there should be a statute preventing designing men from taking the property of people who are easily influenced and misled, on the ground of religious devotion when that devotion is fanaticism and error."[86] These comments were shortly supplemented by Mrs. Kraft's attorney, I. W. Riford, who saw the colony as a "disturbing" element since it "prayed [sic] on the ignorance and credulence and their morals out there are somewhat doubtful."[87] Yet Riford, like Hoffman, emphasized that the Israelites kept to themselves and therefore could hardly be called a public nuisance. Riford added that sanitary conditions were "disgusting" as the colony had been without bathtubs until six months earlier and now had only three for several hundred members. Riford had a client to represent, and Hoffman another faith at heart, yet when taken together the reports suggested to Chase a troublesome situation that required some action.

Throughout the summer of 1907 the disgruntled William Cleveland continued to supply the attorney-general's office with evidence concerning Purnell's past and present activities. By mid-July Chase was able to write to Hoffman, still living in Benton Harbor, a confident note: "We are working on the matter and are going into it with the intention of taking as much action as the facts now stand will warrant."[88] In another letter Chase indicated that he was having some difficulty in getting the "right kind of proof."[89] What kind of proof he was looking for is unclear, and he moved with great caution in the case. In September, 1907 a petition was presented to the secretary of state signed by thirty-five individuals, including the Reverend Hoffman, the pastors of the Congregational Church and Methodist Episcopal Church, and the mayor of Benton Harbor, M. H. Morrow. It requested that no new charter be given the House of David without a public hearing. After consulting with the attorney general, the secretary of state encouraged further investigation, this time to determine whether the colony had exceeded the terms of its charter by buying and selling real estate, by farming, and by its practice of hiring out colony members as day laborers.[90]

In writing to Cleveland, Chase outlined the state's position: "I said to them [the Purnells] that our position was that they were not only violating their corporate charter, but that their teaching was contrary to public welfare, public policy, and destructive to the state and society, and that my judgment was that we would not be satisfied until they conducted their teaching so as to be in harmony with the welfare of society and the government."[91] In October Chase wrote a stern letter to the colony's attorney, H. S. Gray, stating Cleveland's case ("He is a pauper and a cripple") and emphasizing that "Benjamin cannot bring men from foreign countries to Michigan, make paupers out of them, turn them loose upon the public for Michigan to deport them at Michigan's expense."[92] There was no mention in the letter of Cleveland's earlier complaints about Purnell's immoralities. The colony complied with the state's warning by agreeing to maintain the Cleveland family on a weekly stipend, providing them with produce from the colony farms and paying their passage back to Australia; however, Chase did not believe he could press the case beyond the threatening stage because, as he wrote Hoffman, he was unable to "get any specific evidence of immorality against Purnell."[93] Chase further indicated that the colony had changed many of its ways and teachings, though he failed to give Cleveland any concrete evidence of these changes.

The attorney general's office was content to get such a settlement in Cleveland's favor, though it must surely have been difficult to overlook such evidence as Cleveland presented them from another former member, Mildred Giles. In her statement she alleged that:

> When I first came to that place Benjamin met me in the hallway and hugged me; another time he came out to the big farm where I was staying and asked me to go down through the orchard with him to look for mushrooms; as we started he told me to hook my arm in his, and I done so for a few steps, and I made an excuse to get loose and he said, "You are afraid of me" and I said "No," he said "take hold of

me then" but I did not; he said no more to me then so lots of times at headquarters he would meet me on the walks and slap me on the breasts. I don't think that's very becoming for a messenger of God.[94]

Purnell's behavior seemed particularly unseemly for a messenger of God running a celibate ingathering of the elect.

Giles provided Chase with further information about Purnell's conduct toward women in the colony. She wrote:

> Josie Lewis came running down the stairs like someone scared to death and I asked her what was the matter, she said she would tell me when we got home to the big farm. When we got home, I asked her to tell me. She said Benjamin met her in the upper balcony, and grabbed her in a room and closed the door after her and felt of her teats and another time she said he pinched her in the privates.[95]

Many of those alleged offenses were punishable under Michigan law in 1907 but they certainly did not prod Chase into vigilante activity, and he adhered closely to a regulatory role. With large numbers of members leaving the colony in 1908— most of them voluntarily—Cleveland continued his campaign, urging the attorney general to search out an affidavit filed against Purnell in 1896 by one Emma Moore charging him with immoral conduct; however, Chase's office failed to uncover the document after a thorough search. Cleveland's source (a former member, J. Obenauer) believed that "your legal friend from Lansing [Chase] didn't make much of a search of police records" and then provided more information which again failed to substantiate the charges.[96]

There was also considerable pressure on the colony at this time with another case for back pay filed in Benton Harbor and several others pending. During July, 1907 the colony through one of its trustees, M. S. Tyler, agreed to pay both the Clevelands' fares back to Australia. Cleveland accepted reluctantly; though pleased to be heading home, he was sorry that the case against the House of David could not be pressed further. He wrote to his comrade-in-arms Chase: "am always sorry our combined efforts did not oust these vampires from your [Chase's] state they are turning into a veritable Coney Island at their new park."[97] Chase sent a soothing reply, indicating that "everything is quiet in

Michigan. We have not heard from Benjamin and Mary, or about them for some time."[98] But shortly thereafter the governor's office did hear from the Purnells in the form of a request from one of the four "pillars," J. D. Tucker, asking for a letter of recommendation to be used on an expedition to Turkey. "We want," he wrote, "to get to Palestine to search for some ancient relicts [*sic*] supposed to be buried near Jerusalem. Letters of this nature go a long ways with the Turkish authorities."[99] Memories of Richard Brothers's desire to return to Palestine must have remained in the Jezreel legends and were part of the prophetic baggage. The Benton Harbor Israelites did go on an expeditionary trip and relics from that trip are still in Benton Harbor.

Deputy Attorney General Chase may have thought that things were quiet in Michigan, but two colony trips taken in 1909 indicated that Purnell's activities had not abated. These trips later played a prominent part in laying the state's case against the prophet; in 1909 they were just another part of an already developed pattern. One outing, by twenty young girls in a sailboat, involved a trip to Aral on the eastern shore of Lake Erie, just above Frankfort. The Purnells, Cora Mooney, Frances Thorpe, and James Tucker all joined the party, and Purnell reportedly had intercourse with some girls in the group. Another incident occurred when a group traveled to Chicago to take part in a carnival and spread the Davidic gospel. Purnell was later reported to have slept with several girls during the trip. In both cases, these were acts about which a wider circle of community members either knew or participated in. That circle included Mary Purnell, Frances Thorpe, and James Tucker, a prominent trustee. This was not an isolated charge of fanny pinching or lewd behavior, but a serious breach of the law. Purnell (and other colonists) would later charge that Frances Thorpe and Mary Purnell had had an affair, and there is fragmentary evidence of other sexual liaisons in the community. It can safely be assumed that Purnell's own violation of the virgin law was known by an inner circle as early as 1909, probably earlier than that.

While the Cleveland case file grew and an awareness of conditions at Benton Harbor developed at the attorney general's office the state seemed slow to act. True, it had revoked the

View of the administration buildings at the colony, 1912.

colony's charter and had it replaced with a "Voluntary Association Agreement," but it failed to alter practices, as the events of
1909 showed. Between 1907 and 1910 there was constant litigation against the colony by disgruntled members, and rumors
about sexual indiscretions were rife in Benton Harbor, yet the
state stood off.[100] The attorney general's office certainly cannot
be accused of adopting a hostile attitude toward the House of
David because it did allow the colony to pursue its business and
religious activities. Missionaries continued to travel about the
United States, and facilities were improved at the amusement
park. Changes in the articles of incorporation were made which
strengthened the Purnells' hold over community affairs and,
furthermore, additional buffers were constructed against lawsuits. The membership was now at 300, with the bulk of that
group either ignorant of certain practices or so committed to the
seventh messenger that it was inclined to discount any rumors
about his conduct.

By 1910, however, Purnell's pursuit of women brought the
colony perilously close to disaster. In that year another dispute
surfaced that threatened to destroy the society by involving the

community with federal officials on the serious charges of kidnapping and white slavery.

In the seven years since they had come to Benton Harbor, the Purnells had achieved much. Although the millennium Purnell had predicted was still in the future (now 1915), there was considerable evidence that the earthly paradise might serve as an ongoing substitute. For from 1910 until the outbreak of World War I, the colony prospered. The amusement park, zoo, theaters, bands, orchestras, and baseball teams created more than adequate revenue for the ingathering. The baseball team alone eventually brought in $10,000 a year. The amusement complex catered to individuals who crossed the lake from Chicago in search of a quiet, entertaining weekend. Ring Lardner left an account of his visit to the colony for this period: "It sounds like a roadhouse / but / it was even better'n that. You couldn't get nothin to drink, but there was plenty to see and hear, band concerts, male and female, movin' pictures; a zoo, a bowling alley; and more funny looking people than I ever seen at an amusement park before."

Those "funny looking people" also operated several farms in the area, conducted lumbering operations on High Island near Charlevoix, and hired themselves out as day laborers and ticket takers on the city streetcars of Benton Harbor. The House of David was becoming a prosperous settlement, though the eventual extent of its wealth can only be guessed at for this period. There were accounts of Purnell wearing precious jewels and stories about buried treasure on the grounds. During the breakup of the colony in 1927–30, it was estimated that total assets were between $500,000 and $1,500,000 in real estate and real property alone. There was by 1910 more to the House of David than a millennial promise and a two-century tradition of prophecy; there was growing support for it as an ongoing and integral part of the area economy.

CHAPTER FOUR

Chased Like a Fox

Foxes have holes, and birds have nests, but the Son of man
hath nowhere to lay his head.

Benjamin's Travels

Despite growth and success, the House of David began, during
1910, a pattern of evasion and deception in order to avoid the
criminal and civil prosecution of its prophet. That pattern involved the removal of material witnesses from the colony whenever it appeared that an investigation would occur; the flight of
Benjamin Purnell to a secure hiding place whenever there was a
suspicion that he would have to appear in court; and, finally, the
introduction of the group marriages designed solely to cover up
Purnell's sexual escapades and protect him from the charge of
debauchery.

Mary Purnell's role in these strategies was an ambiguous
one. At times she appeared to be Benjamin's coequal and directed the important disciplinarian sweepers in their work. Yet
there was never any hint in the later proceedings against him that
she had pursued the young men with the same fervor that he
expended on the young women.[1] She may have had an ongoing
liaison with Frances Thorpe but that is speculative. She did object
to her husband's activities on at least one occasion, when she was
reported to have told him: "Benjamin, you are running a whore
house." Since Benjamin's philandering occurred with such fre-
quency, she must have tolerated his activities. However tolerant
she was, it was her actions that touched off the first controversy in
1910 when she learned through her physician brother, Dr.

James Stollard, that his examination of some of the girls indicated that Benjamin had "been tampering with them." Mary then "kicked up a row," which immediately led to the marriage of Lillian Davis, age nineteen, to William Hannaford, age 33, on April 30, 1910.[2]

It was the first marriage in the colony and had been hurriedly arranged when news reached Benton Harbor that Lillian Davis's mother, and former colony member Mrs. Elizabeth Fletcher, was coming to take her daughter out of the society. The colony later argued that Hannaford and Davis were in love and wanted to marry, even though the virgin law proscribed anything but the most celestial of love affairs. Whether the colony leadership simply wished to keep Lillian Davis as a member or to hide Purnell's violation of the virgin law is ultimately unimportant, because what the marriage established was the legitimacy of marriage—something that should have shocked the truest believer. Logic of that sort was for unbelievers, however, and the colony accepted the marriage from a prophet whose word was law. That law originated in a tradition where dramatic reversals had revealed themselves before, as in the sudden announcement of Joanna Southcott's pregnancy or in James Jezreel's sudden death paving the way for Esther Jezreel. Although a marriage did take place, certain forms of the old law were continued, and the central principal was upheld, since celibacy was required of the newly married pairs.

Two days after the Davis-Hannaford marriage, an affadavit was signed by fifty-four women members attesting to their collective purity. Each signer swore to membership in the colony, their length of stay at Benton Harbor, and their continued faith in the works of Benjamin. In addition, each attested that

> she had never at any time seen any act on the part of any member of said House of David, or heard any word or suggestion from said House of David, of any improper and immoral nature, that all the teachings and examples shown by the leaders and members of the Israelite House of David are highly religious and moral; and each deponent for herself expressly says that she has not at any time seen or heard any improper and immoral conduct on the part of any member of the Israelite House of David and each deponent for

herself says that she has not at any time told that she has seen or
heard any immoral or improper conduct on the part of the Israelite
House of David.[3]

The affidavit also denied that anyone had written to James
Stollard about immoralities and declared that the primary intent
of the statement was to clear up "rumors and reports which seem
to have been current."[4] These testimonials were drawn up by the
colony's attorney, Humphrey S. Gray, and were intended to
protect the House of David against the current Fletcher-Stollard
charges and to safeguard the society against future charges. Such
affidavits, and others taken later, were kept at colony headquarters and were used to remind the signers that if they had a
change of heart about community life and complained, they
would be perjuring themselves. In addition, an elaborate file was
maintained on each member, containing his or her entering
confession, reports by the sweepers, correspondence from outsiders, and legal documents, usually deeds to property turned
over at entry. Such files were reportedly maintained as a whip
over the membership, and rather than have their private lives
exposed, most members who left kept silent.

Internal disputes continued to cause problems. A serious
one emerged late in 1910, which indicated the continuing fear
that Purnell had of exposure to criminal or civil charges. It
appears that when two faithful members, Frank and Lulu
Baushke, left for Australia on a missionary trip in 1907, they
entrusted their daughter to Purnell. On her return from Australia in April, 1910, Lulu Baushke decided to leave the colony
and signed a release giving custody of her daughter, Harriet, age
fifteen, to the colony for as long as the girl desired to stay at
Benton Harbor. In December, 1910 Lulu Baushke had a change
of heart and returned to claim her daughter. When she arrived
she was told that her daughter had "gone away." In fact, she was
still in the colony and only later was taken to Chicago to prevent
her from telling her mother about Purnell's advances toward
her. Eventually the matter was settled with mother and daughter
united, but the colony leaders had pursued a dangerous course
in taking the young girl out of the state—dressed as a boy—to a
hotel in Chicago.[5]

A parallel case involved a suit brought against the colony by
Emory Swandt to gain custody of his younger brother, Owen,
and possession of some property brought into the society by his
father, Martin Swandt, when he entered in 1906. Martin Swandt
had left the colony without taking the property with him (or had
been prevented from doing so) and when his son Emory brought
suit, Mrs. Swandt (who had remained) and young Owen were
sent to Chicago. Mrs. Swandt died in Chicago and the case was
settled out of court, but during this time the colony had lied to
Emory Swandt about his mother's whereabouts, saying she was at
Hot Springs, Arkansas, for some treatment while in fact she had
been in Chicago. During this same period, Purnell himself had
fled from Benton Harbor rather than accept a warrent issued
against him in civil proceedings over the Swandt property.[6] In
both the Baushke and Swandt affairs, the House of David began
a pattern of evasion, deception, and flight when trouble appeared. Purnell became adept at keeping one step ahead of the
authorities and was successful in maintaining that extra step for
almost twenty years. In this he was supported by at least a coterie
of the leaders and probably by the majority of the membership
who saw the scorpions as trying to wreck the ingathering.

The final event in the string that characterized the continuing crisis of 1910 was an appropriate capstone to these elaborate
self-defense maneuvers. In mid-December of 1910 the colony
moved quickly to correct past errors. Twenty couples were married in group ceremonies contrary to the stated rules of the
society. Under Mary Purnell's direction, each girl chose a husband (or was given a choice of two), and then Mary made the
arrangements with the men involved. Later the state argued that
the marriages occurred to protect Purnell, "so that in case they
should be required to have physical examinations, their condition would be attributed to their husbands." The colony contended that they were marriages of convenience which enabled
couples to travel together as preachers without causing scandal
and to work on the farm as pairs. These group marriages took
place before a justice of the peace at Benton Harbor on successive evenings prior to Christmas, 1910. On December 16, thirteen couples were married. Ten of the brides were under twenty
and their husbands were all considerably older. On December

17, seven more couples married; all of these brides were under twenty-one. According to one source the brides wore white gowns and spent their wedding night separate from their grooms. Of these twenty marriages at least eleven resulted in divorce or separation over the next ten years.[7] The public justification for the marriages was couched in the millennialist tradition that emphasized special years and special days: "According to the Israelite statement this is the 50th year in their way of reckoning time and counts as a jubilee when all shall be free." To the historian this appears a rationalization, to the outsider an incredible flip-flop, but to believing Israelites it was part of their continuing effort to define their millennial place in time and in the Southcottian tradition. If 1861 could be a special year in the House of David calendar then why not 1860?

Irene Pritchard, who had relations with Purnell before her marriage—("He was dressed at the time in his white suit, his preaching clothes. He did not justify the act from Scriptures and I never questioned him about it")—gave an account of the events leading up to the marriages:

> Mary came to us; she said that we should all get married. She told us to get a piece of paper and write who we wanted, pick out someone we would like to marry. I picked somebody else, but he had chosen someone else so I didn't get him. We went to Mary's room the next morning and Edith Meldrim had a list. She read the list, and then I picked Henry Sassman from the list. I had never spoken to him before and had no courtship.[8]

Some couples, like Ruth Wade and Irving Smith, who married under pressure in 1912, forged satisfactory alliances, but these seemed unusual. Ruth had had intercourse with Purnell when she was sixteen and subsequently gave an account of her marriage.

> I had seen Irving Smith around the colony previously and said "How do you do." There had been no courtship and no agreement between Irving Smith and me that we should marry. We didn't have anything to say, only the Justice of the Peace said, "join hands," he said his ceremony, and he said, "you are pronounced man and wife." I walked out and we went home. We went up to Shiloh. I collapsed

there. I didn't know what to do. Benjamin said, "Get out of here. Go back to your father." So I went back with my father, lay there and shook all night, and next morning my father got up and went to my sister, Mrs. Geissler, in Benton Harbor, Benjamin sent for Irving Smith and told him to go down there and tell my father he was my boss, and Irving told him.[9]

Her life with Smith after their marriage was childlike and chaste. They both continued in the faith and traveled together as preachers for the Israelite gospel:

I travelled with Irving Smith for four years but never slept with him. I never had sexual intercourse with Irving Smith. I stayed at the colony until May 24 [1912]. We then started on the road to preach. That was in the year 1912. And I preached the faith for four years.

I travelled with Irving Smith for almost a year and he began to like me pretty well. He worked hard and we sent our money home to Benjamin. We sent $2,275 in sixteen months. I have the receipts for this at home.[10]

While on the road, they had to keep in touch with the central office on a regular basis. On one occasion Ruth's confession resulted in a rebuke from the colony when she returned. Her transgression of the newly defined virgin law came during a period when she and her husband had just begun to warm to one another:

We were at Natural Bridge, Virginia. My husband always took me to see everything there was historically. We went out there to have a good time; and it was confession night. We always had to make confession the last Friday in every month. I always made an honest confession of everything I did. During the month I had kissed Irving Smith. Oh, a couple of times, two or three, I don't know just how many. I says "Irving we have sinned." He said, "I don't see it as a sin to kiss anybody." I said, "Benjamin said if we ever kissed our husbands it is a sin and I have to confess it." Irving Smith said, "If you feel it will do any good I will write it in my confession," that he kissed me and that I kissed him.[11]

On the couple's return to Benton Harbor, Ruth was publicly rebuked by Purnell for her conduct; yet he continued to pursue her as he had before her marriage. With such scrupulous and devoted disciples it is understandable why the colony prospered and why its members were so tractable. Purnell's authority, which he wielded constantly, was unquestionably accepted by the majority.

Rumors about a federal investigation and a visit to the colony by federal officials had prompted the sudden group marriages in late December. From then on, the community began its practice of hanging men's clothing in the girls' rooms in order to simulate a marriage relationship. There was a continuing need for such duplicity since external sources continued to threaten the colony. In 1911 a petition sent to the new governor, Chase Osborne, by some Benton Harbor citizens resulted in a visit to the colony by him.[12] In a graphic letter to his brother John, Purnell outlined the 1911 visit and the charge that the House of David was an immoral place: "They stirred up a few of the lower classes more like themselves and wrote out all kinds of stuff and tried to link us up with M. K. Mills of Detroit and finally got spittoon cleaner [Chase Osborne] to an investigation and found it all to be a lot of false charges and dropped the whole thing."[13] Investigations by federal and state officials were conducted from 1907 through 1920 for one reason or another.

Purnell defended the colony by every available method including such conventional stratagems as using political influence whenever possible. He wrote to then Governor Warner in August, 1910 about a civil suit brought by former member Ethel Brink, which the colony had lost: "Now we have made application for rehearing and if you could in any way use your influence in a private way or otherwise, or could advise me what to do, I would not forget it. We gave you our support in your race for governor. We have not regretted it. You will remember you spoke in our park and would glad have you do so again."[14] Members were given voting instructions about candidates and Purnell could deliver about one hundred votes. There is evidence to suggest that the colony had a good friend in the Benton Harbor supervisor, and M. L. Hamilton, the congressman from Grand Rapids, was open to their influence, or, at least, the leadership believed he would come to their rescue in a difficult situation.[15] There were letters in the local papers against the colony by departing members, but Comstockean fervor failed to seize the Benton Harborers, though there were periodic petitions.

That tolerance continued to be tested during 1914 when the events of 1910 were repeated. It began with the defection of Lena and Augusta Fortney in May or June, 1914, when they publicly charged that Purnell had debauched them. The colony responded with an article by Coy Purnell in the *Benton Harbor Palladium* countering that the girls had lied. The sisters then brought suit against Coy for slander and in the course of the trial testified about their sexual relations with Purnell. Affidavits taken from the women in 1914 charged Purnell with solicitation and the use of force against them:

> I [Lena] went to live at the House of David six years ago. I was fourteen years old when I went there. I came from Charleroi, Pennsylvania. My brother heard them preach on the street and joined the sect. My sister, Augusta, and I joined them afterwards. In about a year we came to the colony at Benton Harbor. We lived in "Bethlehem" a few days and then went to live in the "Ark." I always roomed with three other girls. I have seen Benjamin come into the room a great number of times. . . . Benjamin talked to us and told us he was just like Jesus and had the right to have intercourse with us girls. He then took me into another room and there were two girls in another bed. I protested but he told me he could come to my room where other girls were and I have had intercourse with him and have seen him have intercourse with other girls many times in the same room. The fact is well known among the women of the colony.[16]

Her deposition is interesting for a number of reasons. First, it shows that the pattern of recruitment in 1914 was the same as in earlier years, with itinerant preachers carrying the Israelite message to remote places. Second, it reveals Purnell's self-identification with the Messiah as his justification for sexual intercourse with the women. Finally, the testimony flatly states that his activities were common knowledge among the women, at least for the 1908–14 period. Whether this knowledge was limited to women who lived in the Ark or was, in fact, common currency cannot be answered without further evidence—and would then, obviously, require a radical reinterpretation of Purnell's role—but at the minimum a large circle of women—

possibly thirty—had intimate knowledge about Purnell's messianic prerogatives. When another community member, Edith
Clark, observed him having relations with some of the girls, his
justification to her was that "he was the son of Man and it was our
duty to have sexual intercourse with him in order to be in the
inner court—that every woman must be passed by the king."[17] By
asserting seigneurial rights in this fashion, Purnell was no different from John H. Noyes, who initiated every young woman at
Oneida into the mysteries of complex marriage. But Purnell
went beyond Noyes in that he promised immortality as part of
the bargain. Noyes passed on all the women as a mark of his
religious and spiritual superiority within the colony, in that
sense, like Purnell, acting as a king.

In several cases Purnell used force to rape the young
women, but he was sterile. Hazel Wade was asked in court: "Tell
us now whether when he had sexual relations with you he lost his
seed?" and she answered, "He did not."[18] Two other girls gave
similar testimony. Purnell was reported to have dyed his graying
hair black, parading before the women in the nude, telling sala-
cious stories, and drawing obscene pictures. They had been
instructed to be obedient to him, the Shiloh, and when newly
initiated girls questioned his sexual advances the older girls
defended him. Ione Smith stated: "I became convinced that it
was right, and I went back to Benjamin and apologized and asked
his forgiveness."[19] Furthermore, their faith was so complete that
charges made against him to their parents were not believed: "I
know of mothers who were told by their daughters, but did not
seem to believe it."[20] After the girls were raped they were told not
to have anything to do with other men.

Purnell was prophet, king, life-giver all rolled into one. Only
such a person could both deny and give sexuality and find ready
acceptance for his capricious rules. And conversely, only members who completely accepted the Israelite tradition would—
whether through fear, ignorance, or belief—remain silent for so
long. Some were too young to rebel, others received favors from
the leader, while others accepted his word as law. In nearly all
cases his sexual advances were rooted in and defended by the
Biblical tradition as he interpreted it. As one member stated: "He
would quote scriptures and told us that the flaming sword

spoken of in the scriptures held by the Angel as barring Adam and Eve had been taken away so far as he was concerned and he was purified and had the right to have intercourse with any girl in the colony."[21] Lena Fortney swore that Purnell had managed the group marriages of 1910 because he had relations with all the women in the colony "over the age of twelve."[22] Her sister Augusta confirmed that Purnell not only had relations with the girls in private, but did so in the presence of other girls, keeping the youngest and prettiest in rooms near his bedroom at Shiloh.

The allegations made by the Fortney sisters and Edith Clark in 1914 were serious, yet state officials were content to accept the House of David argument that the women were, in conjunction with their lawyers, trying to extort monies from the colony. The Purnells used a number of strategies to defend themselves from this latest attack. On the one hand, they had already cultivated some friends and turned to them when the charges became known. Writing to his brother shortly after the initial charges were made, Purnell outlined the plan: "Knowing that this would no doubt go to the Attorney-General with their trumped-up charges, I sent for R. L. Hamilton, who was Congressman for this district, and a personal friend of mine and laid the matter before him, showing him their schemes to extort money."[23] In addition, he "had a few articles published" that made fun of his detractors in a "cool" way and turned public opinion in the colony's favor. Although no legal action resulted from the Fortney or Clark suits, they forced the community to use the ultimate defensive weapon: the group marriages. During July, 1914 twenty-five girls were sent to High Island, near the coast of Lake Michigan at Charlevoix, the site of the colony's lumbering operation. The girls were supposedly sent to "pick berries," which might have been a plausible excuse except that the group left at 3 A.M. and the pickers were, coincidentally, all young women who lived at Shiloh house. The girls remained at High Island throughout the summer and their departure conveniently coincided with a three-week trip Purnell took to Canada in the company of some trusted associates.

Clearly the colony was frightened about the possibility of another investigation, presumably from federal officials, since local and state authorities had been placated. In order to meet the situation, a plan was devised by the colony elders. It was decided that Esther Johnson Hansel would go to High Island, make arrangements for a group marriage, and keep Mary Purnell informed. Esther made the trip and induced the girls to write the names of the men they wished to marry and seal them for delivery to Mary Purnell. Mary then spoke to the husbands-designate and arranged to have the marriages take place in early September. When that time came, the Purnells sent a cryptic message to High Island: "Bring the lumber down, leave the green lumber off at South Haven and bring the dry lumber through."[24] Decoded, the message meant that the married and older women were to be returned directly to the colony, while the younger girls were to be "left off" the boat at South Haven. The "green lumber" was met by Frances Thorpe and during the night was driven to the colony. On September 2, 1914 twelve couples were married in a group ceremony and three days later the High Island group was married immediately after its arrival in Benton Harbor. The nuptial contract emphasized at length the voluntary nature of the marriages, reading:

> We the undersigned, do this day of our Lord September 5, 1914, enter into this contract as follows, and fully agree, each of us in taking upon ourselves a marriage of our own choice, and without undue persuasion; we marry with the understanding between ourselves, that in the event of either of us desiring to forsake the faith we now hold and leave the colony of the one, or either one, in the event of leaving shall not disturb the other party of this contract who wish to remain, or try to get the said party to leave with him, nor shall they bother them in any way contrary to the faith we now hold. We furthermore agree to make no trouble or to be the cause of trouble in any way hereafter or forever.[25]

Although Purnell's motive for pressing for the group marriage at this time was sheer expediency, the participants' reasons were mixed. Later some said they married for love, others because they wanted a preaching mate, others because it was part of the faith, and one individual said she married because she wanted someone "she could call her own." Whatever the motives, it was clear that they had entered into unconventional marriages. Primarily their marriage was still with the Shiloh-Christ, Purnell, and with the ingathering they worked toward. Since celibacy was still a stated colony requirement one partner would not "bother another" on this point. And, finally, central to the marriage covenant was the agreement embodied in the last line; it was a promissory note to keep quiet about colony affairs "hereafter or forever." Purnell here succeeded in perpetuating the South-cottian tradition of sealing the membership; in this case, however, the believers sealed themselves into an eternal pact of silence.

Hurried marriages and the signing of binding covenants were defended "in order to save the colony and the faith," as one participant in the marriages of 1910 wrote. Segments of the outside world were hostile, and if given an opportunity, would destroy the colony. Therefore, by agreeing to the marriages, the members reaffirmed their faith in the community's mission. Many of the young people were the children of the Australian Wroeites who had committed everything to Purnell as the true messenger. To repudiate Purnell meant repudiating their parents, their education, and their way of life—repudiations more easily conceived in hindsight than carried out in fact. As studies of the Hutterites show, such complete renunciation of the group is particularly difficult in close-knit communities.

In the long run, these marriages were short-lived, lasting no longer than the marriages of 1910, but they calmed conditions in 1914. In November the recently married pairs defended the action and publicly stated that their marriages had been voluntary and that the Fortney charges were false. At the same time Mary Purnell and Esther Hansel went to Big Rapids, Michigan, and had a lengthy interview with the new governor, William Ferris, apparently convincing him that no investigation was necessary. Ferris promised Mary Purnell that if he were forced to conduct such an investigation he would appoint "non-sectarian and unprejudiced men."[26] State officials did not conduct an inquiry, though federal officials did. In any case, no action was taken against the society.[27]

By December, 1914 it was clear that the defensive measures begun in the summer had worked. Rationalizations about the marriages offered to the press and governor had misled the bloodhounds once again. Between August, 1914 and January,

1915 the colony repeated the defensive maneuvers begun in 1910. By now they were ritual: flight by Purnell from the colony, group marriages, private and public overtures intended to influence opinion. And, as in 1910, it worked. The events of 1914 may have made Purnell somewhat more discreet, but they did not dissuade him from his plan of messianic and sexual ingathering. During 1915 he had twenty-eight girls moved into the printing office so that they could enter Shiloh House without notice by the rest of the membership. Over the next five years, forty-four young girls lived within walking distance of his bedroom. He managed his revels by using the ingenious device of a secret door into the bedroom at Shiloh. Reportedly, his favorite among the girls was Myrtle "Toots" Sassman, who accompanied him on trips and ministered to him during his dying days. Yet he seems to have had an active interest in numerous community women and had relations with many of them just shortly before his death.

Even with all the covenants signed, confessions taken, and marriages performed, individual members continued to leave the colony. When it was suspected that they were scorpions, they were carefully watched and, if necessary, entrapped into incriminating situations so as to maintain control over them even after they left. Just prior to Ruth Wade's departure from the colony in 1916, a plan was outlined to entrap her with a man in Chicago, but the plot failed. After she left and sought legal advice about bringing suit against Purnell, she was opportuned by her husband, Irving Smith, to drop her charges in return for $1,000. Furthermore, Smith, who had remained in the colony, was presented with an affidavit alleging that his wife had relations with men in the colony and he was told to sign it or leave the colony. He left. Ruth Wade attempted to press her case with Justice Department officials in Washington, but nothing came of her efforts. Her attorney believed that Purnell "had such pull" that little could be done about affairs at the colony and that local officials, like Benton Harbor Sheriff William Hogue, were working for the colony in an effort to get her to drop the suit.[28] In addition, Wade discovered that while she was living with relatives in Hammond, Indiana, she was watched by two Israelites (shaved and shorn for the purpose) who reported to the colony about her travels. The Wade defection stirred up a new set of rumors

Draftees from the House of David await induction at Camp Custer in 1916.
Thirty-five colonists were drafted, and all served in noncombatant roles.

within the colony about a raid, and Purnell fled one night when
such an invasion was feared to be imminent; yet, again, nothing
came of the case. Increasingly, the colony must have felt itself
under siege. Rumors about investigations, defections, and raids
became more a part of their affairs.[29] It is no wonder, therefore,
that when public officials moved against them they were very well
prepared and masterful in their deception of federal and state
officials; they had been holding defense alerts since 1910.

Whereas Ruth Wade's defection had been voluntary and
potentially harmful, a larger, involuntary defection took place
the same year which the community turned to its advantage. In
1916 others left the colony for other reasons: they had been
drafted. A determined effort was initially made to have colony
members declared conscientious objectors. After appeals to the
district board in Kalamazoo failed, the colony complied with the
draft laws and never sought thereafter to evade them. Thirty-
five men were inducted into the armed services and all served in
noncombatant roles. Four were sent to Leavenworth, however,

after they refused to handle dead animal carcasses, since the
Israelite injunction against the "dead burying the dead" still
applied. In most cases, the colonists complied with army regulations, though Purnell did make a request on their behalf that
they be given meatless meals and be exempted from carrying
arms. Photographs show the Israelites in dress uniform with long
hair and beards. They suffered taunts and discrimination because of their religious beliefs. Their conscientious objection to
war did not extend to their refusal to serve, and the members
seemingly made the best of their wartime service. Purnell visited
some of them at Camp Custer, near Battle Creek, Michigan, and
lectured them about the necessity of turning over their pay-
checks to the communal economy. There had been some problems with the soldiers getting into the habit of purchasing gifts
for their wives with their pay. What this indicates, of course, was a
growing attachment between pairs that interfered with community spirit and the common treasury controlled by Purnell.
During the war many community members sought occupation-
ally deferred jobs and in almost comic fashion a war-related
group marriage took place in 1917.[30]

This group marriage was no sexual coverup, just simple
greed, as Purnell wanted to obtain dependent relative funds
from the government; soldiers were therefore married so that
their "wives" could claim an allowance.[31] Later the state charged
that the colony was "unpatriotic," was encouraging its members
to become slackers, and was defrauding the government with
false dependent claims. But there were mixed motives in the
colony's actions in this case. The members had a legitimate claim
to conscientious-objector status: and most of them, despite
Purnell's activities, were devout Christians in the pietist tradition.
By exercising that claim they had more to lose than gain in a
heated war situation. By becoming active combatants—American Sikhs, if you will—they could have generated considerable
sympathy for themselves and turned public opinion in their
favor.

Purnell has been depicted as an unscrupulous charlatan who
operated a religious colony for his own benefit. What such an
oversimplification fails to recognize is that he was bound by
certain rules and traditions that limited the options open to him

as prophet. Members retained their visible signature—their long hair—while in the service, maintained a vegetarian diet, and refused work that brought them into contact with dead bodies. This last gesture is most significant since it was Purnell's refusal to bury his daughter which led to his flight from Fostoria, Ohio, to Michigan. Implicit in the refusal to handle dead carcasses was a belief in the immortality of the body; therefore the Israelites had to maintain this external symbol of their undying faith. The long hair and the vegetarianism had historical meanings within the Southcottian tradition, but probably could have been shaped to serve other needs. In the most immediate sense, Purnell was a religious leader bound by certain religious ordinances handed down by the earlier prophets. Obviously, he bent the traditions to serve his own purposes or used sleight of hand to sustain them, as in the case of celibacy being maintained after the group marriages; he did so, however, within the mandate to lead the Israelites into the place foretold by Wroe, Ward, and Jezreel. Under Purnell's leadership the House of David often took the most difficult path—as with the conscientious objectors—and when an obstacle appeared then found a pragmatic and self-serving solution. Once having resisted induction and found that they could not resist, they gave up the principle and adopted the practice of taking wives, a practice once thought abhorrent in the colony, but abandoned in 1910 for other compelling and practical reasons. Yet they maintained certain principles. Much of the colony support for Purnell can be traced to his sense that the society stood for a separated nation, which he distinguished by maintaining external symbols and a belief in the internal purity of their beliefs. It was a nice combination of piety, pragmatism, and deceit—a successful mixture whatever one may think about the individual ingredients.

At the war's end, the colony appeared—to the casual visitor —the epitome of eccentric success. Membership stood at 400, business was good, and the ingathering was progressing at a satisfactory speed, so long as one discounted the earlier predictions of the date of the millenium. Purnell was now fifty-eight and still an impressive figure, particularly when in the company of the handsome Mary. In their forty years together they had accomplished a great deal, achieving wealth, power, and some

dubious fame. Knowing something about the careers of the
earlier prophets, they must have experienced some satisfaction
from the knowledge that they had surpassed the earlier messengers in the accumulation of a material kingdom and had
about them a substantial body of devoted believers. To be sure,
there were problems: dissident members, a fickle press, and
occasionally prying officials who posed a new threat. Indeed,
1919 was no different from the other years. Isabella Pritchard
left the colony, charging that Purnell had violated one of her
daughters, but another set of blanket affidavits signed by fifty
girls and women denied the charges. There were eleven marriages in 1919, one a group ceremony involving young girls who
lived at Shiloh House. By now the Purnells must have thought
they had hit on the magic formula for avoiding conflict with the
authorities. Yet the next year that view was shattered as the
citizens of Michigan were treated to a series of exposés that
destroyed the religious community, drove Purnell into permanent hiding, and effectively ended this growing Anglo-
Israelite empire on Lake Michigan.

The event that precipitated the colony's collapse came as the
result of a routine conflict within the society. Similar conflicts had
occurred before, but this one somehow got out of control and
was not amenable to the usual defensive measures. It centered on
the figure of John Hansel, a disgruntled member, who like many
others before him, decided to leave the community and demanded back pay. Beyond this, Hansel was duped by supporters
close to Purnell into believing that Hansel had sufficient colony
support for starting a competing settlement of his own near
Nashville, Tennessee. Whether the idea originated with Hansel
or with Purnell's advisers when Hansel threatened to leave is
unclear, but Hansel and his family were thrown out of the
colony. This dispute—with all its implications of fraud, deceit,
immorality, and intrigue—wound up in the Grand Rapids courts
in 1921.[32]

Hansel, who was described by the presiding judge in the case
as a "less than average man, a credulous fellow of limited intelligence," had left his home in Logan, Ohio, to join the colony in
1912. His family consisted of his wife Emma, two daughters,
Katherine and Edna, and four sons, Russell, Jerry, Ralph, and

John. On entrance, the Hansels turned over their property and funds to the society, and separated as a family within the society, with John Hansel working as a carpenter. Until 1919 the Hansels appeared satisfied with conditions in the colony, but in that year John Hansel realized that "however attractive the House of David at first appeared, they and their children were doomed to a humdrum life of labor, with no opportunity to improve their condition and no compensation except such food, clothing or sleeping accommodations as the colony afforded."[33]

When it became known to the House of David that the Hansels were going to sue for back wages, an attempt was made to compromise them by involving Hansel in a scheme to overthrow the leadership and establish another colony. Although it is doubtful that such a plot ever existed, Hansel was drawn into mock discussions in which individuals who were likely to join the new colony, as well as potential sources of income, were discussed by the "plotters." During the course of these discussions, someone suggested that blowing up Shiloh House might be a good plan. With Hansel further and further entrapped in the plot, the community leaders hoped to blackmail him into withdrawing his claims against the colony. In late December, 1920 Hansel learned, supposedly for the first time, that Purnell had made advances toward colony women and that the House of David was decidedly an immoral place. His source for these disclosures was his future daughter-in-law, Esther Johnson Hannaford, who had been married in the group marriages of 1914 to someone twice her age. She, too, wanted to leave the colony at this time, and it was her testimony that later would prove so damaging in the civil suit brought by Hansel. But before the Hansels had their day in court, they were forcibly expelled from the colony and threatened with arrest—all on the evening of December 20, 1920. The approach of Christmas seems to have made them edgy since the 1910 group marriages came at the same time.

Hansel's defense attorney gave a vivid account of the dramatic events of that evening:

> Hansel was taken from his bed about midnight and accused of being in another man's room with another man's wife [and] was asked if he had not stolen property in his possession, and was driven to Shiloh, there with his wife to be confronted by a number of zealous hostile

members of the House of David and two deputy sheriffs and the prosecuting attorney of the county. . . . Hansel, at the heated discussion that occurred at Shiloh, without the assistance of any legal adviser, friendless (except for his own children) for aught that appears penniless, and with a family to be provided for, faced accusers of himself, his daughter who was charged with theft, and his thirteen-year-old son, who was threatened with arrest for having in his possession a weapon.[34]

There were other threats, guns were displayed, and it was "made clear that they had to go on the next train." Hansel accepted the tickets, a payment of $100, his carpenter's tools, and then he signed a release absolving the colony of any financial obligation toward him. He was threatened that charges involving robbery, seduction, rape, and conspiracy were going to be brought against him and his family if there was any further trouble from him. Hansel gave none for two months and no charges were brought. The presence of the prosecuting attorney and the sheriff added weight to the threats, which Hansel initially took seriously, as he well might. Yet two months later he recognized that he had been forced into a quick exit and that his entrapment into a plot to overthrow the leadership had been planned from the moment he contemplated a suit against the colony. He then brought suit in federal court to regain his property, back wages, and damages from the colony.

Against the Hansels stood the majority of the Israelite House of David in full support of the Purnells. In November, 1921, 444 members signed an affidavit affirming their "confidence in the messengers Benjamin and Mary Purnell, that we want no change respecting the holding and management of property of the Israelite House of David; that the charges of immorality against the officers and members of the Israelite House of David are absolutely false."[35] Just as the Hansel suit was being filed, the colony heard that Myron Walker, the federal attorney for Grand Rapids, was considering a grand jury investigation.

At this stage the figure of Harry Thomas Dewhirst began to play a major role in the colony's defense. He had entered the colony in 1919 and had the requisite skills necessary to defend the community when all the other defensive moves failed.[36] A lawyer, he had been a judge of the Superior Court in San Bernardino, California, and, on occasion, used his old letterhead and the name of his friend, Hiram Johnson, to impress federal officials to postpone any investigations.[37] After Purnell's death in 1927 Dewhirst headed the main body of the colony, the Israelite House of David, and directed its economic growth through the 1930s and 1940s, though he never made any claims to messianic prophecy. He conducted the colony defense during the Hansel trial and throughout the subsequent legal proceedings against the colony. A man of considerable ability, he came to the colony too late to change the course of its history, yet in time enough to shepherd it through difficult times into a period of reorganization.

It is difficult to know how much someone like Dewhirst knew about the various plots and counterplots that make up so much of the sect's history. There was another plot after he came to Benton Harbor, one resulting directly from the Hansel charges. The suit was brought in October, 1921, and on October 13 a group of young women were sent to High Island and remained there until the following May. It was another effort by the colony to shield itself from prying prosecutors, process servers, and newspapermen, all of whom had a distinct interest in the young girls during the fall of 1921. The girls were told that they were being sent on vacation, and a special cabin was built to house them. A vacation in the middle of a Michigan winter on an isolated island in Lake Michigan was even less plausible than the earlier excuse of a berry-picking expedition. Between October, 1921 and May, 1922 the colony introduced motions to dismiss the Hansel suit; indeed, the girls were returned because the colony leaders did not believe the case would come to trial.[38]

Yet the colony acted prematurely, for in addition to the Hansel suit another claim was being pressed, this time by two sisters, Gladys and Ruth Bamford, who had lived in the colony since childhood. Both women had been intimate with Purnell and knew all the details of the society's inner life, including its finances.[39] Their defection and lawsuit were serious threats, and their eventual testimony, coupled with that of the Hansels, made prosecution of Purnell a certainty. After hearing of the Bamford suit Purnell went into hiding to avoid being served warrants for his appearance in court. He was last seen just prior to Christmas, 1922, and he did not appear until nearly four years later, after a nationwide hunt turned him up at a secret hiding place. During the period he was in hiding from the police, the colony carried on its legal defense against a background of mounting public disclosures and sensational reporting. Even the *New York Times* carried the developing scandal. With each new suit and countersuit the history of the House of David unfolded before an amazed public.

When the Hansel case opened, revelations came fast. Emma Hansel Rosetta testified that Purnell lived in "splendor while his followers lacked plates from which to eat their carrots and turnips." Her husband, Emil, said that colony members had dug a tunnel from the Purnells' home to a vacant lot so that their leader could have a quick escape route. A fast car was reportedly purchased because Purnell believed that "some day the Gentiles will chase me like a fox." As the Hansel trial progressed, the state authorities began to make menacing noises about conditions at the colony; Governor William Groesbeck announced that prosecuting officers in Berrien County would be within their rights to issue warrants against the colony.

Early in April, Attorney General James Daugherty began quo-warranto proceedings in Lansing against the House of David, stating that the colony was "not and never has been a corporation for religious and ecclesiastical purposes." On the contrary, he argued, it had usurped its franchise rights

> by inducing, committing and perpetuating frauds and deceits upon its members; by deluding members into conveying property to the corporation in return for fantastic and absurd promises of immortality and religious spiritual benefit; by setting up within the state by deception and fraud, a temporary kingdom opposed to the constitution and laws of the state and whose avowed principles would subvert and destroy the government of the state; by inducing and permitting acts of an unlawful nature under the guise of religious discipline and spiritual ministration; by inducing and permitting commission of statutory crimes and misdemeanors involving vice and immorality in and about the community known as "Shiloh."[40]

After making the charges, the state served papers on the four pillars, a council of ruling elders consisting of Cora Mooney, Lizzie Tomlinson, Ada Ross Schnieder, and Edith Meldrim, giving the colony until April 22, 1923 to file an answer. Frances Thorpe, now colony secretary, bravely stated to the press that "we have nothing to hide and will meet the state in court confident that the result will prove the House of David and its leaders guiltless."[41] Events moved against the colony with great speed from April to December, 1923, amid rumors of a receivership for the colony, a grand jury investigation, and a nationwide search for Purnell. Just prior to the grand jury investigation at St. Joseph, eighteen couples married in two group ceremonies. The colony denied that the marriages were sudden by suggesting that negative publicity had forced the long-engaged couples to delay their marriages until then. The one-man grand jury went ahead with its work on the Monday following the marriages as Harry J. Dingeman, Michigan's presiding circuit judge, began his inquiry. In the past, hurried defensive measures had staved off an inquiry, but now Purnell's flight, the sudden group marriages, and testimony by the scorpions demanded both official and public attention. There could be no private interviews with the governor now as evidence was being collected from every part of the state for the most sensational exposé of the decade. When six colony pairs applied for marriage licenses in April they were denied them by order of the Attorney General's office. The state of Michigan was strengthening its control over the colony.

In the midst of these diverse proceedings, Judge William Sater handed down his decision in the Hansel case. The trial had been rich in testimony, and several Michigan papers covered it in detail. While over thirty colony witnesses swore to Purnell's innocence and superior moral character, the decision went against the House of David. First, the defense witnesses had made a negative impression on the court and damaged whatever case they might have had against Hansel. They were demonstrative, arrogant about their rights, and disdainful of the court. The judge noted that the "demeanor of some of the witnesses was highly discreditable and unfortunately this may not appear on the record." Several defense witnesses had made such a striking impression upon Judge Sater that he was not at all reticent in allowing his sharp comments to appear in the record: "All concerned were relieved, I think, when Winnie Baushke left the stand. Believing that no intelligent man would regard her evidence, it is here treated in the same manner. The striking characteristic of her husband, Otis Baushke, was his ignorance. The temper, loud tones and general demeanor of Lena Nelson did not commend her to favorable consideration."[42]

Another factor in the court decision was agreement with the widely held belief that colony witnesses had been coached beforehand and had possibly perjured themselves. "Falsification and perjury are unblushingly taught" was the court opinion after looking over colony pamphlets and hearing defense witnesses endlessly repeat the same answers. In fact, mock courts had been established at the colony with pro-Purnell witnesses practicing their lines before they went into court.

The defense argument was also wanting because it was based on a categorical assertion of Benjamin Purnell's purity and innocence in contrast to the criminal trepidations of the Hansels. Such arguments were brushed aside by the court in the face of damning testimony from all concerned and also the fact of Purnell's flight when confronted with the charges. Although the court considered the Hansels' initial demands for back wages and damages excessive, the judge ordered that $24,190.55 be paid to the Hansel family. A countersuit and appeals by the colony were launched, charging the Hansels with a conspiracy to "form a band and gas the Shiloh building of said institution and render the residents therefore unconscious" in order to rob them. It was further alleged that Hansel tried to lure the female cashiers into a new colony, "The League of Nations," with Gertrude Bulley as his "Queen." Hansel was also charged with attempting to undermine the colony by leaving "seditious" notes in the community buildings while a member. Some of the notes included such warnings as "Benjamin chokes babies to death" and other inanities. These appeals and countersuits continued through 1927 and were all denied. The colony ultimately was required to make full payment to the Hansels.[43]

With the Hansel case decided, the newspapers began to fabricate stories (as if that were necessary) and chase the wildest leads in connection with the colony. One news account centered on the tale told by a young gravedigger at the Crystal Springs Cemetery. Charles Pullen related that he had received a casket purporting to contain a sixty-eight-year-old woman from the House of David who had died of apoplexy. As the casket was pushed into the grave the top fell off, "revealing the body of a girl about sixteen, wrapped in an old paper and with three distinct marks on the throat, marks of a kind a strangling hand would make."[44] Of course, Pullen had neglected to mention it to the police at the time of the incident, but current events had sharpened his memory. About fifty other colony members were buried at the cemetery, and the newspapers made the most of the seemingly sinister lack of respect shown to their graves and the indifferent manner of their burial.

What fascinated the papers and the public most was the elusive Purnell, particularly after the two raids were made on the colony in 1923 by the Berrien County Sheriff, George C. Bridgman, from which he came away empty-handed. Reports about the whereabouts of the "King" filtered in from all over the country. The Michigan State Bureau of Criminal Identification led an intensive search between April and November, 1923, following up on leads in Chicago, Phoenix, El Paso, the Pacific coast, and Canada. When the colony was raided in early June, Frances Thorpe told the deputies that Purnell "may be on the seven seas," though speculation favored Australia because of the Wroeite connection. The raid produced a confrontation between the Bamford sisters and their mother, highlighting the intensely personal conflicts which emerged during this period. At this point, most of the colony continued to side with Purnell, although there was a slow exodus of believers shaken in their faith by the revelations. There is clear evidence that at least seventy-five members, including Dewhirst, Thorpe, and Mary Purnell, knew Purnell was hiding in the colony while the police searched the country for him. Throughout his period in hiding, Purnell became progressively more ill with tuberculosis and diabetes; yet he outlived his son, Coy, who died in January, 1924, and whose death failed to bring Purnell out of hiding. Purnell was consistent on one point: he let the dead bury the dead.

Throughout 1924 the state attempted to extend its control over the colony by petitioning that it be put into receivership and

WANTED WANTED

Benjamin Franklin Purnell, charged with the crime of rape committed at Benton Harbor, Berrien Co., Michigan, warrant issued June 3, 1923, age 61, weight 165, height 5 ft.-7 in. eyes brown, hair brown, hair should be grey but dyed brown also whiskers, photo attached.

Purnell is the so called "king" of the Israelite House of David and has been missing from there since January 1, 1923.

A suitable reward will be paid for his arrest, delivery to an officer of the Michigan State Police, who holds warrant for Purnell's arrest on the above charge, wire all communications at my expense.

ROY C. VANDERCOOK
Commissioner State Dept. of Public Safety

MICHIGAN STATE POLICE
Lansing, Michigan

Michigan State Archives

Wanted poster issued for the arrest of Purnell, 1923.

by restraining colony officials from disposing of assets. Court battles over such moves continued through 1925. Mary Purnell now asserted her leadership over the colony. Rumors continued to circulate about the whereabouts of Benjamin Purnell with one report placing him in London where he and a band of followers were supposedly holding meetings.

The following year brought still another suit and the startling assertion that Purnell was still in the colony. Two former members, Arthur and Florence Wright, sought to recover some $30,000 and demanded that the colony be dissolved. The Wrights charged that the House of David was now divided between the forces of Mary Purnell and those still faithful to Benjamin. In this conflict Purnell had declared that Mary was not his wife and that no "spiritual union" existed between them. He had ordered her photos taken down and pictures of Myrtle Tulk substituted. Reportedly 640 members sided with Benjamin and 120 placed their millennial faith with Mary.[45] This vote of confidence in the dying Purnell was a remarkable testimony to his hold over the members. Defections, court trials, and police raids failed to shake their confidence in the Shiloh, even when Mary had openly challenged his authority. The dispute between the two continued after Benjamin's death, resulting in 1930 in the formation of the "City of David" or "The Reorganized Israelite House of David" under Mary's leadership. But because Benjamin was still in hiding and the colony threatened by outsiders, whatever conflicts existed were minimized in public. That situation was to last only a short while, since on the evening of November 16, 1926, Captain I. H. Marnion led a contingent of state policemen to the Diamond House and captured Purnell, still in his nightgown as he fled down a hall toward his secret hiding place. He had eluded capture for nearly four years by the simple guise of staying put—eloquent tribute to the loyalty of his followers and the sway he held over them.

The police were led to the prophet by Bessie Daniels Woodworth, who had left the colony in 1925, and had charged that Purnell had relations with her as late as 1924. The raid was dramatic. The State Police smashed in the door of Diamond House, accompanied by photographers catching the dethroned leader in his slippers, shawl, and nightgown, with his women attendants scattering in all directions.[46] During his confinement at Diamond House, Purnell had been cared for by a contingent of colony women—some old, some young—who ministered to his physical needs. Considering the nature of the offenses against him, there was considerable speculation about the nature of that care. Some expert testimony stated that his diabetic condition would have depressed his sexual activity, while others pointed to the presence of two attractive young women who were present on the second floor as his caretakers when the colony was raided. With their usual ingenious logic, the colony argued that the girls were there to work on a jelly-making project for the whole colony—a variant on the old domestic story. Whatever Purnell

An ailing Purnell outside the courtroom before the opening of the trial of 1927.

did between 1923 and 1926 was essentially irrelevant, but for moralists there was some satisfaction that he was limited to a small section of the colony and that his health deteriorated during the period.

The following day Purnell was released on bonds totaling $120,000. His bond was signed by seven prominent Benton Harbor businessmen, including a city commissioner and a former mayor. The defendant was a shadow of his former self, having lost eighty pounds while in hiding, and he had to be carried from an automobile for his court appearances. "Benjamin was again carried into court by members of his flock. He lay on the stretcher swathed in blankets and wearing his familiar brown overcoat with its closely buttoned fur collar."[47] To add to his problems, his long-lost legal wife, Angeline Brown, suddenly surfaced and issued a statement saying she wanted to see him get a "severe penalty for all his misdeeds."[48]

The state now moved to destroy the ingathering and provided the Michigan press with copy that would last for years. By May, 1927 the preliminary hearings had been disposed of, and the case against Purnell was ready to go to court. During the next four months, 225 witnesses were sworn, 500 exhibits introduced, 75 depositions taken, and 15,000 pages of testimony recorded. At the trial before Judge Louis Fead the state was represented by five attorneys led by George Nichols, and the House of David was represented by three attorneys led by Harry Thomas Dewhirst.

The state amassed a formidable body of evidence about Purnell's activities. This material was condensed into four major charges and twelve minor ones, all directed at proving that the colony was a "public nuisance." The major charges were:

(A) In maintaining a religious system and a system which are, ad initio fraudulent, in that Benjamin Purnell is a religious imposter and that the whole scheme is designed to defraud credulous persons and afford Benjamin an opportunity for immoral practices.
(B) In gross immoralities committed by Benjamin upon the women and girls of the colony, induced by him through his position as spiritual leader and usually upon the representation that sexual intercourse with him was a religious rite.
(C) In that the members are taught to commit perjury for the protection of Benjamin, the colony and the faith.

(D) In that members conspired to obstruct justice in aiding Benjamin avoid the service of criminal process upon him.[49]

Although it is difficult to argue with these charges, the first—from the point of view of a social historian—is clearly false. Benjamin Purnell was not a religious imposter. At the time of his arrest he had hundreds of devoted followers who would, and did, attest to his authenticity as a prophet. In their eyes, their compact with his Shiloh was based on the soundest principles: religious faith and tradition. From a modern or legal standpoint, the Israelites were similar to believers in alchemy: their creed, their worship, and their faith were based on false principles that few in Michigan could accept. The colonists at Benton Harbor had an alchemical faith that gold, or immortality, was possible if they followed the prophet's lead. They accepted as true a premise that no modern mind had the right to accept and they followed their own logic. Their gold may have been iron pyrite in the world at large, but it was accepted as coin of the realm within the religious community. The state and the colony began from sharply different first premises, and the colony had existed within the state because it had been skillful in avoiding any direct confrontation. When that confrontation finally came, the antagonists were not fairly matched. The state looked at the colony and saw a religious faker at work; the colonists believed the scriptures were being fulfilled.

In addition to the major charges there were ancillary problems which the state found with the colony. These matters were more difficult to prove and of dubious standing, but they served to portray the society in the most disreputable manner. In these charges, the state attacked the colony's social life in such a broad way that some of the charges were more emotional than legal in their connotations. They were:

(A) That home life is frowned upon and families broken up.
(B) That the faith requires celibacy and prohibits the reproduction of the species.
(C) That husbands and wives and parents and children are separated and made to live apart.
(D) That the children do not receive an adequate education.

(E) That disloyalty to the government is taught and, during the war, fictitious dependencies were created to mulct the government upon military allowances.

(F) That the members are held in peonage.

(G) That the members are forced into marriage to subvert justice and hide crime.

(H) That they are not provided with sufficient food, clothing, and shelter.

(I) That High Island, a possession of the cult in Lake Michigan off the coast of Charlevoix, is used as a place of punishment and exile.

(J) That Sunday is not observed as a day of rest but used as a particularly profitable business day.

(K) That the members are required to vote as ordered on penalty of excommunication.

(L) That the property is held by Benjamin and Mary in fraud of the members and should be declared a charitable trust.[50]

Much of the testimony given in the *State of Michigan* v. *Benjamin Purnell et al.* was a repetition of the testimony given in the Hansel case. The judge therefore conducted what he called a "judicial inquiry" rather than a trial. What prior investigators had been either unable or unwilling to uncover, Special Assistant Attorney General George Nichols pursued with his thorough and painstaking investigation. From the start of the trial, as the prosecution unfolded the colony's internal history for the previous twenty years, it became obvious that Purnell would hardly survive the onslaught. By now he was a dying man who watched the proceedings from a stretcher.

The first witness was Mary Purnell, who testified that she had been with her husband throughout the years at the colony, had a key to his quarters, and had never seen any girls in his room. Her stout defense of Benjamin could hardly stand for much. The prosecution paraded witness after witness before Judge Fead. Ruth Swanson testified that she "thought she had to submit in order to receive immortality" and Dolly Wheeler said Benjamin represented himself as the second brother of Christ, the archangel Gabriel, and that colony children were taught they belonged to Mary and Ben. Esther Hansel testified that one abortion was performed at the colony by a husband on his wife, though she failed to give any names or dates for the crime.

Hansel admitted to perjuring herself in an earlier trial because she then believed she was "fighting for the kingdom of God and justified in playing the role of Judith." Her most telling remarks came when she described the colony view of itself and its relationship to a hostile and sinful world: "We were taught we were of a separate world, that we must defend our kingdom and our faith the same as if two armies were marching against each other in war. To betray the faith was the same thing as being a traitor." Her belief in the cause was complete and any command given by Purnell was followed without question. On one occasion Purnell explained to her that he was becoming stout because his blood (increasingly purified) "was becoming flesh." Ruth Bamford and Estelle Mills testified that Purnell had forcibly raped them. Bamford was ten when the rape took place, and one of his favorite women, Edith Meldrim, was in the room at the time. In all, some seventy-seven witnesses took the stand for the prosecution over a six-week period. The court adjourned for two weeks in late June before hearing the defense arguments.

Throughout the whole of the trial the court was packed with colony members (present and former), and the best of Benton Harbor society reveled in the sensational testimony. When the colony came to defend itself in mid-July there were few new disclosures. The defense presented Benjamin Purnell as a pure Shiloh who had the trust, respect, and confidence of the House of David. Colony members Gladys MacFarlane Jeffries, Violet Tucker, and Annie Faust Lanier all swore to his purity. Edward Johnson denied any charges that Purnell was immoral, thereby contradicting his own daughters' testimony. And twenty-two young women between the ages of thirteen and nineteen took the stand to swear to their own purity and, of course, that of Benjamin. Several local politicians took the stand to defend themselves against charges that they had neglected to prosecute the colony while they were in office when they were, in fact, on the colony payroll. John Sterling, one-time prosecuting attorney in Berrien County and later attorney for the House of David, and Chester O'Hara, county prosecutor from 1913 to 1917, were both eager to clear their names before Judge Fead. Several physicians testified that Purnell was too weak to have done all that he was charged with doing because of his diabetes, and Dr. C. N.

Suvers stated that Purnell had tuberculosis and only had a year to live.

In August, for the first time in any courtroom, Purnell took the stand to defend himself against his accusers. He was on a stretcher, obviously ill, but a reporter noted that "a huge diamond ring set in yellow gold, shimmered brilliantly on his little finger."[51] His only admission of guilt came when he was questioned about his bigamist marriage, but to all other damaging assertions he answered "no." His second day before the court (he was still on a stretcher) brought forth a startling admission: namely, that he feared that Mary Purnell, in league with Frances Thorpe, was undermining the colony. During the raid on the colony the state had obtained some notes written by Purnell to the faithful in which he attacked Mary as a "wicked person."

Written in a rambling and almost incoherent style, the letter charged Mary with compromising the faith by associating with defectors. "She is a vulture and an unjust bird," he wrote, "and I want it understood that I sanction nothing that she does—she is a deceitful reprobate, how can Frances have excuses? Working with Mary and the scorpions in open and rank rebellion and how could there be a better proof that they never was in the faith?" Benjamin thought that Mary's real goal while he was in hiding had been to gain control of the colony's wealth: "Her intention is to fool them until she can get money and property in her hands then she doesn't care what becomes of them." In another note he continued his attack on her by stressing her relationship with Thorpe. He wrote about "her bold [association with] Frances and she says she does not care who knows it."[52] The collapse of the dual leadership was now a public fact and further division of loyalties within the colony inevitable.

When the trial came to a close in late August, there was considerable speculation about the remedy that Judge Fead would prescribe for the nuisance. Governor Fred Green and Attorney General W. W. Potter attended the final court sessions to hear the attorneys give their final arguments in the case. In its summation the defense argued that disgruntled members had plotted against the society and had perjured themselves in open court. But the core of the defense argument lay in Thomas Dewhirst's description of the religious compact forged by the believers with their leader. That compact was a secure one, and the state had failed to prove that Benjamin Purnell was the sex maniac leader of a bizarre cult: "That no lunatic or fanatic could surround himself with such a large body of people of divers trades, labors, and professions and retain the respect of the large majority is evident. That no charlatan as leader under the pressure that has been brought to bear in the last four years could retain the love, honor and respect of his parishoners is equally evident."[53]

On November 10, 1927 the judge issued his decree, declaring that Benjamin and Mary Purnell should leave the colony. The court granted that the colony should be placed in receivership, to be appointed by the state. There was more to the House of David than Benjamin Purnell's ingathering, as holdings were reported in excess of one million dollars and membership was at 700. A summary dissolution would therefore have thrown many innocent victims out into the world and disrupted the local economy. Under Fead's decree the members could remain at the colony for as long as they wished, and the colony's financial affairs were placed in competent hands.[54]

Yet the Shiloh escaped from the law once again. His expulsion from the ingathering place never took effect, for on December 16, 1927, Benjamin Purnell, the seventh messenger of the House of David, died of tuberculosis. Many in the colony waited for his resurrection: "They believe Benjamin will undergo a resurrection as Christ did and they are holding the body for three days," said the attending physician.[55] When the final miracle failed to occur, he was embalmed "with a non-poisonous fluid" so that his resurrection might be effected at a later day. According to press reports, Mary Purnell wept, saying that his enemies had crucified him. Plans were discussed but never carried out for the construction of an impressive mausoleum, and rumors circulated in Benton Harbor that Purnell was buried with a cache of wealth and jewels.

Divisions continued within the colony. Open warfare broke out in 1929 when Mary Purnell was locked out of the auditorium by followers of Thomas Dewhirst. She countered by filing a suit that asked for the colony's dissolution and property distribution among the members. She alleged that when Purnell went into hiding in 1923, he took with him one million dollars in gold and currency and secreted it in Diamond House. She also charged that the colony's wealth, secretly swollen by jewels and gifts given to Purnell by wealthy believers, was considerably more than the court believed. In 1930 an out-of-court settlement was reached that ended the litigation between the two sides. Mary Purnell accepted her exile across the street from the original colony site and took possession of some colony buildings and $60,000. She was ready to lead her new "City of David" congregation, while Dewhirst took Purnell's place as the true Israelite leader. Despite the compromises, legal disputes persisted, along with stories about buried treasure at the House of David.[56]

By 1936 the controversy had faded considerably, and the colony was increasingly identified in the public mind with its traveling teams. It was in that year that Ray Doan, a former member, offered Babe Ruth $35,000 to play with the House of David team. According to Doan: "The Babe won't be required to wear whiskers either."[57] The Babe declined and the teams continued to travel about the country until 1953, though the players were primarily nonbelievers in mufti. They still wore the beards as their trademark. One colonist recalled playing before 22,000 fans at Shibe Park in Philadelphia against the Bacharach Giants of Atlantic City.

It had all begun around 1912 after some colony boys had played some local Benton Harbor teams, and had won. Then they worked out with a semipro team, the Benton Harbor Speed Boys, and were soon beating local factory-sponsored teams in western Michigan. The team branched out to take on teams like Rube Foster's Chicago American Giants and to tour the east. According to Jerry Kirshenbaum: "A couple of colony players— Pitcher/Outfielder Jesse (or Doc) Talley and Shortstop Walter (Dutch) Faust—were as good as most minor leaguers and maybe even a few major leaguers."[58]

In the beginning there were only a few outsiders on the team, but as their popularity grew so did the number of ringers. Grover Cleveland Alexander actually played for them in 1930; during one cross-country tour with the black Kansas City Monarchs, Alexander regularly pitched against Satchel Paige. The colonists exhibited their flair for the dramatic to complement the

The House of David baseball park, shown in a colony postcard, seated 3,500.

appearance of famous stars with them. They tucked their long braided hair under their caps and entertained the crowds with lightning-fast pepper games. Posters scattered about a town announcing their arrival touted the pepper game as being "worth the price of admission alone."[59]

During the 1930s there were several teams that toured the country calling themselves the House of David. Among the bogus teams was a black team (presumably the Sons of Gadreal, the beast serpent who deceived Eve, according to colony literature about the races). The bona-fide Israelite nines represented the two factions that emerged after Purnell's death in 1927. One team was led by Thomas Dewhirst and the other by Frances Thorpe, the leaders of the rival factions. The Dewhirst group often had as many as three House of David teams on the road at one time, so it is not surprising that so many Americans have memories of seeing the bearded baseball teams play in the 1930s. The City of David team even played under the House of David name because by the 1930s it was that name that attracted the crowds.

House of David baseball players. At one point in the 1930s, there were two House of David teams and one from the City of David touring the country and playing exhibition games.

The Israelites drew crowds at home since they had their own stadium that seated 3,500. While the first-string teams were on the road there were three other nines that entertained fans at Benton Harbor. There was a girls team, a boys team, and another men's team. Baseball, both at Benton Harbor and on the road, was good business. During the Depression the teams entertained the crowds by playing donkey baseball. They also played night baseball by using a portable lighting system borrowed from the Kansas City Monarchs. By the late 1930s Dewhirst decided to stop sending teams out because there were too few Israelites left to give credence to the team name emblazoned on their uni-

House of David basketball player. The colony toured a basketball team for about ten years but by 1955 all sports teams had been discontinued.

Benton Harbor Herald-Palladium

forms. That left the field clear for the City of David team, and they continued to play till 1953.

During the 1940s and 1950s the City of David promoted a basketball team and they toured, for a time, with the Harlem Globetrotters. George Anderson, a City of David member who had played baseball, organized the basketball team, but its history was less noteworthy than the baseball teams. In 1955 Anderson shaved his beard and left the colony. That was the last year that the American public saw a sports team that had Benton Harbor Israelites—real or bogus.

Harry Thomas Dewhirst and his followers had, by 1937, become the "biggest industry in Benton Harbor," according to the *Detroit News*.[60] There were still 300 members associated with the House of David in 1937. Dewhirst supervised the society's activities from a splendid home on St. Joseph's "Gold Coast" where he had a direct line into a Chicago brokerage house. The Grande Vista Tourist Court was run by the Dewhirst-led House of David. It had twenty-six cabins, a cocktail bar that featured a floor show, and had a large service area for automobiles. Ample grounds surrounded the cottages, and one highlight at the motel was four electric-powered fountains previously on display at the Chicago World's Fair of 1933. *Motor News* called it "one of the most beautiful motels in America" and recommended it as a "delightful place to spend a weekend."[61] In Benton Harbor the colony built a three-story fruit warehouse with storage space for 300,000 bushels. Two automobile agencies and the House of David Hotel thrived in the area: "Israelite drivers, their hair done up in Psyche knots, bring fleets of used cars and trucks to a sales lot in Detroit while other cult members raise fruit or fancy dahlias, turn out lumber in the north, or tour the land with the several House of David teams and musical organizations."[62]

The colony property on High Island was known in the days of Purnell's rule as a penal colony for dissenting members, but by the 1930s it had been turned into a potato farm and center for commercial fishing. Eden Springs, the amusement park that Purnell started in 1908, was rededicated in 1933 and was in full operation, particularly for the summer season. Tourists flocked to ride the miniature railroad, to stroll in the zoo, to listen to the concerts by the colony band, and to enjoy a leisurely meal at the vegetarian restaurant. The *Detroit News* estimated that the colony's annual income was in excess of a million dollars and that the profits were enormous since all the labor was donated by colony members who worked long hours and remained devoted to the principle of the ingathering, even without the Shiloh. Over the years the colony found itself on both sides of a controversy concerning its relationship to New Deal legislation concerning Social Security laws. In 1944 a federal court declared that the members were employees of the colony and therefore subject to the Social Security Act. The colony successfully appealed the decision on the grounds that the members were indeed the owners of the colony properties. They preferred at that point not to pay the Social Security payments, instead remaining secure in the bosom of the colony. But by 1951 they had experienced a change of heart and sought admission into the Social Security system; some began to draw pensions. In 1955 an administrative ruling went against them and the pensions were stopped only to

Benton Harbor Herald-Palladium

Mary Purnell preaching in her City of David, late 1930s.

be reinstated in 1963 after the colony brought suit. By that time over two-thirds of the then 118 members were over the age of sixty-five. Their relationship with the welfare state was symptomatic of their changing economic circumstances during that period. The colony could provide for its own in the 1930s, but by the 1950s it had an increasingly dependent and aging population to care for, a population that sought the aid of a state that helped crush the colony's millennial dream.

Mary Purnell's City of David operation was considerably smaller than the House of David, and its income was a "mere trickle" compared with the Dewhirst operation. Mary Purnell preached on the radio and continued to send missionaries out to spread the word about the ingathering, although one disgruntled Israelite complained in 1938 that Mary had abandoned the faith and adopted the teachings of the mystical St. Germaine and the "I Am" movement. Her group operated a hotel in Benton Harbor and held an interest in a sewage disposal business. Mary died in 1953 and Judge Harry T. Dewhirst in 1947. The last convert to join the House of David arrived in 1957. George Wacklyn was attracted to the colony for the same reasons as earlier converts: "I was living in South Carolina when I saw some literature from the House of David and I believed." When interviewed in 1977 he said: "We expect a revival. We look for a time when people will start coming here again." People did come to the colony grounds for a time in the late 1960s and early 1970s when the auditorium was turned into a dance palladium and the baseball field converted into a trailer park. But over the years both the House of David and the City of David sold off their properties and reduced their business enterprises so that now both colonies are, in effect, retirement homes for the believers.

Today the two colonies—with a combined membership of fifty—support themselves through the rental of their extensive properties and by the sale of wood and plaster-of-Paris items. They represent a dying faith in a decaying site, still shrouded in as much secrecy as fifty years ago. It is difficult to imagine a revitalization of the colony. The membership is old, the tradition has been discredited by revelations about Purnell, and the Shiloh is dead. Yet in the past the Israelite tradition has sustained itself and there is always the faint hope that somewhere there is a prophet or prophetess who will revive the old stories, infuse them with some new myths, and announce that the true messenger has come.

In the course of a suit in the 1950s, a City of David member echoed the optimism that had sustained the colonists in England, Australia, and Michigan for 150 years: "We put our trust in God that everything will come out all right. Benjamin told us that there would be times when we would be sorely tried. He said the day might come when we would be down to our last two cents."[63] Any visitor to Benton Harbor today can see that the House of David and the City of David still exist. The remaining members will courteously hear out the inquiries of a visitor and indicate that they are not interested in the past, but only in the future ingathering. They will state that they still believe that Benjamin was the Shiloh and the charges against him false. They are, like the few remaining Shakers, on the verge of history rather than prophecy.

CHAPTER FIVE

The Social Compact

These people constitute a little world within a world. The large world is not even aware of their existence while they have the advantage of knowing their own world perfectly well. This network, interwoven with all manner of curious, intersecting influences and lines of intercommunication, constitutes what we may term the Communistic World, for lack of a better designation.

Albert Shaw, *"Kindred Social Experiments," Icaria*

What does it mean? That question must be asked about every historical movement, but particularly about communal settlements like the House of David. Such colonies are easy to ridicule, or to offer easy generalizations about, or to dismiss because they lack a convenient place in our historical literature.[1] Often lumped together as part of "freedom's ferment" or the "small sects of America," they are more often than not seen as misguided and transient responses to conditions beyond the comprehension of their leaders and followers. On occasion they are seen as precursors of significant social movements, or as harbingers of social change that are directed by rational and political forces and only understood in retrospect.[2] Rarely are they seen on their own terms and with a view toward understanding the social dynamic that created them and the consequences that followed for individuals involved in the venture.

The earliest histories of the communal tradition were written by the participants themselves, the most noteworthy of which is John H. Noyes's *History of American Socialisms* (1870), which took the Scottish Owenite A. J. Macdonald's notes and shaped them into the first substantial narrative.[3] Noyes saw the

Shakers, the Owenites, and the Fourierists as part of a large providential design that drew upon the twin forces of revivalism and sócialism to shape America in the antebellum period. For Noyes, individual community experiments were incidental to the greater forces at work in the spiritual awakening of the age, best exemplified by the revival of 1831; therefore, the success or failure of a single community was largely unimportant since it only indicated a momentary adjustment in larger historical patterns. Naturally, Oneida was an exception to this generalization since it alone among the experiments was providentially conceived. Though it is valuable for the sources it presents, Noyes's history was limited by his view that divine providence worked through history and by his own conviction about the central role Oneida played in that process.

The first "outside" historian of communal societies was the newspaperman Charles Nordhoff, whose *The Communistic Societies of the United States* was published in 1875.[4] Like Noyes, Nordhoff had a particular reason for writing his account: he was opposed to the then developing labor unions and wanted to show how success was possible through "associated" labor instead of militant trade union activities. Whereas Noyes's bias had been toward the revival tradition that nurtured Oneida, Nordhoff's sympathies lay with the cooperative movement, wherein laborers "thus become the owners of capital" and class conflict can be avoided. He catalogued and visited a wide range of communities, and his observations were sound, though limited by his desire to show that a cooperative economy could work without trade union organization.

Another nineteenth-century historian was William Hinds, an Oneida community member, who in 1878 published *American Communities and Cooperative Enterprise*. Because of his work with the Oneida periodicals, *The Circular* and *The American Socialist*, Hinds developed numerous contacts with other communities over the years, and his work has proved most valuable, particularly the 1908 edition.[5] It is especially valuable because it reflected the existence of a wide variety of communal settlements (there was a section on the House of David in the last edition) and their programs.

All of these writers had to depend on the colonists themselves for information and on occasion were able to visit a few
communities to flesh out their data. Such information as they
received was invariably self-serving, and although such documents as community constitutions, membership requirements,
and pamphlets were assembled, they were rarely explored for
their meaning. And, of course, none of these works offers much
information about the internal dynamics of community life. To
be sure, there are accounts by insiders: the Shaker apostate
Thomas Brown and the dissatisfied Owenites Paul Brown told
tales after their colony experiences, and Nathaniel Hawthorne
and Louisa May Alcott drew inspiration from their disappoint-
ing communal experiences, but it was not until Albert Shaw
presented his study of the Icarians that the internal aspects of a
society were systematically studied.

Shaw's is the first modern history, written with detachment,
adequate documentation, and synthetic insight. In his study
Shaw hoped to be scientific: "Too little diligence is given today to
searching for the facts of history and to studying with minute
attention the actual experiences of men." By presenting the
history of a single communal society, he hoped to explain its
origins, to follow the external facts of its history, and "to picture
its inner life as a miniature social and political organization." In
sketching the history of the Icarians Shaw tried to move away
from both the romantic and censorious approaches and onto a
new ground of investigation. By reading the literature produced
and read by the Icarians and by personalizing their lives through
sketches, Shaw rightly believed that he had entered a "new and
very curious field of sociological inquiry."[6] Shaw's mentor in this
inquiry was Richard Ely, of Johns Hopkins, who had pioneered
with a new social history with his *French and German Socialism in
Modern Times*, which has been called the "first objective and
impartial account of socialist doctrines to be published by an
American scholar."[7] Since the publication of Shaw's work there
has been an uneven stream of monographs about individuals and
communities complemented by an increasing number of mem-
oir accounts and collections of letters by and about participants in
settlements.

Yet it was not until after World War II that substantial progress was made in defining the nature and promise of communal history. With the publication of the impressive two-volume *Socialism and American Life*, edited by Stow Persons and Donald Egbert, a whole new range of subjects was suggested for researchers.[8] In short, the study of communal experiments had moved from Shaw's "curious field" to a substantive body of potential subjects that touched on numerous facets of community life. The publication in 1950 of Arthur Bestor's *Backwoods Utopias* confirmed what the Egbert and Persons volumes had suggested: namely, that there was a varied and complex history to be explored in relation to such colonies and that their development threw light on national developments.[9] Such colonies were, as Bestor elaborated on in an article in the *American Historical Review*, "Patent Office Models for the Good Society," part of the frontier thrust for egalitarianism and an open society.[10] According to Bestor, such communities were quintessentially American in their experimental attitudes. What both *Socialism and American Life* and *Backwoods Utopias* had shown was the pervasive influence that such colonies had on American intellectual and social life—particularly in the ante-bellum reform agitation. Communal ventures continued largely unabated in the post–Civil War period but were overlooked because they failed to explain conveniently the larger thrusts toward industrialism, urbanization, and centralization. Emphasis was placed instead on the utopian fiction of the period, suggesting that the idealistic drive found an outlet in dreams rather than actual community settlements.

Although there were substantial studies done during this period (Charles Andrew's Shaker studies are the most notable) there was both a popular and scholarly conviction that such communities were relics of the preindustrial age and, in fact, Bestor's analyses supported such a view. Then, supposedly out of nowhere, or at least left field, came the commune movement of the 1960s, which repeated all the contradictions of the 1840s. Historians were suddenly at a loss to explain the phenomenon. Sociologists were having a field day interviewing, collating, and classifying, and historians slowly began to reexplore the communal tradition with an eye on understanding the present. The task was now to go back and look at the experiments to see what they offered their members and how they reflected trends and needs within the American experience.

Some recent studies move beyond this limited and idiosyncratic view of communal movements, toward a comprehensive understanding of both the individuals and the colonies. Nicholas Riasanovsky's study of Charles Fourier and Laurence Veysey's analyses of cultural radicalism and communal societies both go to the heart of the question about meaning. Fourier's erratic career and imaginative writings long escaped serious study, and his philosophy was obscured by the quaint story that emphasized his lifelong vigil for a patron to finance his timely scheme for social improvement.[11] Yet what attracted men and women into Fourierist phalanxes was his social critique, which offered an alternative to the prevailing economic and social discord while at the same time retaining individual choice and liberty. Riasanovsky bored from within with a detailed examination of Fourier's writings. Veysey began with a wider concern, that of cultural radicalism, and what the anarchist and mystical traditions had contributed to it.[12] Resisting the temptation to use previous communal experiments simply as precursors to the cultural radicalism of the 1960s Veysey saw the anarchist colony of Stelton, New Jersey, and the Vedanta ashrams on the east and west coasts as part of a continuing effort to define a radical cultural perspective within the American experience. Essentially what both books did—in contrast to other studies—was to approach the communities on their own terms and then to delineate the forces, motivations, and purposes that molded such movements.

Such colonies offer significant areas for social, cultural, and philosophical investigation. There are several traditions available for approaching any colony history: the historical, the social scientific, and the one used in this study, the "social compact" approach. The social compact approach combines elements of the case-study method with the traditional assumptions of intellectual history. It tries to move beyond seeing such communities merely as fragments, cultural oddities, or footnotes in our social history, but rather sees them as integrated units with purposes, programs, and possibilities that deserve our attention on their own terms and in the light of their own developing history. Such an approach—to paraphrase John Hostetler's description of the

Amish—emphasizes that the House of David was, at once, a
commonwealth ruled by the law of love and redemption in the
theological sense; a sectarian society rejecting established religious authority and separated from the larger society; a face-to-
face community holding onto its distinctiveness while it confronted the outside world; and a high context culture in which
the members were deeply involved with one another.[13]

One comparative study using American sources is Rosabeth
Kanter's *Commitment and Community*, which compares the commitment mechanisms used in successful communities (those lasting longer than twenty-five years) with the binding devices, or
lack of them, in unsuccessful groups. She concludes that successful communal societies had instrumental, effective, and moral
commitment mechanisms that involved six processes: sacrifice,
investment, renunciation, communion, mortification, and trans-
cendence. Unsuccessful groups were ideologically diffuse, sustained a conventional marriage pattern, and had an eclectically
drawn membership. When one applies Kanter's scheme to the
House of David, it becomes apparent why this group was a
success: it lasted for twenty-five years and used all the appropriate commitment mechanisms in order to achieve that long
life. Was it successful for the membership? Did they lead religiously satisfying lives or did they, when the colony began to
disintegrate, regret the time spent at Benton Harbor? On balance the colony can be called a success since most of its members
who stayed seem to have found what they sought: an earthly
kingdom that satisfied their yearnings for religious security within a prophetic tradition. However, for some it was a fraud because Purnell's sexual advances, the dreariness of colony living,
the failure of the millennial prediction, and the funds lost all
showed that the seventh messenger was for them a religious
faker.

But the colony's success or failure cannot be measured solely
in survival years nor solely in terms of member satisfaction.
There are other standards available, and by these the colony
failed in great measure. It contributed little to enrich the members' lives beyond the sustenance of millennial hope; education
was denied, individual choices were severly limited, and
"worldly" ideas were systematically excluded.[14] It was a parochial

colony intent on its own aims, turned in on its own problems, and unconcerned about its fellow man except for the purposes of recruitment for the ingathering or when that fellow man threatened the colony. Clearly the society looked outward in terms of business interests, and Purnell's entrepreneurial talents were considerable. Benton Harbor benefited economically from the colony's presence, and the colony added color and vibrancy to the eastern shore of Lake Michigan. But it left no substantial legacy in buildings or ideas, particularly when one considers what the Shakers, Oneida, and the Harmonists left behind in architecture, crafts, scientific work, and inventions. In fact, the House of David's major success was that it did last so long and seemed to satisfy so many with so little. The same obviously can be said about the early Mormons, the current Children of God commune, and other groups, in that they sustained a common life—but at the cost of human possibilities and autocratic practices. Yet the debate about the success or failure of communal societies is, in the long run, a futile one, since it necessarily directs our attention away from communities and toward some set of general principles that determines the context of success or failure.[15] The relevant question remains: what did the colony "mean," regardless of its duration, organizational structure, or goals. For it is the community that matters, rather than any moral or political principles that its history refutes or sustains.

How, then, should the House of David be characterized and viewed? The most comfortable category for it is as a sect, as outlined by Troeltsch and others; yet this study shows that it was a part of the Southcottian "church" with a theology, a century of tradition, and a substantial body of believers.[16] Sect histories have emphasized their volatile nature, their connection with socio-economic upheaval, and their transient nature. Such connotations are appropriate if one sees such groups without a substantial history or without a basis for ongoing religious legitimacy: without a history because they are eruptions that break the surface at occasional moments, and without religious legitimacy because they are deflections away from major religious tendencies. These groups can be seen as part of a stream with a constant force, vitality, and a life all their own. Unfortunately, the recent proliferation of sociological studies has turned attention away from the continuity of sect and communal development and away from an appreciation of the dynamic historical qualities that sustained them. Only recently have we come to appreciate the impact of Perfectionist ideas on American thought far beyond the confines of a few eccentrics like Noyes.[17] Much the same can be said for the communal and prophetic charismatic traditions rooted in millennial expectations.[18] The approach taken here has been to focus on a single community—a church unto itself—which operated within that communal and prophetic tradition and to examine its roots and internal history as far as the records allow. That history is unique to the tradition from which it emerges.

Yet there are some legitimate areas of comparison because other communities spoke to similar conditions, generated a following that had millennial expectations, formed societies that were cooperative in economic matters, were restrictive in sexual theory, charismatic in leadership, and were part of an underground sect tradition. Three other case studies immediately present themselves for comparison: the Oneida Community, the Koreshan Unity, and the Children of God movement. Oneida, the most celebrated and analyzed American community, was led by the impressive John H. Noyes, who, like Purnell, ruled his followers with an autocratic hand. His membership was drawn to Oneida because of the reassuring intermillennial message he preached, which emphasized security from sin in the Perfectionist tradition, a shared life based on communal principles, and a sexual regime that promised control over destructive sexual urges.[19] Although Noyes's theory of complex marriage allowed for sexual intercourse without orgasm (coitus reservatus), it was, according to Noyes, closer to the Shaker position than to the theories of Robert Dale Owen. If the Shakers had been "right" on certain theological matters, Noyes would have joined the group early in his career, but his belief in a Perfectionist, sinless faith kept him separated from Mother Ann's millennial church.[20] The communists at Oneida placed great faith in their ability to conquer sin, sickness, and death. To that end they practiced faith healing, seeing it as an integral part of man's willful ability to transcend death in life. Although they did not believe in the

immortality of the body, they had a firm faith in mankind's ability
to perfect and purify both physical and spiritual states.[21]

Members who joined both Oneida and the House of David
had clear millennial expectations when they joined. Both societies were founded on the belief that the community was preparing the way for the true millennium, one based on a redefined
social and religious ethic. At Oneida Noyes was considered a
prophet (like Saint Paul), and his writings were seen as divinely
inspired. When the community moved from Putney, Vermont to
Oneida, New York, they moved as a persecuted minority bound
together by their faith in Noyes's leadership, their Perfectionist
faith, and a unique sense of mission. That "mission to the world,"
as they called it, was to establish a place where a Perfectionist elect
would, by example and good works, spread the system of Bible
Communism. That system had been outlined in a heavenly message, and there was little that was "experimental" about the
model:

> So the true plan of association, about which many in these days are
> busily scheming, is not a matter of future discovery and experiment.
> The church of the first born has been for ages working out in theory
> and practice all the problems of the heavenly science. If Fourier has
> had access to the heavenly model and based his motives on the actual
> experiments of the citizens of the New Jerusalem, his system will
> stand. If not it will be consumed when the fire shall try everyman's
> work.[22]

That "heavenly system" had been developed by Noyes during his wandering years from 1834 to 1848 when he tested his
religious convictions, married for convenience and money, and,
like Benjamin Purnell, experimented with new sexual relationships. In terms of their interests, aspirations, and social practices,
"Father John" and "King Ben" differed in many ways, but their
common ground was substantial. Both were self-announced
prophets, both demanded and received total obedience from
their followers, and both gathered-in converts under a theocratic
rule. Noyes's attraction to and command over the young women
of the colony was evidenced by his seigneurial practice of introducing young women into the complex marriage arrangement
and his fathering of almost a fifth of the stirpiculture children.

His preeminent position in the colony was challenged only in the mid 1870s, when he was in his sixties, but throughout most of the colony history he had complete power over some 300 believers. As prophet, leader, and founder of this Eden in central New York, Noyes demanded attention, respect, and obedience from community members. He often isolated himself from colony life, though he sustained his influence through a system of internal regulation (mutual criticism) and helped build an economic structure that kept the community solvent. Like Purnell, he was seen by the popular press of his day as a "freelover"; on the other hand, historians have viewed the group at Oneida as a collection of progressive, pure freethinkers, neglecting its darker and autocratic side. What we see in the House of David is a different reflection of that dark side, since both colonies drew and held their membership by offering the same promises: a system of sexual regulation that had religious legitimacy, a millennial theology, and, eventually, an economic and social life that satisfied some basic needs.

A closer parallel to the life and times of the House of David is the exotic and fascinating Koreshan Unity colony led by Cyrus Teed. Located first in Chicago (1888), then at Estero, Florida (1894), it prospered under Teed's theory of "Cellular Cosmogony," which held that the world was a concave sphere closed at both ends with men living on the inner surface.[23] Teed, an eclectic physician, started his career in Noyes's burned-over district of central New York after an 1869 revelation told him he was "Cyrus the Prophet" or "Koresh," the Hebrew word for Cyrus. He was, in fact, a Swedenborgian mystic who tried to reconcile science and theology by constructing a cosmogony that promised immortality of the body, an ingathering for the elect, and a "universal science from which every problematic and doubtful question has been eliminated, because of the final revelation of the mysteries in which it is no longer occult or hidden."[24] To gain immortality one had to accept a celibate life because the "greatest of all the sins was sexual excess." Like Purnell, Teed expected to gather in the 144,000 elect, and he did succeed in establishing a 400–member colony in Florida, which lasted from 1894 till his death in 1908.

Whereas Noyes sits on the communal left wing because of his progressive attitudes toward sexuality, one finds Teed far to the right with a regressive pre-Copernican view that turned inward; whereas Noyes attempted to reconcile science and religion by adopting complex marriage and advancing his eugenics scheme, stirpiculture, Teed rejected that science and emphasized a static world where energy was limited and recycled. Like Purnell, Teed emphasized celibacy and economic and social cooperation, and he was held in God-like reverence by his followers. Teed described himself as a "type of the seventh messianic potential" and "reflex of the presence of the Messiah in the world since 1839"—the first year of the Millerite upheaval.[25]

Teed had dreams of starting a university to spread the message and saw Estero as the center of a great religious revival, the "vitellus of the great cosmic egg." Similarly, Noyes wanted a university with roots at Oneida. The Koreshan people carried the notion further by setting up a "college of life science" with a curriculum of religious and aesthetic studies. Teed's grandiose plan swept away old belief systems, substituting a new vision of the world, "limited, integral, balanced." After the elect 144,000 were gathered at Florida, there would be a purified race on earth. That ingathering at Florida was hastened by the society's persecution in Chicago when fraud charges were leveled at Teed. Their move to the west coast of Florida was similar to Noyes's flight to Oneida from Putney, Vermont, and Purnell's move from Fostoria, Ohio, to Benton Harbor. By moving to a new location all three prophets were able to create a new environment for their followers and new landscapes for their millennial dreams.[26]

New community converts had to break away from old ties of family and faith in order to embrace a new religion based on messianic prophecy and communal organization. The move to a new site was both dramatic and necessary: it created a common bond that helped hold the colonies together during periods of stress. This separation of the elect from the degenerate world gave visible hope to the followers that a new age was beginning. Working to usher in that new commonwealth was a central function of each community. With each new building or new family of converts the fabric of the new empire was strength-ened. In the same way each attack on a colony made the bond stronger, particularly for those who had fled from earlier social or religious persecution. Furthermore, all of the prophets began their first communal societies when they were in their early thirties; each took a new female helpmate after rejecting their original marriage partner; each then imposed a restrictive sexual theology on their followers; each established the ingathering at a new place and with a theological system emphasizing religious security for the membership. To be sure, they were different men working within different traditions and appealing to dis-crete segments of that tradition: Noyes, the Perfectionist tradi-tion; Teed, the mind-cure tradition; and Purnell, the South-cottian tradition. Similarly, Thomas Lake Harris and George Baker, better known as Father Divine, constructed societies based on celibacy, cooperative economics, and a higher law that demanded total obedience from a body of believers.[27]

The recent controversy surrounding the "Children of God" commune led by David Berg and his family runs parallel to certain aspects of Koreshan, Oneida, and the House of David. Like the earlier groups, the Children of God represent the "Way" and are lead by a charismatic male leader; they reject the world and its corruption; they lead a communal life; they de-mand the rejection of an old sexual pattern and the adoption of a new one under community counsel. Berg, called "King David" and "Moses" by his followers, formed the group in 1969, basing it on a philosophy of Biblical fundamentalism and his personal theories about group marriage. Individuals who joined were asked to turn over all their possessions, reject their families in favor of the commune, make a confession about their sinful past, and accept a sexually open life.

According to a report issued by the New York State Attor-ney General's Office, members were instructed in five basic areas: (1) relationship with the world; (2) discipleship; (3) finan-cial responsibility; (4) obedience to leadership; (5) behavior and community agreements (called the "revolutionary sheet").[28] Followers were indoctrinated into total subjection to Berg's phi-losophy with the result that new recruits became alienated from former friends and family and a deep hatred of conventional society followed. After being accepted into the communes, most members—young and without families—identified totally with Berg's message. "Moses Letters," or lesson plans for new members, stressed the necessity for a complete break with the past, particularly parents, with scatological instructions for his followers: "The parents have filled them so full of houses and cars and education and all that shit—it's like making them eat their father's dung—and now the kids want to kill them for it! You can hardly blame them! I've felt like that myself sometimes! May God deliver me from being around these systemites! I hate to think what I might do if I had a tommy gun sometimes—I might have been tempted to mow them down—I would have made a hell of a communist."[29]

"Prophetic" marriages occurred in the Children of God communes when individuals "spontaneously" (under group pressure) chose a mate and went through a "betrothal" ceremony performed by a Church of God minister, or, on occasion, a local minister. Such marriages were casual affairs, directed at providing marriage partners and children to "increase the tribe." The taking of several wives was encouraged because monogamous marriage arrangements strike at the root of the community.[30] Dedication to the community was so great that when young people left the Berg communes, it took a lengthy period of time for them to renounce their faith. Berg's followers are true believers in his prophetic leadership, not unlike the Koreshan members who trusted that they lived on the inside of the globe, or the followers of the House of David who refused to acknowledge any taint of evil in Benjamin Purnell. Charges leveled at the Children of God communes stress that they encouraged draft evasion, obstructed justice by disregarding court orders, and engaged in educational fraud. They are portrayed in the press as a deviant, manipulative, and self-serving group that first attracts and then corrupts its members. Press accounts and parental outrage have driven the group leaders undergound, and it is doubtful that they will achieve a substantial following, particularly after the 1974 Attorney General's report and the attendant publicity.[31]

What constitutes another link between the earlier traditions and the Children of God is the self-absorbed dedication to Berg's prophetic leadership, the group's ability to attract members (5,000 at this point), and the hostility that their sexual doctrines encounter. As a "totalist" community, they demand full allegiance from their members, a belief in Berg's prophetic message, and a commitment to this new sexual ethic. Some argue that members are physically coerced into the communes and kept there against their will by a corrupt leadership. That assertion may be true (only further studies will substantiate it), but there is another explanation: namely, that the members are held in the colony by a social compact similar to that in effect at Oneida, Estero, and Benton Harbor.

The career of James Warren Jones was also erratic, a tortuous path that led him from his birthplace in Lynn, Indiana, to a jungle clearing and a violent death in Guyana. Along the way he gathered about himself a solid body of believers. A large contingent of blacks joined his People's Temple in San Francisco and found in Jones's philosophy a mixture of Marxism, millennialism, faith healing, social protest, and evangelism that approximated the earlier gospel of Father Divine, whom Jones admired. The bond formed between Jones and his followers was astoundingly powerful—so powerful that the adults at Jonestown committed suicide and allowed their children to be murdered. The details surrounding Jones's career and the faith he inspired in his followers are still unknown, but one clear fact emerges: the members were united in their common dedication to the colony at Jonestown and unswerving in their faith that the life they led there was preferable to life in the United States.

However imperfect these comparisons may be, they suggest a way of understanding the dynamic social compact that holds together the prophet, the members, and the theology within a developing framework of historical circumstances. Those circumstances differ with each colony, but the lines separating a Noyes, a Teed, a Purnell, a Father Divine, a David Berg, and a Jim Jones should be drawn finely.

What is essential in each case is that we look at the colony and its internal dynamic rather than simply using a category into which such groups are slotted. In the case of the House of David, the interaction between Purnell, the members, the Southcottian tradition, and local circumstances molded that dynamic. Clearly

Benjamin Purnell was central; but his message—a combination of Southcottian, Wroeite, and Jezreelite prophecy—fell upon ears already attuned to the meanings implicit in that prophecy. Just as Noyes had spread his Perfectionist theology to believers in central New York where there was a history of Perfectionist activity, so the House of David settled in Michigan, a seat of Jezreelite missionary work. Just as Harlem, and later Philadelphia, were to be natural ingathering spots for Father Divine, so Benton Harbor became the chosen seat for the new commonwealth because of prior local interest.

Purnell's personality was a determining factor since he was, like Joseph Smith, a curious mixture of religious enthusiast and secular opportunist. A self-assured prophet secure in both the revival and communal traditions, he offered a haven for his religiously anxious followers. One gathers that he had charisma, but he needed something more than that to sustain a career, namely the Anglo-Israelite prophetic tradition, which emphasized the messenger's role and the prerogatives that flowed from that role. As it were, he stepped into the shoes of some of the earlier prophets while his helpmate, Mary Purnell, took on the regal qualities left as a legacy by female prophetesses. That historical role gave the leader effective control over the religious and sexual lives of his or her followers. Earlier, Joanna Southcott's sudden pronouncement of the impending birth of the Shiloh established a precedent that joined the prophetic, religious, and sexual roles into one person. Prophets like John Wroe and Esther Jezreel expanded that role to include some questionable religious and sexual practices. Purnell's elaboration of the "virgin law" to include cohabitation with the prophet was amply justified by tradition. His sexual escapades may have been sheer personal adventurism, but they were accepted by his young followers as a reasonable extension of his divinely given authority. That authority—which was unquestioned—was one of the reasons why families joined the colony. That some members doubted his sanctity and grew disillusioned seems natural enough given Purnell's erratic career; many individuals stayed, however, suggesting that the prophetic mandate—in both personal and theological terms—held the membership in sway even during periods of profound change. The hold of the Mormon churches over the membership from the days at Nauvoo until Utah's admission to the Union, for example, demonstrates the strength of the prophetic tradition.

More than just Purnell's charismatic character and the assumption of prophetic authority held together the ingathering at the House of David. There was the full force of millennial theology that outlined a prophetic past, an ingathering present, and a coming kingdom. As with many other social experiments, the members entered first a religious, second a communal, and third a sexual experiment. Since the early 1790s communities of believers had organized around figures like Purnell in the hope that their leader would provide them a secure religious future. As the early history of the Southcottian movement shows, members came from varied backgrounds, including radicals, distinguished scholars, parsons, and illiterate peasants, and that pattern of religious faith continued throughout the nineteenth century, regardless of economic or social conditions.[32] The House of David drew its members from diverse geographic areas, during a period of economic and social peace, but from a body of Southcottian and Wroeite believers.

Although the colony failed to offer complete financial security to its membership and, in fact, demanded a tribute on entry, it did give an inestimable gift—one that offers the key to understanding its history. As part of the compact the members were to receive immortality of the body and soul; a secure home away from the corrupt and corrupting world; a working faith that explained the past through Biblical exegesis and messianic revelation; a present life worth working for through cooperative labor; and an assured future in the presence of that seventh messenger, Benjamin Purnell, and his queen, Mary. In short, they entered into a compact that was religious, social, and historic in nature. There was much to be gained in such an arrangement and little to be lost. To an outsider, the compact appeared the most fragile of bargains: here was no established church, no priesthood, no sacraments, only a curious sect with a crude theology, an eccentric leader, and a fragile future. What could it promise in the bargain?

For many if offered a place to await the predicted millennium, even though successive prophecies reinterpreted that date. For the large contingent from Australia who came in 1905, it was the culmination of a century's ferment that began with Joanna Southcott's prophecies and continued with John Wroe's missionary activity in Australia. These members had come from an established sect with established roots in Australia, and when they accepted Purnell they had nowhere else to turn. For the Wroeites it was the final social compact, one not easily shaken. The religious logic was unassailable. They might modify their beliefs, have some doubts and, in some cases, even leave; but for the majority there was no recourse, nowhere else to turn. As the history of the colony shows, he was successful as a prophetic leader, but in the most perilous fashion. By combining equal parts of greed, guile, and audacity he stayed one step ahead of the law and one prophecy ahead of the membership. Of course, by 1907 the original disciples had as much invested in the colony as did Purnell since they were now part of an ongoing, thriving business concern as well as the destiny of the Israelite House of David. Threats from outside agencies tended to heighten their sense of mutual dependency and define their special place in the world. During all this period Purnell remained at the center, with Mary Purnell complementing his prophetic stature. Their trips, their clothes, their isolation from the membership—and even Purnell's peccadilloes—reaffirmed that special place that Shiloh's messenger played in their lives. He may have lived high, but that's what kings did in the Wroeite and Jezreelite traditions; he may have been an autocrat, but theocracies are not democracies.

Individuals came to the House of David sure of their expectations; yet it was a dynamic social contract that they made, dynamic in that it was open to reinterpretation, redefinition, and elaboration if the prophet so wished it. Earlier prophets had introduced new elements into the theology and social practices so that marriage, though never implicit in the early doctrinal statements, was acceptable when offered in the face of outside pressure. Their compact with Purnell permitted a one-way flow of change, and they accepted abrupt shifts in their practices that shocked outsiders. Their hierarchical society bound them to a common purpose, and that bond was sufficient to absorb certain contradictions that are most apparent. Devoted to celibacy, the gathering gained notoriety as a promiscuous colony; devoted to an ingathering of 144,000 it never grew beyond 800; devoted to immortality and regeneration, it lives on today in decaying buildings after the death of its leader.

Sixty Propositions

These sixty propositions were published by Mary Purnell in 1932 and represent a brief sketch of the colony's theology. This same set of propositions had been published by the Jezreelites, but according to the House of David "little was fulfilled," until the appearance of Benjamin and Mary. The latter-day Philadelphians saw and emphasized their English roots.

Sixty Propositions

Philadelphian Church Whithersoever Dispersed as the
Israel of God.

This article, called the Sixty Propositions, was written A.D. 1699, about 300 years ago, by Jane Lead, of England, which is having its fulfillment today, in Israel of this Visitation.

1. There shall be a total and full redemption through Christ.

2. This is a hidden mystery, not to be understood without the revelation of the Holy Spirit.

3. The Holy Spirit is at hand to reveal the same to all holy seekers and loving inquirers.

4. The completion of such redemption is withheld and obstructed by the apocalyptic seals (7).

5. Wherefore as the Spirit of God shall open seal after seal, so shall the redemption come to be revealed both particularly and universally.

6. In this gradual opening of the mystery of redemption in Christ doth consist the unsearchable wisdom of God, which may continually reveal new and fresh things to worthy seekers.

7. In order to which, the ark (of God's testimony in heaven) shall be opened. Before the end of the world (age) and the living (144,000) testimony which is herein contained be unsealed.

8. The presence of the divine ark will constitute the life of the Philadelphia church, and wherever that is, there must of necessity be the ark.

9. The unveiling of the living testimony within the ark of the Lord must begin the promulgation of the everlasting Gospel of the Kingdom.

10. The proclamation of this testimony of the Kingdom will be as by the sound of a trumpet to alarm all nations of the earth, especially all professors of Christianity, because attended with the power of working all wonders.

11. There shall be an authorative decision given forth immediately from Christ to put an end to all controversies concerning the true church.

12. This decision will be the actual sealing of the members of this church with the name of God, giving them a commission to act by virtue of the same. This new name will distinguish them from the 7,000 names of Babylon.

13. The election and preparation of this church is after a secret and hidden manner, as David in his minority was elected and anointed by the prophet of God, yet was not admitted to the outward possession of the kingdom for a considerable time afterward.

14. Of the stem of Jesse, a virgin church which hath known nothing of man or of human constitution, is yet to be born.

15. And if it be yet to be born, it will require some considerable time before it gets out and arrives at the full and mature age.

16. The birth of this virgin church was visionally typified to John the revelator by the great wonder in heaven, bringing forth her first-born that was caught up to the throne of God.

17. For as a virgin mother brought forth Jesus, the Christ, after the flesh, so likewise a virgin woman is designated by God to bring forth the firstborn after the Spirit, who shall be filled with the Holy Ghost and with power.

18. The virgin that is here designated must be as a pure spirit, so also of a clarified body, and all over impregnated with the Holy Ghost.

19. This church so brought and signed with the mark of the Divine name shall be adorned with miraculous gifts and powers beyond what has been.

20. Hereby all nations shall be brought into it so that it shall be the catholic church according to the genuine sense and utmost latitude of the word.

21. It must be an anointed church whereby it may bear the name of Christ or Christian, being with Him anointed to the priestly prophetical and royal dignity.

22. Hence there will be no bonds or impositions but the holy unction among the new born spirits with all and in all.

23. This catholic and anointed church must be perfectly holy so that it may worthily bear the name of the Lord, our righteousness.

24. Until there be such a church made ready upon earth so holy, catholic, anointed, without spot or wrinkle or any such thing, so that it is adorned as a Bride to meet the Bridegroom, Christ will not personally descend to soleminize this marriage and present the same to His Father.

25. But when this bridal church shall be made ready and thoroughly cleansed and sanctified from every spot of defilement through the blood of Christ then He will no longer delay His coming.

26. There is not this day visible on all the earth any such holy catholic anointed church, all others being found light when weighed in the balance, therefore they are rejected by the Supreme Judge.

27. Which rejection and condemnation will for this end take out of them a new and glorious church in whom there shall be no fault to be found.

28. Then shall the glory of God and the Lamb rest upon it, as the cloud upon the typical tabernacle, that it shall be called the tabernacle of wisdom.

29. Though this Philadelphia church is not known in visibility, yet it may be hid at the present in the womb of the morning.

30. Notwithstanding it will be brought forth into visibility out of the wilderness in a short time.

31. Then it will go on to multiply and propagate itself universally, not only as to the number of the firstborn (144,000) but also to the remnant of the seed (aliens), and strangers, against whom the dragon shall make war.

32. Therefore the spirit of David shall most eminently revive in this church, and more especially in some or other selected member of it, as the blossoming root is to precede the day of Solomon in the millennium. These will have might given to them to overcome the dragon and his angels, even as David overcame Goliath and the Philistines.

33. This will be the standing up of Michael the great prince of Israel, and will be as the appearance of Moses against Pharoh, in order that the chosen seed may be brought out from their hard servitude.

34. Egypt being a figure of this servile creation Babylon, under which each one of Abraham's seed groans, but a prophetical generation will the Most High raise up, who shall deliver His people by the mere force of spiritual arms.

35. For which there must be raised up certain head powers to bear the first offices, who are to be persons of great eminence and favor with

the trinity, whose dread and fear shall fall upon all nations, visible and invisible, because of the mighty acting power of the Holy Ghost which shall rest upon them.

36. For Christ before His own distinct and personal appearance will first appear and represent Himself in some chosen vessels, anointed to be leaders unto the rest, and to bring into the promised land the new creation state.

37. Thus Moses, Joshua, and Aaron may be considered as types of some upon whom the same spirit may come, yet to rest in greater proportions, whereby they shall make a way for the ransomed of the Lord to return to Mt. Zion.

38. But none shall stand in any considerable office under God, but they who are tried stones, after the pattern of the chief corner stone, Christ Jesus.

39. This will be a thorny trial which very few (144,000) will be able to pass, or bear up in, wherefore the waiters for the visible breaking out of this church are strictly charged to hold fast that which they have, and wait together in unity of pure love, praying in the Spirit according to the apostolic pattern, that they may be sent forth to multiply universally.

40. This trial must be of absolute necessity to everyone in particular and to all in general for the constituting and cementing of the church of Philadelphia together, by the clearing away of all the remaining infirmities of nature, and burning up all the hay, stubble, and dross which may have been added to the Word of the Lord.

41. For nothing must remain in this church but what can remain in the fire, Holy Ghost. For as a refiner will the Lord purify the sons and daughters of the living God, and purge them into perfect righteousness.

42. Through the operation of the Spirit in these waters, they may for a long time contend with many infirmities and evils, yet if it be kept continually warm and watched it cannot at last but work out a perfect cure and bring a full and complete redemption from the earth.

43. There may be some at present living who may come to be thus fully and totally redeemed having another body put on them, i.e., after the priestly order.

44. This priestly, anointed body will render them impregnable, and qualify them for that high degree of spiritual government to which they are called.

45. Wherefore it requires on our part to suffer the spirit of burning to do upon us the refining work, fanning us with His fiery

breath, searching every part within us until all be pure and clean, and we thereby arrive to His fixed body from which wonders are to flow out.

46. This body will be the sealing character of the Philadephia church.

47. Upon this body will be the fixation of the Urim and Thummim, that are to be appropriated to the Melchisedecan order whose descent is not to be counted in the genealogy of that creation (under the fall), but is another genealogy which is from the restoration.

48. Hence these priests will have a deep inward search, and a divine insight into the secret things of the Deity, and will be able to prophesy on clear ground, not darkly and enigmatical, for they will know what is couched in the first originality of all being and the eternal arch type of nature, and will be capacitated to bring them forth according to the divine council and ordination.

49. The Lord, whose hand is lifted up, sweareth in truth and righteousness that from Abraham's loins, according to the spirit, there shall arise a holy priesthood.

50. Abraham and Sarah were a type of that which should be produced and manifested in the last age of the world.

51. The mighty spirit of Cyrus is appointed to lay the foundation of the true temple and to support it in its building.

52. These are such characteristics, or marks, whereby the pure virgin church, so founded, shall be certainly known and distinguished from all others, and whereby the action and true sound of the Holy Ghost shall be discerned from that which is false, base, counterfeit.

53. There must be a manifestation of the Spirit whereby to edify and raise up this church suitable to the ascension of Jesus Christ.

54. This manifestation must be the absoluteness of power and in the beauty of holiness, so bringing down heaven upon earth and representing here the new Jerusalem state.

55. In order to which, spirits that are thus purely begotten, conceived and born of God, can ascend to Jerusalem above, where their head in great majesty doth reign, and there receive such a mission whereby they shall be empowered to bring down to this world its transcendant glory.

56. None but those arisen in Christ in the regeneration (reformation) can thus ascend and receive of His glory; can descend again to communicate the same, being thereby His representatives upon the new earth and subordinate priests under Him, the Lord of lords, and King of kings.

57. Now He that ascended and glorified has made Himself our debtor, consequently He will not be wanting in qualifying and furnishing certain high principal instruments who shall be most humble and as little regarded as Daniel was, whom he will dignify with great knowledge and priestly sovereignty for the drawing together in one, the scattered little flock into one fold, coming out of all nations.

58. Therefore, there should be a holy emulation and ambition stirred up among all true lovers of Jesus so that they may be the first fruits unto Him that is risen from the dead, and so be made principal agents for Him and with Him that they may be, if possible, members of the firstborn of Jerusalem above, our Mother.

59. All lovers of Jesus and true waiters for His Kingdom (in spirit) under whatsoever professions or forms that are dispersed, ought to be members among the Philadelphia Spirit to whom this Message pertains.

60. The society is not the church of Philadelphia, but consists of those who are associated to wait and hope in the unity of the Spirit for its appearance and manifestation, wherefore there is such a strict charge given them throughout this Message to be watchful and quicken up their pace.

Colony Membership List

This partial list of colony members contains 427 names. The bulk of the information was taken from court records and petition lists presented as affadavits in court proceedings. The date of birth is estimated, the place of last residence prior to entering the colony noted where available, the date of entry into the colony and the date of departure included in many cases.

Name	Birth	Prior Residence	Joined	Left
Achterberg, Hilda Pritchard	1893	Melbourne	1906	1919
Adams, Grace Goodwin	1893		1907	
Adkins, Thomas	1880	California	1903	1927
Adkins, Mary Ranger	1871	Michigan	1904	
Ailes, Harriet Bond	1901	England	1921	
Ailes, Charles				
Anderson, Joseph				1920 (died)
Askerlund, Annabelle Wheeler		Arkansas		
Bailey, Annie Bond		England	1921	
Bailey, William				
Baker, Homer			1913	1918
Bamford, Eliza		Australia	1905	1925
Baushke, Albert			1903	
Baushke, Theodore				
Baushke, Otis		Michigan	1903	
Baushke, Eliza Murphy		Australia	1905	
Baushke, Frank			1903	
Baushke, Lulu		Indiana	1903	1910
Baushke, Harriet				
Baushke, George			1903	

Name	Birth	Prior Residence	Joined	Left
Baushke, Helen				1921
Baushke, Emma			1903	1922
Baushke, Henry				1922
Baushke, Stanley				
Baushke, Dwight			1905	1926
Baushke, David			1903	1927
Baushke, Cora Bell		Australia	1906	
Baushke, Winifer Murphy		Australia	1905	
Bell, Andrew				
Bell, Sarah		Australia	1906	
Bell, Gladys		Australia	1906	
Bell, Leslie				
Bell, Marie Falkenstein		Germany	1911	
Benstead, William		England	1906	
Blackburn, James		Australia	1905	
Blackburn, Rachel Bulley		Australia	1905	
Blakenship, Gladys			1905	1916
Blume, Emily		England	1913	
Blume, Max				
Boltz, Henrietta			1919	1920
Bond, Raymond		England	1921	
Bond, Mary		England	1921	
Boone, Clifford				
Boone, Helen Perroud		Washington		1920
Bowers, Elise			1916	
Boyersmith, Clovis	1903		1918	
Boyersmith, Margaret Vieritz			1916	
Boyette, Thomas			1903	1910
Boyette, Clara				
Boyette, Cliola				
Boyette, William	1894		1903	1911, 1917
Brison, William			1922	1923
Brown, William				
Brown, Anna				
Bulley, John	1873	Australia	1905	
Bulley, Edmund		Australia	1905	
Bulley, Percy		Australia	1905	1924
Bulley, Myrtle Hartman				

Name	Birth	Prior Residence	Joined	Left
Burkland, Lillian				
Bush, Helen Goodwin	1903		1907	1923
Cady, Fred				
Cady, Mary Estes			1914	
Caudle, John	1878		1903	1923
Caudle, Mary	1901		1917	1923
Caudle, Charles			1903	1925
Caudle, Jessie Wheeler				
Chesters, Albert John	1883	Philadelphia	1903	1910
Chesters, Edith				
Chesters, Ruth			1903	1910
Clark, Moses	1871	Australia	1905	
Clark, Edith				
Clark, Frank				
Clark, Norman				
Clark, Sidney				
Clark, Zilla				
Connon, John				
Connon, Laura		Texas	1914	
Couch, Elizabeth		North Carolina	1910	
Couch, Deaver			1910	
Couch, Edgar				
Couch, Job				
Couch, Jewell			1912	
Crow, Glen				
Crow, Esther Widders			1905	
Crow, Gay				
Crow, Lois			1914	
Crow, Ruth			1914	
Dalager, Agnes			1918	
Dalager, Violet			1918	
Daniels, John			1915	
Daniels, Effie Landcaster			1915	
Dewhirst, Thomas			1920	
Dissen, Charles	1861	Missouri	1903	
Dissen, Lizzie	1874		1903	
Drake, Pulaski				
Drake, Louisa		Alabama		
Estes, Ruth	1906	Arkansas	1914	

Name	Birth	Prior Residence	Joined	Left
Essex, Alice			1903	
Everett, Veda	1912	Arizona	1917	
Falkenstein, Albert				
Falkenstein, Ruby Baushke	1900	Michigan	1903	
Falkenstein, David				
Falkenstein, Freda	1899	Germany	1911	
Falkenstein, Gladys	1903	Australia		
Faust, Louis			1904	
Faust, Margaret Matter			1904	
Fenn, Ella Hurd		Michigan	1903	1905
Flake, Claudra		Illinois	1919	1923
Flake, Pearl				
Fletcher, Elizabeth			1903	
Flynn, Elizabeth Fortney	1891	Pennsylvania	1907	1921
Forrester, Larkin	1895	Texas	1916	
Forrester, Clara	1899		1920	1924
Frye, William				
Frye, Edith Meldrim	1890	Colorado	1903	
Glover, William		Texas	1904	
Glover, Jane	1881	Texas	1904	
Glover, Kate			1904	
Goodwin, Mary	1877	Pennsylvania	1907	
Goodwin, Eunice			1907	
Groves, William				
Groves, Laura Plank	1878	Colorado	1903	
Hall, Percy	1873	Australia	1916	1927
Hall, Adele	1882	Australia	1916	1927
Hall, Audrey	1909	Australia	1916	1927
Hannaford, Rachel	1878	Australia	1905	
Hannaford, Joseph		Australia	1905	
Hannaford, Horace		Australia	1905	
Hannaford, Miriam	1883	Australia	1905	
Hannaford, William				
Hansel, John		Ohio	1912	1920
Hansel, Margaret			1912	
Hansel, Edna				
Hansel, Katherine				
Hansel, Ralph			1912	1920
Hansel, Russell			1912	1920

Name	Birth	Prior Residence	Joined	Left
Hansel, John				
Hansel, Jerry	1898	Ohio	1912	1920
Hansel, Esther Johnson			1903	
Harrison, William Franklin		Australia	1905	
Harrison, Jacob		Australia	1905	
Harrison, David	1905	Australia	1905	
Haynes, Elverse	1911	North Carolina	1916	
Hebertson, Dons		Australia		
Hebertson, Gladys	1910	Australia		
Hill, Gladys		Canada	1905	
Hill, Richard	1879	Canada	1905	
Hill, Rosie Plank	1879	Colorado	1903	
Hill, Dora				
Hill, Lillian David				
Hilton, Wilson	1859		1904	1905
Holliday, Allan				
Holliday, Roxie				
Hornbeck, Ray	1892	Missouri	1903	
Hornbeck, Geneva Goodwin	1895		1905	
Hornbeck, Frank				1920 (died)
Hornbeck, Bertha Bell	1897	Australia	1905	
James, Martha	1867		1907	
James, Hubert	1896		1907	1922
James, Myrtle	1897		1907	1922
James, Mabel	1890		1907	1921
Jeffrey, Charlie				
Jeffrey, Gladys McFarlane	1887	Australia	1905	
Jeffrey, Rueben				
Johnson, Edwin		Sweden	1903	
Johnson, Anna Adkins				
Johnson, Bert				
Johnson, Catherine				
Johnson, Esther				
Keenan, Amanda	1895		1903	1919
Keenan, Richard	1898		1913	1919
Keiser, Anna				
Kester, Elizabeth Shuttle		Canada	1903	1907
Kester, Roy				

Name	Birth	Prior Residence	Joined	Left
Kirkham, James		Australia		
Kirkham, Henry Ernest	1886	Australia	1909	
Kirkham, Vetra Drake		Georgia	1918	
Koehler, Alfred	1892		1912	1926
Koehler, Cora	1898		1912	1926
Lane, Solon				
Lane, Vernie Reed			1908	
Lanier, Forest	1873	Missouri	1903	
Lanier, Annie Faust			1904	
Larson, Grave Reeves		Missouri	1903	
Lumen, Ruth		Oregon	1918	1924
Lynch, Silas				
Lynch, Cora Rein	1905		1907	1923
McCaslin, Florence			1918	
McFarlane, James		Australia	1905	
McFarlane, Leslie	1905	Australia	1905	
McFarlane, Miriam		Australia	1905	
McFarlane, Violet		Australia	1905	
McFarlane, Cyril	1901	Australia	1905	1922
McFarlane, Ellice	1899	Australia	1905	1924
McFarlane, Ernest		Australia	1905	
McFarlane, Doria		Australia	1905	
McFarlane, Herman	1896	Australia	1905	1922
McFarlane, Grave Lane				
Maderes, M.				
Martin, Setven Ray				
Martin, Maretta Winifred	1903		1910	
Martin, W. H.	1881	Texas	1920	1926
Martin, Annie Lewis	1901	California	1906	1919
Martin, William		Texas	1920	
Matthews, Earl	1885	Texas	1916	
Meldrim, Wilbur	1900		1905	1919
Mergenthaler, Herman				
Mergenthaler, Lillian	1889	Australia	1905	
Mills, Percy				
Mills, Estelle Meldrim	1892		1903	1913
Mitchell, May			1914	1919
Mooney, Silas			1903	
Mooney, Cora			1903	

Name	Birth	Prior Residence	Joined	Left
Moore, James	1878	Georgia	1906	
Moore, Etiodorpha	1902		1911	
Moore, Walter	1898	Alaska	1917	1925
Moore, Dora Hill				
Moore, Minerva	1905		1914	1921
Murphy, Daniel	1828	Australia	1905	
Murphy, Winnie		Australia	1905	
Nelson, Arthur				
Nelson, Lena Johnson	1900			1919
Ohrn, Gus Sr.			1907	
Ohrn, Gus	1905		1907	1924
Ohrn, Lavinia Woodworth	1890		1911	
Olsen, Josephine	1889		1905	1910
Pritchard, Isabella	1858	Australia	1906	1919
Purnell, Benjamin	1878	Kentucky	1903	
Purnell, Mary		Kentucky	1903	
Raft, Estella Meldrim	1870	Colorado	1903	1920
Raft, Edith				
Raft, Wilbur				
Raft, Estell				
Rains, Atta			1903	
Rains, Lillian				
Reed, Leslie				
Reed, Leslie H.	1896		1908	
Reed, Elta Noron	1897		1908	
Reed, Warren	1899		1908	1919
Reed, May Vaughan			1910	
Reed, Robert				
Reed, Ruth Bamford			1905	1922
Rein, William			1907	
Rein, Pearl			1907	
Rein, Edith		Arkansas	1907	
Reynolds, Ed		Pennsylvania	1916	1923
Reynolds, Ila	1891	California	1916	1923
Robertson, General				
Robertson, Ida				
Robertson, Henry				
Robertson, Linnie				
Robertson, Mamie	1891	North Carolina	1905	

Name	Birth	Prior Residence	Joined	Left
Robertson, Oscar				
Robertson, Phoebe				
Robertson, Roy				
Roe, Jalmar			1916	1923
Roe, Stella			1914	1923
Rogers, Frank	1867	Colorado	1904	1905
Rosetta, Adolph				
Rosetta, Ethel Tucker	1890	California	1903	
Rosetta, Theresa				
Rosetta, Emil	1888	Kansas	1907	1916
Rosetta, Leona		California	1903	1919
Rosetta, Dolphine				
Rosetta, Frank	1894	Kansas	1907	
Rosetta, Ione Smith	1892		1906	1916
Rowe, Thomas	1864	Australia	1903	
Rowe, Emma	1871	Australia	1903	
Rowe, Leonard		Australia	1913	
Rowe, Elizabeth Stroup	1901		1918	
Rubel, Ben				1920
Rubel, Gladys Bamford	1903	Australia	1905	1920
Salin, Martha		Illinois	1918	1922
Sanderson, Joseph	1859	British Columbia	1910	
Sassman, George	1865	Illinois	1905	
Sassman, Charity		Texas	1903	
Sassman, Oscar	1904		1907	
Sassman, Mellie Edmunds			1916	1926
Sassman, George	1895		1907	1919
Sassman, Henry		Illinois	1907	1919
Sassman, Irene Pritchard	1892		1906	1919
Schaeffer, Edna		Colorado	1912	
Schwartz, Edith Clarke		Australia	1905	1911
Schnieder, John		Ohio	1903	
Schnieder, Wesley		Ohio	1903	
Schnieder, Ada Ross	1882	England	1906	
Schnieder, Olive Craig				
Smiley, Sam	1881			1924
Smiley, Ruth Lumen				
Smith, John F.	1874	Kansas	1909	

Name	Birth	Prior Residence	Joined	Left
Smith, Josie	1886	Kansas	1909	1924
Smith, William Emmett		Alabama	1906	
Smith, Ariana				
Smith, Virgil			1911	
Smith, Mary			1911	
Smith, Ruby Glover	1901	Texas	1903	
Smith, Ruth Wade				
Smith, Virgil D.	1907		1911	
Spalter, Dorothy Wade	1898		1907	1912
Staubach, Stephen	1894		1917	1922
Stott, May Webster				
Stroupe, Henry H.				
Stroupe, Carrie Rockefeller				
Stroupe, Albert	1904		1917	1918
Swanson, Christian	1891	Florida	1913	1914
Swanson, Ruth	1892		1914	
Swant, Elizabeth				
Swant, Martin				1911
Swant, Owen	1897	Minnesota	1907	1911
Tally, Jessie Lee				
Tally, Edith Walker	1898		1916	
Thomas, Daniel	1898		1919	1921
Thomas, Eva			1919	
Thorpe, Frances	1876	Iowa	1904	
Tucker, James	1866	North Carolina	1903	
Tucker, John Ogden	1900		1903	1917
Tucker, Violet McFarlane	1893	Australia	1905	
Tucker, Carl				
Tucker, Viola Sassman	1901		1907	1920
Tucker, Earl			1903	
Tucker, Robert				
Tucker, Rosie	1906		1913	1926
Tulk, Samuel	1866	Australia	1905	
Tulk, Eliza	1868	Australia	1905	
Tulk, Florence	1889	Australia	1905	
Tulk, Lillian	1890	Australia	1905	
Tulk, Violet		Australia	1905	
Tyler, Marcus	1846	Australia	1905	
Vaughan, Hix			1910	

Name	Birth	Prior Residence	Joined	Left
Vaughan, Mary				
Vaughan, Adelaide				
Vaughan, Elsie Rowe				
Vaughan, Hubert				
Vaughan, Otis				
Vaughan, Velma				
Vaughan, Virdo			1910	1925
Vieritz, Cliola Bagette	1901		1903	1919
Vogler, Herbert	1901	Illinois	1914	1922
Vogler, Mildred Vaughan	1903		1910	1923
Wade, Richard H.		Oklahoma		
Wade, Cletis		Oklahoma		
Wade, Dorothy		Oklahoma		
Wade, Edna		Oklahoma		
Walker, Hugh		Pennsylvania	1917	
Walker, Marie Boyersmith		Australia		
Walmer, Al	1875	Colorado	1904	
Walmer, Ida Caudle	1887	Texas	1903	
Walstrom, Gustaf	1891	Sweden	1919	
Walstrom, Tiflis Drake			1918	
Warner, Annie Olive			1912	1918
Wheeler, Virginia	1895	Alabama	1908	
Wilkerson, Bert		Oregon	1915	1926
Williams, Austin	1896	Texas	1913	1922
Williams, Miriam McFarlane		Australia		
Williams, Clay				
Williams, Preston				
Williams, Sidney A.			1913	1918
Wilson, Thomas	1876	Texas	1906	
Wilson, Millard	1899		1906	
Winiborg, John	1878	Sweden	1908	
Winiborg, Lucy Caudle		Texas	1904	
Woodworth, Ami	1889	Oklahoma	1911	1926
Woodworth, Countess Drake				
Woodworth, Emerald			1911	1925
Woodworth, Bessie Daniels	1905		1915	
Woodworth, Manna	1896			
Woodworth, Annie Robertson	1896	North Carolina	1905	
Wright, William	1876	Australia	1905	

Name	Birth	Prior Residence	Joined	Left
Wright, Leah	1881	Australia	1905	
Wright, Vera	1903	Australia	1905	1918
Wuerth, Hazel Wade		Oklahoma	1907	1916
Wulff, Elna Hill	1899		1915	
Wylands, Frank				
Wylands, Della Martin	1883		1906	
Zerrer, Freda	1885	Germany		

APPENDIX C

Biographical Information

Material about the membership of most communal colonies is difficult to obtain. A few communities, like Brook Farm, had members who reflected on their experiences after they left while some communities, like Oneida, asked their members to assess their past lives on entry. The following biographical information was taken by a prosecuting attorney and his staff in search of evidence to put Benjamin Purnell in jail. Some of this information was given freely by disgruntled and disappointed former members while others had to be subpoened and their life stories taken from them.

Such biographical information gives up a glimpse of the families who came to the ingathering at Benton Harbor. We know a great deal about Benjamin Purnell and his life and these sketches allow us to see his followers. This material appeared in rough form in Nichols's notes and has been edited with an eye toward providing personal detail rather than legal evidence.

Frank Baushke Family. "Frank Baushke, wife and baby girl, Harriet, joined the colony selling their little home in Benton Harbor, at first of ingathering. Frank and Lulu traveled on the road as preachers at various times and were finally sent to Australia. . . . Lulu returned from Australia with Mary McDermott, leaving Frank Baushke and John Snyder over there. Lulu was discouraged with the place when she returned, and after listening to Harriet's story left the colony. Harriet Baushke is in Cleveland and bears an unsavory reputation. Frank Baushke is in the House of David and Lulu Baushke is in California."

Meldrim Family. "Tom Meldrim, father, with wife, two daughers, Edith and Estelle, and one son, Wilber, came to the colony in 1904 or 1905 from Cripple Creek, Colo. They brought some property. The oldest of these children was 13 and 14. . . . They lived in the Ark for a time, then the mother was moved to the farm with the boy and Estelle, and Tom lived in another place. When Benjamin moved to Bethlehem I was moved with him and Mary and went on the road preaching shortly after. While on the road Mary Purnell wrote me Benjamin had moved Edith to Bethlehem and she was eating at their table. After I came home, in a day or two, Mary Purnell told me to watch Edith Meldrim because she thought she was getting pretty soft with Benjamin and asked me if I had ever seen Benjamin feeling her legs or breast. . . . At one time Benjamin told Edith in my presence that the mother had made a confession showing that she was nothing but an ordinary trollop . . . and advised her not have anything to do with her mother. . . . On one occasion while sleeping in a room with Edith I was awakened by hearing voices in some bed, and Benjamin was there. The next day Edith said she had taken covenants and said, 'I have taken the covenants. You have passed them and could take them too.' On second or third conversation on subject he came to room and had intercourse with Edith right before me. Tom Meldrim died at House of David. Mrs. Estelle Mills Rouse, her mother, and Wilber Meldrim live at Niles."

Vaughan Family. "They entered the House of David in 1910. The family consisted of husband, Hicks Vaughan, wife, Mary Jane Vaughan, and children, Elsie, Velma, Hubert, Zula, Tommie May, Mildred, Otis, and Verdo, ranking from one to fourteen years. Vaughan turned into the colony at that time $4,400. They were not there more than a week or two before the entire family was separated. . . . The girls were put under Emma Rowe, among a bunch taken over in 1915, and from there they were moved up to Shiloh and then over to Benjamin's house. They were married in group marriages in 1914 and 1919."

Chester Family. "Albert and Ruth Chester came to the colony in 1904, after having read some of the books of the faith. They sold all their property and turned everything over to the House of David. There was $22,000 of this property. The children used every effort to keep them from going to the House of David. . . . They lived in the colony for some considerable time, but finally the house in which they were living burned and it was rumored they had set the fire. After the fire they were sent to Aral: that is, Chester and his wife and daughter, Edith. The mother wrote a letter to her son stating the conditions they were living under and begging for help, and he brought the family out by paying their expenses himself."

Edward Johnson Family. "My father got Benjamin's faith through Mary McDermott in San Francisco. Mary McDermott wrote and told Benjamin my father was a contractor and builder, and about that time Benjamin came to Benton Harbor and he wrote my father, calling him to the ingathering. My mother was not in the faith, very much against it, but my father proceeded to make preparations to go and leave her. In the meantime my uncle, Tom Adkins, wrote and informed Benjamin that my mother's health was poor and her mind not right. Benjamin Purnell wrote a letter to my father, telling him inasmuch as his wife was not in the faith, he would have to come to some agreement with her before he could join the colony, but he said, 'If I am correctly informed that her mind is unbalanced, the easiest way to get rid of her would be to put her in an asylum.' He also wrote instructions to this effect to my Uncle Tom. . . . My father had me write a letter and tell Benjamin the authorities would not take her but that he could make satisfactory arrangements with her, and Benjamin wrote him to come on."

Stritch Family. "It is claimed that Elizabeth and her sister, Alvina, came from Vancouver, B.C. and brought with them $50,000 or $100,000. The husband of Elizabeth came also. He was in poor health and finally died at the Ark after he had been in the colony a short time. After he died, Mrs. Stritch got queer, and she and her sister were sent to High Island."

The Fleming Family. "Came from New Zealand, Malcolm Fleming, wife, and daughter Sophie. They brought some property, money, and stock. The daughter Sophie lived in Jerusalem, and it is uncertain as to whether Benjamin had anything to do with her. The girl went insane and made certain outcries or charges against Benjamin and she was sent to Kalamazoo, October 8, 1919 and released October 13, 1922; later was sent to New Zealand, where she is now in an asylum. Some of the Fleming family now live in Benton Harbor. They were kicked out of the colony without a cent."

Markham Family. "James Markham and his wife came from Kentucky about 1904 or 1905. He brought some property. He went mentally wrong and claimed he was to have brides. His wife left him before that and got a divorce and married some other man later on. . . . Benjamin kept him in a barn until Richard, his son, objected, and then he was shipped back to Kentucky, but during this time Benjamin put up a fake marriage for the amusement of the girls. Ray and Estelle Hornbeck took part of Leah and Rachel. They were dressed in white, etc. . . . Edith Meldrim, after he left, wrote him for money. . . . Some time afterward Richard, who was a watchman, was killed on a railroad near Paw Paw. He was found with his hair in his pocket, also money, and was brought back to the House of David for burial. Benjamin took money off his person, and he was buried in Crystal Springs Cemetery."

The Widders Family. "Lige Widders and Hettie Widders and four children, Jessie, Mabel, Albert and Esther. They brought in considerable money. They were all separated. She was put to cook in one house and the old man worked on one of the farms. The daughter Mabel was moved to live in Jerusalem and Esther stayed with her mother most of the time—she wasn't very bright. Either through her relations with Ben or by reason of his talk with her, Mabel got delusions in regard to that matter and would write in her confessions concerning same. These confessions were read by Esther, Benjamin, and others. When it looked as if there were charges against him, Ben directed that they be sent to the office instead of going to Mary, as was the usual course. This girl eventually got into poor health and was sent out to one of the farms and died there. After Mabel's death her father went insane, and the burden of his cries was concerning the daughter and the way she had been wronged. In fact he got so bad that they tied him to a tree in the orchard and when the girls passed back and forth he took on terrible. He was eventually disposed of; don't know if anybody knows about it. He died at the House of David.

His son Jesse was held mentally unbalanced for some reason—possibly on account of his sister or his father. He escaped and went somewhere.

The other son, Albert, who was a bright boy, left and went back to Ohio. Later on the other sister went to him.

The mother went insane and was sent to the asylum at Kalamazoo on August 14, 1922, where she died on July 14, 1926."

The Pate Family. "Pate was a contractor from Henderson, North Carolina. Through reading the writings he got into the faith and when Hazel Weurth was on a preaching trip she met him and at that time he wanted to turn over checks in blank dollars to her for all the money she wanted. This he didn't do, but he bought Hazel and himself tickets and came to Benton Harbor where he was taken in. Just how much money he turned over I don't know but it was a large amount. It was learned through an order that went into the office that Pate had syphillis, and Benjamin finding this out started in to drive Pate out of the colony, and all manner of little persecutions were used to that end. Finally he went down to Benton Harbor and either jumped off or fell off a building and was killed. They gave Pate nothing when he left and his family was broken up before he came to Benton Harbor."

The Veen Family. "Simon Veen came from British Columbia or Washington to Benton Harbor. He left his family behind him but brought quite a sum of money with him. After being there a time he got batty and Benjamin attempted to send him back to his home, but he refused to go on account of the Biblical saying about 'Putting your hand to the plow,' etc. He got so bad that they were going to send him to the island but he slipped out and got away when he learned what they proposed to do with him and went home. He had delusions so that he claimed he was the Seventh Messenger and created a scene at a public meeting in 1917 or 1918."

The James Family. "Martha James left her husband who lived in Kansas City. She got into the faith which caused separation and divorce from her husband, and she and one son Hubert and one daughter Mabel came to the colony. This daughter roomed with Hazel Weurth, and Hazel saw Ben having intercourse with Mabel. Mabel was forced to marry George Hendrickson in 1914. She went insane over this marriage and Ben sent her to High Island. He sent George with her and they were there some time. She wrote letters down from the Island telling that she was in love with her husband, and these letters were read in the parlor before all the girls. She wrote about having intercourse with her husband. Dr. Sowers said she had dementia praecox. Her relations with her husband or something else finally cured her of her delusions, and she returned to the colony and was there when Esther left but subsequently moved away and is now in Cleveland."

The Bamford Family. "George and Eliza Bamford lived in Melbourne, Australia. He had considerable property, and he and his wife were induced to come from Australia to Benton Harbor bringing with them one daughter, Gladys. Ruth, another daughter, was born about thirty days after they reached the colony. Both of these children were brought up in the faith. Bamford turned in all his property. He was one of the gentry in Australia and retired, but when he went to the colony he was put at hard labor, such as mixing concrete. While acting as watchman without sufficient clothing he was exposed and took pneumonia and died after he had been in the colony several years. The two girls were taken to Shiloh and both of them seduced by Benjamin. Gladys left in 1920 and Ruth in 1922. The mother still stayed, refusing to believe the story of the two girls."

The Meyers Family. "George Meyers and his wife came into the colony about 1907 and their son-in-law came with them. They brought about $30,000 or $35,000. The son-in-law after being there a time advised the old people to leave as he thought that Benjamin was illiterate and was not what he represented himself to be. This statement he made to Esther who reported it to Benjamin who called the old man in and said to him, 'That son-in-law of yours just wants to get you back home when he will get your money and do away with you.' This took place after the old man had told Benjamin he thought he would go back to his son-in-law. The son-in-law was an osteopath and had treated his father-in-law, and Purnell in his argument to keep the old man from returning told him what he needed was exercise, and he finally persuaded the old man and his wife to stay and the son-in-law left. Afterward Benjamin got the old man performing on the trapeze from which he fell and broke his neck, but before he died Frances Thorpe got him to sign the roll and Hazel Weurth heard Ben tell Frances Thorpe to go over and get his signature before he died because they could not fake any signatures. Thorpe got it and shortly after the old man passed away. The old lady, his wife, is still in the colony."

The Ryan Family. "Peter Ryan and his wife came to the colony and turned in what they had. He drew quite a large pension. He brought a niece with him by the name of Carrie Ryan. She got mixed up in a mess with Jim Stollard, Mary's brother, along with Elizabeth Fletcher, and on account of this trouble Ben got Carrie Ryan married off in the 1910 group to Bob Gray. Bob and Carrie left and went back to the colony, and the old man began showing doubts. This was learned through reports that came into the office as they had a reporting or spy system. The old man then refused to turn in his pension, and he was rebuked at an open meeting and threatened with expulsion. Benjamin said he could not compel them to turn in their pensions but he could cut them off. A week later Ryan dropped dead while carrying a heavy stove, and Benjamin got up in a public meeting and said this was another case of Ananias and Sapphira."

The Hoskins Family. "Ben and Emma Hoskins came from California and brought some money with them. They were separated. A short time after their arrival a forty-day fast was declared. At the end of the fast Ben Hoskins and some others nearly died and Hoskins never recovered. He was sent back to California. His wife, Emma, stayed at the colony but for some reason she never menstruated after that, and she got the delusion that she was the tree of life and that her blood was leaving her according to the *Star*. At the direction of Benjamin, Esther Hansel, Jane Glover, and Florence Craig sprinkled red ink in her bed to make her believe she was alright and had menstruated. But that made her worse, and she claimed that this was an indication of her return to the flower of her youth. She was taken in an automobile and was sent to 30 Acres under guard, but she got away and was found in the streets of Benton Harbor in an automobile. She was taken in an automobile to the asylum at Kalamazoo on Benjamin's directions.

Upon her recovery she was sent back to California where her husband had gone and died. She now lives in Los Angeles."

Lane Family. "This old man Lane came with two daughters, one a schoolteacher and the other a bookkeeper. His object in coming with them was that he had heard tales about the place and he wanted to know if it was a suitable place for his daughters to come. I talked to old man Lane, and Benjamin talked with him in my presence. The two girls and the old man were royally entertained, special effort being put forth to entertain them. The old man left and returned later with his wife and younger son, a married daughter and her two sons. The daughter left her husband to come. They turned in some property, just how much I don't know. They were girls in their twenties when they came, the boy probably fourteen or fifteen. After they came in the old man and lady were moved to the farm; the two girls were eventually moved to Shiloh. Eva Lane worked in the office as bookkeeper, and Flora Lane taught school. The group marriages came on then, and Eva Lane married Clarence Bell September 2, 1914. She became discouraged with the thing because of Ben's actions both toward herself and particularly his actions with Ruth Swanson. Eva Lane Bell and her husband were divorced. She went away with Dave Perrin, and they are now living in New Zealand and have two children. The other sister is still in the House of David. Old man Lane and wife are still in the House of David. The daughter and two foolish children were shipped to High Island."

The Winfrey Family. "Edgar and Ole Winfrey came from Fort Worth, Texas, about 1912. They had just completed a new home, and Esther on one of her trips stayed with them. Family consisted of mother, father, and baby and another yet to be born. Esther upon her return was questioned about their property. She told Ben that they had considerable and that the mother was pregnant. Under Ben's instructions they were informed to await coming to the colony until after arrival of the baby, and Benjamin named the baby Adina. They came after the baby was born and turned in their property. There was some trouble between husband and wife over a confession the husband made while he was separated from his wife, and because of this they were both sent back to Fort Worth. Benjamin did this through Esther Hansel, and the husband's confession was held over their heads with the threat that if they tried to get any of the property back it would be used against the husband in prosecuting."

The Klienknect Family. "Lena and Paul Klienknect, brother and sister, came from Germany. They could hardly speak the English language. They turned in a considerable sum of money. Benjamin moved Lena to Shiloh to cook for him. He had relations with her according to his own story to Esther Hansel. Lena lost her mind or became unbalanced on the question of sex involving the faith; thought she was the tree of life. She had to be moved out of Shiloh and put under guard. Benjamin told Esther Hansel it was a funny thing to him that all the German girls went batty as soon as he had anything to do with them. Benjamin said to Esther Hansel, 'I am afraid Lena is in the family way; told her what to do but you can't get anything into their heads.' Shortly after this Lena and Paul were shipped back to Germany, and Benjamin caused the story to be told around the colony that Paul had intercourse with his own sister."

The Smith Family. "Mr. and Mrs. Virgil Smith and two daughters, Etidorpha and Marrietta, and a small son came to the colony from Kentucky and turned in a considerable amount of money. Mrs. Smith herself was never in the faith but joined because of her husband. The mother was very much in love with her husband, and when he was sent to High Island to take care of dentistry work one winter, the wife became very blue and despondent and wrote very pathetic letters of love and endearment to her husband. This being contrary to the faith and considered a sin, the letters were read at Benjamin's instructions to the girls in Benjamin's parlor or they were commented upon by Benjamin and laughed at and made fun of by the girls.

The mother died of tuberculosis, and she was not in her grave before the two young girls under fifteen years of age were moved to Benjamin's house and under Benjamin's guardianship. Etidorpha Smith a short time after this became mentally unbalanced. This girl gave birth to a child, and it is claimed Benjamin is the father of the same."

The Darst Family. "William Darst and wife came from Zion City and turned in considerable money. Husband and wife were separated, Darst considered to be foolish. Always in trouble because he wanted to live with his wife. This man was terribly mistreated both by Benjamin and the officers. Esther Hansel has seen Frank Wyland, Edmund Bulley, Frances Thorpe, and Tom Adkins beat and abuse Darst because he would argue and refuse to do as they wanted him to do. He was finally sent to the island, and when he tried to get on the boat he was thrown into the icy water and nearly drowned."

Notes

Chapter One

1. Norman Cohn, *The Pursuit of the Millennium*, p. 3.
2. Ibid., p. 14. Kenneth Rexroth in *Communalism* begins his survey of communal history with a chapter on the Essenes, the Egyptian Therapeutae, and the community at Qumran. "As Renan said, Christianity was an Essenism which succeeded—more or less." Ibid., p. 23.
3. See Robert Lerner, *The Heresy of the Free Spirit in the Later Middle Ages*.
4. W. H. G. Armytage, *Heavens Below*, p. 14.
5. Christopher Hill has emphasized the impact that religious enthusiasts had during the 1640–60 period: "It is impossible to exaggerate the social significance of the religious and intellectual revolution of the sixteen forties and fifties. . . . Sects hereto illegal, whose members were drawn mainly from the lower classes, now met and discussed in public, and their views were printed. . . . The long term liberating effects of the competition of rival religious views, as against the monopoly which the established had enjoyed in 1641, is impossible to calculate." *Reformation and Revolution*, pp. 190–91. See also Hill's *Society and Puritanism*, chapters 5 and 14.
6. Keith Thomas, *Religion and the Decline of Magic*, p. 143.
7. For an excellent collection of essays on English millenarianism see Peter Toon, ed., *Puritans, the Millennium and the Future of Israel*.
8. Quoted in Armytage, *Heavens Below*, p. 19.
9. Norman Cohn has characterized this select group as the "righteous remnant" that read the prophetical books and saw their special role in history to establish a "rebuilt Jerusalem, A Zion which has become the spiritual capital of the world and to which all nations flow." Cohn, *The Pursuit of the Millennium*, p. 2.
10. Ronald Matthews, *English Messiahs*, p. xv.
11. Thomas, *Religion and the Decline of Magic*, p. 137.
12. See T. L. Underwood's essay "Early Quaker Eschatology" in Toon, ed., *Puritans, the Millennium and the Future of Israel*, pp. 91–103.
13. Matthews, *English Messiahs*, pp. 3–42.
14. Thomas, *Religion and the Decline of Magic*, pp. 139.
15. See Christopher Hill, *The World Turned Upside Down: Radical Ideas During the English Revolution*.
16. Quoted in Armytage, p. 34.
17. Nils Thune, *The Behmenists*, pp. 68 ff. Thune also mentions a German religious community led by Eva von Butlan, who claimed she was the second Eve, p. 146.
18. Clarke Garrett devotes a full chapter to the "Mystical International" in his *Respectable Folly*, pp. 97–120.

19. Henri Desroche, *The American Shakers*, stresses the importance of international influences on the development of Shakerism; he writes: "At any rate Europe's fading millennial vision, which had its last blaze in the Cevenne's, would soon receive new life from an unexpected encounter with another millenarian movement, this one in full bloom: American millenarianism" (p. 56).

20. See Desiree Hirst, *Hidden Riches* (New York: Barnes and Noble, 1964) and Robert Hindmarsh, *Rise and Progress of the New Jerusalem Church*. For the most complete exposition of the forces that molded eighteenth-century mystical thought see J. F. C. Harrison's *The Second Coming*.

21. Cecil Roth, *The Nephew of the Almighty*, p. 20.

22. Clarke Garrett doubts that Brothers ever visited Avignon, but was told about the society by Wright. Clarke Garrett, "Jacob Duche," in *Proceedings of the American Philosophical Society*, 119, no. 2 (March, 1975): 143–55. J. F. C. Harrison documents that Brothers knew about Avignon independent of Wright, *The Second Coming*, p. 72.

23. William Bryan, *A Testimony of the Spirit*, p. 27.

24. Ibid.

25. The sources for Brothers's life are Cecil Roth, *The Nephew of the Almighty* and G. R. Balleine, *Past Finding Out*. Both Roth and Balleine fail to cite any sources for their studies and therefore are difficult to trust at times. The recent Harrison study, *The Second Coming*, is an exemplary work that covers the details of Brothers's life, particularly Chapter 2.

26. Roth, *Nephew of the Almighty*, p. 20.

27. See John Lacy, *The Prophetical Warnings of John Lacy, Esq.* In the pamphlet Lacy states he had no anticlerical or antimonarchical sentiments and had simply been seized by the spirit to perform healing work. For an account of the French prophets in England see Desroche, *The American Shakers*, pp. 16–27.

28. Roth, *Nephew of the Almighty*, p. 38.

29. Ibid.

30. Ibid, p. 44.

31. Ibid., p. 46.

32. See Garrett, *Respectable Folly*, pp. 164–74.

33. Matthews, *English Messiahs*, p. 96.

34. E. P. Thompson, *The Making of the English Working Class*, p. 117.

35. *Dictionary of National Biography (DNB)*, 8:119, "Nathaniel Halhead."

36. In the margin of his engraving of Brothers, Sharp wrote: "Fully believing this to be the man whom God has appointed, I engrave his likeness." W. S. Baker, *William Sharp*, p. 79.

37. G. R. Balleine, *Past Finding Out*, p. 33.

38. See Garrett, *Respectable Folly*, pp. 186–87.

39. Matthews, *English Messiahs*, p. 101.

40. John F. C. Harrison, *The Second Coming*, pp. 66–67.

41. The full title was *The New Covenant Between God and His People; or the Hebrew Constitution and Charter; with the Statues and Ordinances, the Laws and Regulations and Commands and Covenants. By the late Mr. Brothers.*

42. Ibid.

43. Matthews, *English Messiahs*, p. 109.

44. A. M. Hyamson, *A History of the Jews in England*, p. 302.

45. The reference to her "aboral rhyme" is in a biographical sketch in the *DNB*, 18:685. There is no substantive modern biography of Southcott and researchers would do well to consult James Hopkins, "Joanna Southcott: A Study of Popular Religion and

Radical Politics, 1789–1814," Ph. D. dissertation, University of Texas at Austin, 1972. I am indebted to John F. C. Harrison for this reference and for his helpful comments on this chapter.

46. Harrison, *The Second Coming*, p. 88.

47. For a discussion of Pomeroy see Matthews, *English Messiahs*, pp. 55 ff.

48. Balleine, *Past Finding Out*, p. 26.

49. Matthews, *English Messiahs*, p. 59.

50. Ibid., p. 60.

51. Harrison, *The Second Coming*, p. 94.

52. Balleine, *Past Finding Out*, p. 55.

53. Matthews, *English Messiahs*, p. 72.

54. Harrison, *The Second Coming*, p. 97.

55. Cited in Balleine, *Past Finding Out*, p. 66.

56. See F. Anthony Wallace, "Revitalization Movements," *American Anthropologist*, 58, (1956): 264–81.

57. Clarke Garrett suggests that the notion that women could free the human race from Satan's bond was prevalent in sixteenth-century France. Garrett, *Respectable Folly*, p. 91.

58. Balleine, *Past Finding Out*, p. 72.

59. Ibid, p. 78.

60. Ibid.

61. Ibid., p. 70.

62. According to one source, Carlile described Ward as "the most philosophical Irishman I ever met with, and he is not the worst because risen from the lapstone." C. B. and A. B. Hollingsworth, eds., *Zions Works*, 5:37.

63. See J. F. C. Harrison's assessment of Ward in his *Quest for the New Moral World* (New York, 1969), pp. 112–13 and *The Second Coming*, p. 159.

64. Ward tried to instill some robust spirituality into Greaves, but found the Transcendentalist too ascetic: "Mr. Greaves lives upon bread and water; he finds it best for his health, he says. Very well, that's all right. I do not find fault with him for that; and I am at liberty to eat a little meat and to fare in common with other people, in moderation; and who is there that ought to chide me." Hollingsworth, *Zions Works*, 5:256.

65. Balleine, *Past Finding Out*, p. 103.

66. *DNB*, 21:1073, "John Wroe."

67. The major source for Wroe's life is the anonymous work, *The Life and Journal of John Wroe* (Gravesend, 1859).

68. Ibid. See also Tess Van Sommers, *Religions in Australia*, pp. 54–57, 84–86.

69. Allan Stewart, *The Abominations of the Wroeites*.

70. Ibid.

71. Armytage, *Heavens Below*, p. 276.

72. Harrison, *The Second Coming*, p. 140.

Chapter Two

1. *New York Sun*, August, 20, 1841.

2. Sylvester Bliss, *Memories of William Miller*, p. 142.

3. J. L. Bishop, *A Brief History of a Church Surnamed Israel*, p. 6.

4. Daniel Milton, *Revelation and Vindication*, p. 1.

5. *New York Sun*, January 28, 1845. Cited in Daniel Milton, *Messiahs Universal Kingdom, First, Sixth and Seventh Seal Opened with Thunder and Lightnings From the Pen of Daniel Milton*, p. 3.

6. *New York Sun*, July 31, 1858.

7. The Israelites sent a letter to the editor of the *Sunday Mercury* in January, 1862, with this message: "Will you please inform your readers that he is not our minister neither do we believe that any sin born man can be the promised Shiloh. Some years Mr. M. was a member of this church; he had also been a member of some Christian Church before uniting with us. It is several years since we had to expel him from the church for claiming these Divine Titles."

8. G. R. Balleine, *Past Finding Out*, p. 113.

9. P. G. Rogers, *The Sixth Trumpeter*, pp. 11–12.

10. Balleine, *Past Finding Out*, pp. 111–12. One study emphasizes the larger proportion of women over men in the Southcottian movement. "God had selected a woman, not a man, through which to reveal himself. . . .Joanna herself recognized that a remarkable number of women were flocking to her cause. 'This appears marvelous in my eyes,' she said, 'more so than all my writings.' " James Hopkins, "Joanna Southcott," p. 184.

11. Rogers, *The Sixth Trumpeter*, p. 7.

12. James Jershom Jezreel, *Extracts From the Flying Roll.*

13. Letter, J. J. Jezreel to "Lottie & William," Boston, August 30, 1882.

14. Rogers, *The Sixth Trumpeter*, p. 53 ff.

15. James F. Findlay, *Dwight Moody*, p. 177.

16. Harrison, *The Second Coming*, p. 79.

17. In October, 1891, Mills claimed to have undergone a physical change in which he "suffered great agony, and by which the evil was burned out of his body." Newspaper clipping, n. d., Michigan Historical Commission.

18. Harrison, *The Second Coming*, pp. 124–26.

19. *The Detroit Free Press*, April 24, 1892. Membership at the Detroit colony was about 120.

20. "A Copy of a Report Relating to the Israelite House of David," Michigan Historical Commission, Governors' Papers, 1958.

21. *Detroit Free Press*, April 24, 1892.

22. Ibid.

23. Ibid.

24. "Petition to the British Consul, D. H. Paunceforte" May 12, 1892, Public Record Office, London. They also received threatening notes stating that "if you and your heathenish tribe do not get out of town inside of two weeks you will be dealt with in a manner not to your liking. Remember there are several large trees in the neighborhood." Signed "By Order of the Committee." March 31, 1892, Public Record Office, London.

25. *State of Michigan* v. *Michael Mills.*

26. Ibid.

27. Ibid.

28. See "Prince Michael and the New Eve" in Rogers, *The Sixth Trumpeter*, pp. 111–28. A Detroit paper noted his passing with a headline: "Death Recalls 'Holy Rollers,' " *Detroit News*, January 23, 1922.

Chapter Three

1. *The People of the State of Michigan* v. *The Israelite House of David.* The Circuit Court for the County of Berrien. Louis H. Fead, Circuit Judge. Hereafter cited as Fead, *Michigan* v. *Israelites.*

2. House of David publication, *Brief Points of Benjamin's Travels*, p. 2.

3. House of David publication, *The Testimony of Benjamin.*

4. Milo Quaife, *Lake Michigan*, pp. 262–78. According to Purnell's own court testimony he married Mary Stollard on August 3, 1880.

5. In the colony literature Purnell's public career begins in 1894. See *Benjamin's Travels*, pp. 4–14.

6. House of David publication, *Brief Points of Benjamin's Travels*, p. 4.

7. Fead, *Michigan v. Israelites*.

8. John Pelton Statement, n. d., Michigan Historical Commission.

9. Ibid.

10. Fead, *Michigan v. Israelites*.

11. Property Deeds, Berrien County, Michigan, Vols. 153–57 (June, 1905–February, 1906).

12. James Pender, *History of Benton Harbor*.

13. J. S. Morton, *Reminiscences of the Lower St. Joseph River Valley*.

14. *Census of the State of Michigan: Population, I* (Lansing, 1904).

15. Orville Coolidge, *A Twentieth Century History of Berrien County, Michigan*.

16. Material about the Alphadelphia Phalanx can be found at the Michigan Historical Commission, University of Michigan and in N. Gordon Thomas, "The Alphadelphia Phalanx," Ph.D. dissertation, Michigan State University, 1970.

17. David C. Byers and Willis Dunbar, "Utopia in Upper Michigan," *Quarterly Review* (1955):171.

18. *Detroit Evening News*, April 13, 1897.

19. *Coming Nation*, March 20, 1895.

20. Joseph Cohen, *In Quest of Heaven*.

21. Fead, *Michigan v. Israelites*.

22. Alexander Cruden, *Unabridged Concordance to the Old and New Testaments and The Apocrypha* (Philadelphia, 1838 ed.).

23. House of David publication, *Shiloh's Coming and a Brief Explanation of the Time and Dates*, p. 10. Although England was the site of the earlier messengers, the United States became the favored spot. "Israel must first be gathered in America—the land of the free—They shall fly toward the land of the west while England goes through her judgments, and is purged. Then—and not till then—will Israel be gathered back to England. And when Israel is taken out of America, she will be purged, and great shall be her judgments because of the rejection of the message of life offered by Israel, even as Jesus offered life to the Jews! And from England they will be gathered to Palestine." *The Book of Wisdom, The Flying Roll*, 2:50.

24. Ibid., p. 12.

25. Ibid., p. 26. See P. Gerard Damsteegt's *Foundations of the Seventh Day Adventist Message and Mission* (Grand Rapids, 1977) for a discussion of the concept of sealing as debated by the American adventists.

26. House of David publication, *The Star of Bethlehem*, pp. 267–68.

27. Ibid, p. 709.

28. "He promises to cleanse the blood and take the evil away; and so it is written that a cleansing fountain shall be opened in the House of David for sin and uncleanness, and a new convenant—not like the old which was broken; and the new covenant is when I shall take away their sins—more than forgiving." *The Book of Wisdom, The Flying Roll*, 2:25.

29. "So I appear again, if we sow to the flesh, we shall of the flesh reap corruption—reap the wages of sin, which is death; but if we sow to the spirit, we shall of the spirit reap life everlasting." *The Book of Wisdom, The Flying Roll*, 3:89.

30. *The Star of Bethlehem*, p. 277.

31. "There shall be a fountain opened in the House of David for sin and unclean-

ness. A garden enclosed is my sister, a spring shut up, a fountain sealed:—now unsealed by the law of Christ. The paradisical laws will roll the stone away and the spring and fountain of life will be a refreshing stream from the presence of our Lord and his Christ. He that believeth in me as the scripture hath said, out of his belly shall flow rivers of living water; and it shall be in him a well of living water springing up into everlasting life. Behold the springtime has come! The voice of the turtle is heard in the garden of the bride! The winter is past, and we see the sunrise of the millennial day; and the time is rolling on, and soon the approach of the millennium morn." *The Book of Wisdom. The Flying Roll*, 4:31.

32. The chief prosecutor for the state during the trials was George Nichols, appointed by Governor Groesbeck in 1921. Nichols kept elaborate trial notes based on investigative reports and information from informers. Much of this information did not appear in the trial record, but, fortunately, his notes were kept by the attorney general's office at Lansing. Hereafter, they will be referred to as Nichols Trial Notes.

33. Nichols Trial Notes.

34. "Declaration of Incorporation," May 29, 1903. The opening statement in the 1905 revision acknowledged the Purnells' central role in the society: "Christ Jesus and Jerusalem with Benjamin and Mary Purnell, the anointed Heads by Shiloh of the Christian Israelite Church of God." The colony's pacifist stand was clearly stated in Article XII: "Therefore we could not carry the sword and gun in one hand to slay our fellow man."

35. Ibid.

36. Nichols Trial Notes.

37. See Appendix C for biographical sketches of some members, taken from the Nichols Trial Notes.

38. Deposition of Sally Humphrey, June 22, 1927.

39. Harry Williams's Statement, Nichols Trial Notes.

40. Two missionaries had come to England in July, 1905 and preached from a base in North London. They reportedly traveled to Ireland and Scotland and had about fifty followers in London. In May, 1906 nineteen men and women (mostly couples) sailed for Benton Harbor from England. "The trumpet is blowing and we go to the ingathering of Israel, for Benjamin and Mary, our leaders in Michigan, have spoken. We believe in the immortality of the body and those who live with us shall remain unchanged when the end comes, and the earth is restored to its Eden state." "The New Eden," *Daily Mail*, May 15, 1906. In 1906 missionary teams were sent to Australia and Alaska. The Australia visit resulted in twenty-one converts coming from Victoria in February, 1906 while the local newspapers reported that the Alaskan group had "found a gold field." *Benton Harbor News-Palladium*, Feb. 22, 1906.

41. According to one report, the majority of Australians were "well along in years though there were 25 children among the group." Newspaper clipping, n.d., Michigan Historical Commission.

42. Tess Van Sommers, *Religion in Australia*, p. 54.

43. *Detroit News*, April 2, 1905.

44. Ibid.

45. Ibid.

46. Ibid.

47. Ibid.

48. Ibid.

49. Ibid. Emphasis mine.

50. Ibid.

51. Ibid.

52. That estimate is from a pro-colony legal deposition and cannot be verified except to note that many members did turn over large sums on entry. See Appendix A.

53. *Benton Harbor News-Palladium*, March 29, 1905.

54. Their visit to London was in August, 1905. Margaret Bryan Affidavit, Michigan Historical Commission.

55. Mary Chew Statement, Michigan Historical Commission. In addition, Mary Chew was told that unless she gave up all her money and property she would not be saved.

56. *Benton Harbor News-Palladium*, June 8, 1927.

57. Sally Humphrey, June 22, 1927.

58. Isabella Pritchard, *Echoes of Life*, p. 10.

59. Ibid.

60. Ibid., p. 12.

61. Ibid., "Benjamin A Second Noah." "He is gathering together specimens of the animal kingdom from all over the world to insure their preservation after the coming of the millennium." *Benton Harbor News-Palladium*, April 27, 1906.

62. Ibid., p. 14.

63. House of David publication, *The Preachers Book*, n.p.

64. House of David publication, *Dialogue #44*, n.p.

65. Pritchard, *Echoes of Life*, p. 18.

66. "Declaration of Incorporation; The Israelite House of David," May 29, 1903, Michigan Historical Commission.

67. "Articles of Association and By-Laws," October 3, 1907.

68. "Articles of Voluntary Religious Association," January 1, 1908.

69. For an illuminating discussion of the female role in Shaker communities see Henri Desroche, *The American Shakers*, pp. 77–79.

70. "Amendment #1" to "Rules and By-Laws of the Israelite House of David," December 29, 1911.

71. Ibid.

72. Helen Kraft Deposition, March 9, 1906.

73. Ibid.

74. Ibid.

75. Ibid.

76. H. M. Williams, *Mysteries, Errors and Injustice at Mary and Benjamin's Israelite House of David*.

77. Nichols Trial Notes.

78. *Hansel v. Purnell*, II, 392.

79. Ibid., p. 34.

80. William Cleveland to Wilfred Powell, May 15, 1907.

81. William Cleveland to Wilfred Powell, April 27, 1907.

82. Ibid.

83. Charles E. White to Henry E. Chase, May 2, 1907.

84. Ibid.

85. Henry E. Chase to Reverend Elisha A. Hoffman, May 11, 1907.

86. Reverend Elisha A. Hoffman to Henry E. Chase, June 4, 1907.

87. I. W. Riford to Henry Chase, May 23, 1907.

88. Henry E. Chase to H. M. Williams, July 5, 1907.

89. Henry E. Chase to Harry Williams, August 20, 1907.

90. Petition to secretary of state, Lansing, Michigan, September 10, 1907. Purnell

when interviewed said: "They're nothing but lies, all lies. It is perfectly filth and rot," in his "familiar blue grass tongue." *Benton Harbor News Palladium,* September 6, 1907.

91. Henry E. Chase to William L. Cleveland, September 25, 1907. At a mass meeting on September 30 the colonists deeded all their property to Mary and Benjamin to show support. One member said: "This is our faith. If it were not we would not be here." *Benton Harbor News-Palladium,* October 1, 1907.

92. Henry E. Chase to H. S. Gray, October 18, 1907.

93. Henry E. Chase to Reverend Elisha A. Hoffman, November 6, 1907.

94. Mildred Giles Statement, n.d.

95. Ibid.

96. William L. Cleveland to Harry E. Chase, May 23, 1908.

97. "I thought I would just drop you a few lines to let you know of one young lady, an Australian named Ethel Williamson who went from here to Benton Harbor with us in 1905 in the Mary and Benj. sect, and has now returned here after a stay in that colony of a little over 4 years, during which time she tried several times to get away, but her plans were found out, and her object frustrated each time through being so closely watched. . . .She avers that M & B row and wrangle very much between themselves, after this style. M to B; You ought to go back where you came from, B to M: You give the money and I'll go quick enough and charge each other with undue familiarity with the brothers on Mary's part and with the young girls on Ben's part, thereby showing they are not a happy pair in themselves and are jealous of each other.

2ndly. Then Mary when not well, which is very often, has two of the brothers, viz. Frances Thorpe and Wm. Hannaford to bath her and won't have females to do it.

6thly. Benj. would often come into the women's bedrooms when they were bathing. . . .

7thly. On one occasion he tried to force a young girl named Gladys Hill aged about 18 yrs. old backwards onto a bed and endeavored to pull up her clothes." William L. Cleveland to Henry E. Chase, July 1908.

98. Henry E. Chase to William L. Cleveland, November 19, 1909.

99. J. D. Tucker to Fred Warner, December 1, 1909.

100. George Shoemaker, a former member, complained to local, state and federal officials for fifteen years and was dismissed as a crank. Another member, E. S. Peissert later joined another colony venture, Koreshan Unity, at Estero, Florida. His complaining letter of August, 1909, gives some interesting insights into the Australian Israelites' journey from their home to Grand Rapids in 1905: "It cost $15,000 to bring them to America via Suez Canal, to make a big splurge before the public. Mr. Lyles and I were delegated to meet them at N.Y. City and imagine my disgust to find that Benjamin had made them fast and even took their pin money from them, after they sailed." Peissert also stated that the eighty-three converts brought $100,000 with them. Rev. E. S. Peissert to Gov. Warner, August 19, 1909.

Chapter Four

1. Writing from Australia in late 1909 William Cleveland charged that Benjamin and Mary were "not a happy pair in themselves and are jealous of one another." William Cleveland to Henry E. Chase, December 21, 1909.

2. Nichols Trial Notes.

3. Ibid.

4. Ibid.

5. Nichols Trial Notes. It was reported that Purnell disguised himself as a woman

when Mrs. Baushke's attorney visited the colony. Nichols's notes fail to indicate how Purnell was able to disguise his flowing beard.

6. Ibid. At the same time they were denying any interest in relocating the colony: "While it is true that we have offers of free land for park purposes . . . we have no intention of moving our headquarters." *Benton Harbor News-Palladium*, November 26, 1910.

7. The marriages were between: Percy Mills-Estelle Meldrim; Adolph Rosetta-Ethel Tucker; Emil Rosetta-Ione Smith; Leslie McFarlane-Miriam Croft; Robert Gray-Carrie Ryan; Wesley Snyder-Olive Craig; Jesse Hornbeck-Lena Faust; Otis Baushke-Eliza Murphy; Walter Trotter-Manda Johnson; George Holliday-Roxie McDavid; Frank M. Wayland-Della Merlin; Charles Jeffrey-Gladys McFarlane; Quinto Rosetta-Leon Johnson; Mark Wheeler-Virginia Smith; Estelle Hornbeck-Geneva Goodwin; Alan Holiday-Augusta Fortney; Henry Sassman-Irene Pritchard; Ernest McFarlane-Lena Fortney; John Faust-Minnie Robertson. Nichols Trial Notes.

8. Irene Pritchard Affidavit, n.d.

9. Ruth Wade Affidavit, n.d.

10. Ibid.

11. Ibid.

12. Petition to Governor Chase Osborne, September, 1911.

13. Benjamin Purnell to E. A. Purnell, March 4, 1915.

14. Benjamin Purnell to Governor J. Warner, August 30, 1910.

15. Nichols Trial Notes.

16. Lena McFarlane Affidavit, July 30, 1914.

17. Edith Clark Affidavit, July 30, 1914.

18. *Hansel v. Purnell*, II, 308.

19. Ibid., 365.

20. Ibid, 283.

21. Augusta Holliday Affidavit, July 30, 1914.

22. Ibid.

23. Benjamin Purnell to E. A. Purnell, March 4, 1915.

24. Nichols Trial Notes.

25. Ibid.

26. Mary Purnell to Honorable Governor Ferris, December 30, 1914.

27. Nichols Trial Notes. Ferris reportedly told Mary Purnell that "he did not think there would be any federal investigation as Myron Walker [U.S. Attorney in Grand Rapids] was a personal friend of his." Ibid.

28. Ruth Wade's attorney was John Sterling of Benton Harbor.

29. During this period Mary Purnell outlined a plan which involved "sending all the girls into the cupola of Shiloh and nailing them in so as to prevent them being discovered when the raid they expected to take place would be made. When Esther talked with Benjamin she advised not to do anything of the kind and stop Mary from doing it, but to get the girls around with their intended husbands and pick up all the douche bags and put men's clothes in different rooms so as to make the appearance of husband and wife living together as a better plan to head off any investigation or trouble that might come up." Nichols Trial Notes.

30. Nichols Trial Notes.

31. Six couples were married on December 18, 1917.

32. *John W. Hansel and Margaret Hansel v. Benjamin Franklin Purnell*, U.S. District Court, Western District of Michigan. Hereafter cited as *Hansel v. Purnell*.

33. Ibid.

34. *Hansel* v. *Purnell.*

35. Affidavit, November 7, 1921. It was signed by 444 colony members.

36. H. T. Dewhirst to Department of Justice, November 24, 1921.

37. H. T. Dewhirst to Postmaster General, September 14, 1921. "I am writing my personal friend, Hon. Hiram W. Johnson, directing his attention to the conspiracies, and respectfully refer you to him for any information regarding my prestige and standing while in California."

38. Sixteen girls were sent to High Island. Nichols Trial Notes.

39. *Ruth Bamford Reed* v. *Benjamin Purnell*, Circuit Court, Berrien County, Michigan; *Gladys Bamford Rubel* v. *Benjamin Purnell*, Circuit Court, Berrien County, Michigan.

40. *New York Times*, April 5, 1923.

41. Quoted in *New York Times*, April 4, 1923.

42. *Hansel* v. *Purnell.* Judge William Sater, June 26, 1923.

43. *The Israelite House of David* v. *John W. Hansel, et. al.*, February 19, 1923.

44. *New York Times*, April 29, 1923.

45. Interview, Robert Gregg, City of David, September, 1980.

46. Seven colony members (Joseph Couch, Millard Wilson, Thomas Wilson, Leonard Rowe, Myrtle Ross, Annabelle Ashland, Helen Boone) were later arraigned on charges of concealing Purnell, but they were never prosecuted. *Benton Harbor News-Palladium*, January 6, 1927.

47. *Benton Harbor News-Palladium*, January 12, 1927.

48. *New York Times*, April 29, 1923.

49. Fead, *Michigan* v. *House of David.*

50. Ibid.

51. *Benton Harbor News-Palladium*, August 12, 1927.

52. Nichols Trial Notes.

53. *Benton Harbor News-Palladium*, September 21, 1927.

54. Fead, *Michigan* v. *Israelites*, p. 186.

55. *Benton Harbor News-Palladium*, December 19, 1927.

56. *Benton Harbor News-Palladium*, November 14, 1927.

57. *New York Times*, May 24, 1934.

58. Jerry Kirshenbaum, "The Hairiest Team of All," *Sports Illustrated*, (April, 1970): p. 113.

59. Ibid.

60. *Detroit News*, January 17, 1937.

61. *Motor News*, November, 1950.

62. *Detroit News*, January 17, 1937.

63. *Detroit News*, September 1, 1954.

Chapter Five

1. The only available non-colony account of the House of David is Milo Quaife's *Lake Michigan*, in which the author summarily dismisses the group as a "community of crackpots." And, of course, there are newspaper articles about the colony, particularly in the local paper, the *Benton Harbor News-Palladium*.

2. This is, of course, the classic Marxist indictment found in Frederich Engels, *Socialism—Utopian and Scientific* and in Karl Mannheim's *Ideology and Utopia*. Mannheim, however, understood the dynamic behind the chiliastic mind and tried to explore its significance, whereas Engels was scornful of the earlier religious utopians.

3. John H. Noyes, *History of American Socialisms*.

4. Charles Nordhoff, *The Communistic Societies of the United States*.

5. William Hinds, *American Communities and Cooperative Colonies*.

6. Albert Shaw, *Icaria*, p. 175.

7. Donald Egbert and Stow Persons, eds., *Socialism and American Life*.

8. Ibid., I, 472.

9. Arthur E. Bestor, Jr., *Backwoods Utopias*.

10. Arthur E. Bestor, Jr., "Patent Office Models for the Good Society," *American Historical Review*, 57 (April, 1953):526.

11. Nicholas Riasanovsky, *The Teaching of Charles Fourier*. Robert Heilbroner's essay "The Beautiful World of the Utopian Socialists" in *The Worldly Philosophers* is a good example of a conventional treatment of Fourier's thought.

12. Laurence Veysey, *The Communal Experience*. Veysey's work is particularly noteworthy since it attempts to throw light on the current communal settlements by reflecting on earlier antique commonwealths. See my essay-review "Their Place or Your Place: Comparative Communal Etchings" in *Reviews in American History*, 2, no. 4 (December, 1974):504–9 for a longer discussion of *The Communal Experience* and also Rosabeth Moss Kanter's *Commitment and Community*.

13. John Hostetler, *Amish Society*.

14. For an interesting discussion of contrasting value systems in communities see Paul Conkin's *Two Paths to Utopia*.

15. This debate about the long-term impact of the utopian or socialist dream occupies a central place in political science literature. See Judith Sklar, *After Utopia*; George Kateb, *Utopia and Its Enemies*; Frank E. Manuel, ed., *Utopias and Utopian Thought* (Boston: Houghton Mifflin, 1965).

16. For the continuing discussion about the use of sect typology see Vatro Murvar, "Toward a Sociological Theory of Religious Movements," *Journal for the Scientific Study of Religion*, 1975, 14: 229–56.

17. Lewis Perry, *Radical Abolitionism*.

18. The best general accounts of the community remain Robert A. Parker, *A Yankee Saint* and Maren Lockwood Carden, *Oneida*.

19. The attractions that the colony offered new recruits are outlined in Robert S. Fogarty, "Oneida: A Utopian Search for Religious Security," *Labor History*, 14, no. 2 (Spring, 1973): 202–27.

20. See John H. Noyes, *Confessions of Religious Experience* and his *Essay on Scientific Propagation*.

21. This connection between physical health and spiritual perfection is treated in Robert Thomas, *The Man Who Would Be Perfect* and Robert S. Fogarty, "The Oneida Community, 1848–1880," Ph.D dissertation, University of Denver, 1968.

22. "Fourierism," in *The Perfectionist and Theocratic Watchman*, 4, no. 13 (September 7, 1844).

23. See Robert S. Fogarty, "We Live on the Inside," Introduction to *Cellular Cosmogony*. There are two unpublished master's theses on the Koreshan people, but no full history is available.

24. Koresh, *The Messianic Appearing and Personality*, p. 1.

25. Koresh, *The Immortal Manhood*, p. 46.

26. For an examination of the physical design elements of such groups see Dolores Hayden, *Seven American Utopias*.

27. See Herbert Lawton and Herbert Schneider, *A Pilgrim and a Prophet* for information about Harris. See Sara Harris, *The Incredible Father Divine* for the details of Baker's life.

28. Herbert J. Wallenstein, "Interim Report on the Activities of the Children of God," January 8, 1974; "Final Report on the Activities of the Children of God," September 30, 1974. I am indebted to the Attorney General's Office, State of New York, for these reports.

29. Wallenstein, "Interim Report," pp. 6–7.

30. "In other words, *partiality towards your own wife or husband or children strikes at the very foundation of communal living—against the unity and supremacy of God's family* and its *oneness* and *wholeness!* What you're doing when you do that is whittling away and chopping off little chips and bits of *the* Family to separate them in spirit, and even sometimes in actuality, from the *rest* of *the Family*, just because they're *yours*" (emphasis in original). Quoted in Wallenstein, "Final Report," p. 46.

31. For the Children of God see Shana Alexander, "A Lust for Leadership," *Newsweek*, January 7, 1974; "Children of Moses," *Newsweek*, October 28, 1974; Calvin Redekop, "A New Look at Sect Development," *Journal For the Scientific Study of Religion* (September, 1974), pp. xiii, 3.

32. The thesis that there is a clear relationship between prophetic leadership and social unrest is explored in Vito Lantennari, *Religions of the Oppressed* and E. P. Thompson, *The Making of the English Working Class*.

Bibliography

Note on Sources

Court Records

Court records represent the most abundant body of records since there was so much litigation, particularly in the 1920s. The state records are at the Michigan State Historical Commission, Lansing; cases tried in the federal courts can be found at the Federal Archives Center, Chicago.

John W. Hansel and Margaret Hansel v. *Benjamin Purnell and the House of David*, #1949–1. U. S. District Court for the Western District of Michigan.

Ruth Bamford Reed v. *Benjamin Purnell*. #3035, Circuit Court for the County of Berrien, Michigan.

Gladys Bamford Rubel v. *Benjamin Franklin Purnell*, #3036, Circuit Court for the County of Berrien, Michigan.

The People of the State of Michigan, ex rel Andrew B. Dougherty, Attorney General v. *The Israelite House of David*, Circuit Court, Berrien County, in Chancery, State of Michigan, #33522.

Horace Hannaford v. *Esther Hannaford*, #3923, Circuit Court for the County of Berrien, Michigan.

Joseph Bulley and Gertrude Bulley v. *Esther Hansel and others*, #2993, Circuit Court for the County of Berrien, Michigan.

Gertrude Bulley v. *John W. Hansel*, #3038, Circuit Court for the County of Berrien, Michigan

Investigatory and Trial Records

These records constitute the largest single primary source for this study. When the state decided to move against the colony in 1923 after the Hansel trial, it put together a prosecuting team led by George

Nichols. Nichols and his staff interviewed former members, solicited affidavits from interested parties, probed the colony's war record—in short, investigated any likely source in order to document the case against Purnell. In a preliminary report to Governor Fred Green and Attorney General William Potter, Nichols outlined his approach: "It is going to be necessary to send investigators to different parts of the country and interview important witnesses and arrange either to take their depositions or bring them to Michigan. Shall I go ahead regardless of expense (which of course I will keep down to the minimum) or shall I not?" The answer was yes.

Nichols roughed out an investigatory strategy, and by the time he was ready to go to trial against the colony he had amassed an enormous amount of data including sworn depositions, membership lists, articles of incorporation, religious practices, family histories, and even a list of deaths in the colony. Much of this detailed information failed to appear in the trial transcripts, but was used as background by Nichols's staff in preparing the case. Fortunately, all of these preliminary trial notes, including two sets of Nichols's actual trial plan, were kept by the attorney general's office in Lansing.

Attorney General's Records, R653–5–A (Boxes 9–11).
Attorney General's Records, R653–7–A #357.
Attorney General's Records, State Records Center, Boxes 159–60 of Lot 1. "Nichols Trial Notes."

Colony Literature

Documents published by the colony, including Mary Purnell's later City of David group, consist of pamphlets, tracts, and manifestoes. Much of the pamphlet material is undated and often went through several revised, though undated, printings. When citing such sources I have relied on Robert G. Hayman's *Catalogue Fifty-Nine Americana* (Carey, Ohio: 1960) which is an annotated seller's guide to a special collection "From Joanna Southcott to the House of David" offered for sale by Mr. Hayman, an antiquarian bookseller, from the estate of Noah Drew, a Michigan Israelite believer. I examined colony literature at the Michigan Historical Commission and the Michigan State Library, both in Lansing, and at the British Museum, London.

Benjamin's Last Writings. Benton Harbor: 193–[?].
Book of Dialogues. Benton Harbor: 1912.
The Book of Jasher from Adam to the Flood. Benton Harbor: n.d.
The Book of Wisdom, The Flying Roll, vols. 1–7. Benton Harbor: n.d.

Brief Points of Benjamin's Travels. Benton Harbor: 1926.
Cain's Wife. Benton Harbor: n.d.
Debate References: Earth and Sun. Benton Harbor: n.d.
Dialogue #44. Benton Harbor: n.d.
Eden's Paradisical Liberty: Prohibition (?)-Temperance (?). Benton Harbor: 1915.
Elocution. Benton Harbor: n.d.
The Flaming Ball of Fire. Benton Harbor: 1925.
The First Rudiments of Israels Faith. Benton Harbor: n.d.
Fun in a Vaudeville Agency. Benton Harbor: n.d.
House of David Song Book. Benton Harbor: n.d.
Jane Lead. Benton Harbor: [1932?].
The Key of the House of David. Benton Harbor: 1912.
The Little Book. Benton Harbor: n.d.
Mary and Benjamin's Travels. Benton Harbor: n.d.
Patriotic Songs by Benjamin. Benton Harbor: 1918.
Poetry by Benjamin. Benton Harbor: n.d.
The Preacher's Book. Benton Harbor: n.d.
Preachers Reference Book. Benton Harbor: n.d.
Prove All Things, Hold Fast to the Good. Benton Harbor: n.d.
The Rolling Ball of Fire, vols. 1–3. *Benton Harbor: n.d.*
The Royal Seed. Benton Harbor: 1947.
Rules and Regulations. Benton Harbor: n.d.
Shiloh's Coming and a Brief Explanation of the Time and Dates. Benton Harbor: n.d.
Shiloh's Wisdom, The Living Flying Roll, vols. 1–3. Benton Harbor: 1933–34[?].
The Star of Bethlehem. The Living Roll of Life. Benton Harbor: 1910.
Subject Texts to the Rolling Ball of Fire No.1. Benton Harbor: n.d.
Subject Texts to the Rolling Ball of Fire No.2. Benton Harbor: n.d.
Subject Texts to the Seventh Book of Wisdom and Images and Likenesses. Benton Harbor: n.d.
The Sword of the Spirit of the House of David. Benton Harbor: n.d.
The Testimony of Benjamin. Benton Harbor: 1928[?].
Vegetarian Cookbook. Benton Harbor: 1951.
What is the Soul? Benton Harbor: n.d.
The What? When? Where? Why? and How? of the House of David. Benton Harbor: n.d.
Where Did Cain Get His Wife? Benton Harbor: n.d.

Thorpe, Frances. *Crown of Thorns.* Benton Harbor, 1929.
             Gabriels Vision. Benton Harbor, n.d.

The Beautiful Mantle of Shiloh Immanuel. Benton Harbor, n.d.

Correspondence

There is very little correspondence in public depositories. The only open collection is in the hands of Don Allen, a Three Oaks, Michigan bookseller, who has patiently gathered material from colony sources over the years. In 1958 the Michigan Historical Commission gathered all of its correspondence files pertinent to the colony into a single volume titled *The House of David.* The earliest correspondence begins in 1892 with the "Prince Michael" case and ends with a 1910 letter to Governor Warner. Included in this volume are letters from British consular offices to the U. S. secretary of state about harassment charges and others pertinent to early state investigations. There is a brief correspondence file at the Public Record Office, London, concerning the harassment of the Mills colony in 1892, but no record of any materials pertinent to the House of David.

In addition, there is some correspondence in the Department of Justice files at the National Archives and Records Center, Washington, D.C., regarding government prosecution of colony members for alleged violation of the War Risk Insurance Act when community men took wives to gain additional dependent benefits. Those records are of minor interest:

"House of David." Xeroxed correspondence. Michigan Historical Commision, Lansing.

General Services Administration, National Archives and Record Service, Cases # 17–38–1; 27–109; 27–209. Governors' Papers, Box 31, #3.

Public Record Office, London, FO 115/942–43.

Newspapers: *Benton Harbor News-Palladium, Detroit Free Press, Detroit News, Lansing State News, Lansing State Journal,* and *New York Times.*

Books

Armytage, W. H. G. *Heavens Below: Utopian Experiments in England, 1560–1960.* London: Routledge, Kegan, Paul, 1961.
Baker, William S. *William Sharp.* Philadelphia: Gebbie & Barrie, 1875.

Baldwin, R. A. *The Jezreelites.* Orphington, Kent: Lambarde Press, 1961.

Balleine, G. R. *Past Finding Out: The Tragic Story of Joanna Southcott and Her Successors.* London: Macmillan, 1956.

Beal, Vernon L. *Chase Salmon Osborn.* Ann Arbor: Historical Collection, University of Michigan, 1950.

Becker, Howard, ed. *Family, Marriage and Parenthood.* Boston: D. C. Heath, 1955.

Bestor, Arthur Jr. *Backwoods Utopias: the Sectarian and Owenite Phases of Communitarian Socialism in America, 1663–1829.* Philadelphia: Univ. of Pennsylvania Press, 1950.

Bishop, J. L. *A Brief History of a Church Surnamed Israelites.* New York: Herald Building, 1843.

Bliss, Sylvester. *Memories of William Miller.* Boston: J. V. Himes, 1853.

Block, Marguerite. *The New Church in the New World.* New York: Holt, 1932.

Brothers, Richard. *The New Covenant Between God and His People.* London: A. Snell, 1830.

———. *Prophetical Passsages.* London: M. Ritchie, 1795.

Carden, Maren Lockwood. *Oneida: Utopian Community to Modern Corporation.* Baltimore: Johns Hopkins Press, 1969.

Caesar, Gene. *King of the Harem Heaven.* Derby, Conn.: Monarch Books, 1960.

Cohen, Joseph. *In Quest of Heaven.* Reprint. Philadelphia: Porcupine Press, 1975.

Cohn, Norman. *The Pursuit of the Millennium.* New York: Oxford Univ. Press, 1961.

Conkin, Paul. *Two Paths to Utopia: the Hutterites and the Llano Colony.* Lincoln, Univ. of Nebraska Press, 1964.

Coolidge, Orville. *A Twentieth Century History of Berrien County.* Chicago: Lewis & Co., 1906.

Damsteegt, P. Gerard. *Foundations of the Seventh-day Adventist Message and Mission.* Grand Rapids: William P. Eerdmans, 1978.

Desroche, Henri. *The American Shakers: From Neo-Christianity to Pre-Socialism.* Amherst: Univ. of Massachusetts Press, 1971.

Duche, Jacob, pseud. Tamoc Caspipina. *Observations on a Variety of Subjects.* Philadelphia: Robert Bell, 1774.

Egbert, Donald Drew and Stow Persons, eds. *Socialism and American Life.* 2 vols. Princeton: Princeton Univ. Press, 1952.

Ellwood, R. S. *Religious and Spiritual Groups in Modern America.* Englewood Cliffs: Prentice Hall, 1973.

Engels, Frederich. *Socialism: Utopian and Scientific.* New York: International Publishers, 1935.

Findlay, James F. *Dwight Moody.* Chicago: Univ. of Chicago Press, 1969.

Finlayson, John. *The Last Trumpet and the Flying Angel.* London: n.p., 1849.

Gardner, Hugh. *The Children of Prosperity.* New York: St. Martins, 1978.

Garrett, Clarke. *Respectable Folly: Millenarianism and the French Revolution in France and England.* Baltimore: Johns Hopkins Press, 1975.

Gerth, Hans and Mills, C. Wright, eds. *From Max Weber: Essays in Sociology.* New York: Oxford Univ. Press, 1946.

Greaves, James Pierrepont. *Letters and Extracts From Ms. Writings of James Pierrepont Greaves.* Ham Common: The Concordium, 1843.

Harris, Sarah. *The Incredible Father Divine.* London: W. H. Allen, 1954.

Harrison, J. F. C. *Quest For the New Moral World.* New York: Scribners, 1969.

————. *The Second Coming: Popular Millenarianism, 1780–1850.* New Brunswick: Rutgers Univ. Press, 1979.

Hayden, Dolores. *Seven American Utopias.* Cambridge: MIT Press, 1976.

Heilbroner, Robert. *The Worldly Philosophers.* New York, Simon & Schuster, 1961.

Hill, Christopher. *Reformation and Industrial Revolution.* New York: Pantheon, 1967.

————. *Society and Puritanism.* London: Schocken, 1964.

————. *The World Turned Upside Down.* New York: Viking, 1972.

Hindmarsh, Robert. *Rise and Progress of the New Jerusalem Church in England, America and Other Parts.* London: Hodson & Son, 1861.

Hinds, William. *American Communities and Cooperative Colonies.* Chicago: Charles H. Kerr, 1908.

Hine, Robert. *California's Utopian Colonies.* New Haven: Yale Univ. Press, 1966.

Hirst, Desiree. *Traditional Symbolism From the Renaissance to Blake.* New York: Barnes & Noble, 1964.

Hollingsworth, C. B. and Hollingsworth, A. B., eds. *Zions Works.* 5 vols. London: John Mcqueen, 1899.

Holloway, Mark. *Heavens on Earth.* New York: Dover, 1966.

Hostetler, John. *Amish Society.* Baltimore: Johns Hopkins Press, 1980 ed.

Hyamson, A. M. *A History of the Jews in England.* London: Chatto & Windus, 1905.

Jerome, Judson. *Families of Eden.* New York: Seabury, 1963.

Jezreel, James J. *Extracts From the Flying Roll.* 3 vols. Grand Rapids, n.p., 1879.

Judah, J. Stillson. *The History and Philosophy of Metaphysical Movements in America.* Philadelphia: Westminster, 1967.

Kagan, Paul. *New World Utopias.* New York: Penguin, 1975.

Kanter, Rosabeth. *Commitment and Community.* Cambridge: Harvard Univ. Press, 1972.

Kateb, George. *Utopia and Its Enemies.* New York: Free Press, 1963.

Koresh. *The Immortal Manhood.* 2nd ed. Estero, Florida, 1909.

———. *The Messianic Appearing and Personality.* Estero, Florida, n.d.

———. *Cellular Cosmogony.* Reprint. Philadelphia: Porcupine, 1974.

Lacy, John. *The Mighty Miracle.* London: n.p., 1774.

———. *The Prophetical Warnings of John Lacy, Esq.* London: B. Bragg, 1707.

Lane, Charles. *Life of Joanna Southcott and Bibliography of Joanna Southcott.* Exeter: Devonshire Association for Advancement of Science, 1912.

Lantennari, Vittorio. *Religions of the Oppressed.* New York: Knopf, 1963.

Laurence, Richard. *Ireland's Great Future.* Glasgow: John Thompson, 1912.

———. *The Book of Enoch.* Glasgow: John Thompson, 1912.

Lawton, Herbert and Schneider, Herbert. *A Pilgrim and A Prophet.* New York: Columbia Univ. Press, 1942.

Leff, Gordon. *Heresy in the Late Middle Ages.* Manchester: Manchester Univ. Press, 1967.

Lerner, Robert. *The Heresy of the Free Spirit in the Later Middle Ages.* Berkeley: Univ. of California Press, 1972.

Mannheim, Karl. *Ideology and Utopia.* New York: Harcourt Brace, 1936.

Matthews, Ronald. *English Messiahs.* London: Methuen, 1936.

Milton, Daniel. *Judgment of Daniel Milton, the Promised Shiloh.* Wrenthorpe: The Hebrew Press, n.d.

———. *Messiahs Universal Kingdom, First, Sixth and Seventh Seal Opened With Thunder and Lightnings From the Pen of Daniel Milton.* New York: Christian Israelite Press, 1863.

———. *Revelation and Vindication.* New York: The Hebrew Press, 1863.

Nordhoff, Charles. *The Communistic Societies of the United States.* New York: Harpers, 1875.

Noyes, John H. H. *Confessions of Religious Experience.* Oneida: Leonard & Co., 1849.

———. *Essay on Scientific Propagation.* Oneida: Oneida Community, 1875.

————. *History of American Socialisms*. Philadelphia: Lippincott, 1870.

Noyes, George W. *The Religious Experiences of J. H. Noyes*. New York: Macmillan, 1923.

Orvis, Marianne. *Letters From Brook Farm*. Reprint. New York: Porcupine, 1973.

Parker, Robert A. *A Yankee Saint*. Reprint. Philadelphia: Porcupine, 1973.

Pender, James. *History of Benton Harbor*. Chicago: Braun, 1915.

Perry, Lewis. *Radical Abolitionists*. Ithaca: Cornell Univ. Press, 1973.

Pope, Liston. *Millhands and Preachers*. New Haven: Yale Univ. Press, 1944.

Pritchard, Isabella. *Echoes of Life*. Benton Harbor: n.d.

Quaife, Milo. *Lake Michigan*. Indianapolis: Bobbs-Merrill, 1944.

Rexroth, Kenneth. *Communalism*. New York: Seabury, 1974.

Riasanovsky, Nicholas. *The Teachings of Charles Fourier*. Berkeley: Univ. of California Press, 1969.

Rogers, P. G. *The Sixth Trumpeter*. London: Oxford Univ. Press, 1963.

Roth, Cecile. *The Nephew of the Almighty*. London: E. Goldston, 1933.

Schwartz, Gary. *Sect Ideologies and Social Status*. Chicago: Univ. of Chicago Press, 1970.

Sharp, William. *An Answer to the World*. London: S. Rousseau, 1806.

Shaw, Albert. *Icaria*. Reprint. Philadelphia: Porcupine, 1973.

Sklar, Judith. *After Utopia*. Cambridge: Harvard Univ. Press, 1953.

Southcott, Joanna. *The Book of Wonders*. London: Marchant & Galabin, 1813.

————. *Divine and Spiritual Communications*. London: Marchant & Galabin, 1809.

————. *The Third Book of Wonders*. London: Marchant, 1814.

Stewart, Allan. *The Abominations of the Wroeites*. Melbourne: Abbott & Co., 1850.

Thomas, Keith. *Religion and The Decline of Magic*. London: Scribners, 1971.

Thomas, Robert. *The Man Who Would Be Perfect*. Philadelphia: Univ. of Pennsylvania Press, 1976.

Thompson, E. P. *The Making of the English Working Class*. London: Hammondsworth, 1968.

Thune, Nils. *The Behmenists and the Philadelphians*. Uppsala: Alquist & Wiksells, 1948.

Toon, Peter, ed. *Puritans, the Millennium and the Future of Israel*. Cambridge: Cambridge Univ. Press, 1970.

Troeltsch, Ernest. *The Social Teachings of the Christian Churches*. 2 vols. New York: Macmillan, 1939–49.

Tuveson, Ernest. *Redeemer Nation*. Chicago: Univ. of Chicago Press, 1968.

Van Sommers, Tess. *Religions in Australia*. Adelaide: Rigby Ltd., 1973.

Veysey, Laurence. *The Communal Experience*. New York: Harper & Row 1973.

Warner, Robert. *Chase Salmon Osborn*. Ann Arbor: Univ. of Michigan, 1960.

Waterman, William. *Frances Wright*. Reprint. Philadelphia: Porcupine, 1972.

Weber, Max. *Theory of Economic and Social Organization*. New York: Oxford Univ. Press, 1947.

Williams, H. M. *Mysteries, Errors and Injustice at Mary and Benjamin's Israelite House of David*. Benton Harbor: H. M. Williams: n.d.

Wilson, Bryan. *Magic and the Millennium*. London: Beekman, 1978.

————. *Religious Sects*. New York: McGraw Hill, 1970.

Wright, Eugene. *A Catalogue of the Joanna Southcott Collection at the University of Texas*. Austin: Univ. of Texas Press, 1968.

Wroe, John. *Guide to the People Surnamed Israelites*. Boston: V. N. Bradley, 1847.

————. *Life and Journal*. 2 vols. Gravesend: W. Deane, 1859.

Yinger, Milton J. *The Scientific Study of Religion*. New York: Macmillan, 1970.

Index

Achterberg, Hilda Pritchard, 64
Alphadelphian Association, 49–50
Avignon Society, 6–7

Bamford family, 107–8, 168
Bateman, Mary, 17
Baushke, Albert, 48, 56
Baushke (Frank) family, 90, 164
Benton Harbor (Michigan), 48–49
Berg, David, 140–42
Bestor, Arthur, 132
Bickle, Bernice, 39–40
Bishop, John, 28–29, 30
Boehme, Jacob, 4, 5, 6
Boon, Mary, 22
Brothers, Richard, 7–8; creed, 10; fol-
  lowers, 10–12; incarceration of, 12–13;
  influence of Avignon Society on, 6–7,
  173 n.22; and prophetic tradition, 19;
  visions of, 8–10
Brown, Angeline, 43, 115
Bryan, William, 7
Bryson, Mary, 63
Bulley, William, 59–60

Carpenter, Elias, 16, 37
Chase, Henry E. (Deputy Attorney Gen-
  eral), 81–85
Chester family, 165
Chew, Mary, 63–64, 178 n.55
Children of God commune, 140–42
Cleveland, William, 80–85
Court, Eliza, 39, 40

Darst family, 171
Davis, Lillian, 89
Dewhirst, Harry Thomas, 106–7; as de-
  fense attorney for colony, 107, 115,
  119–20; as leader of House of David,
  125
Diggers, 3
Drew, Noah, 33–34
Duche, Jacob, 6–7

Eden Springs Park, 67–68, 125. *See also*
  House of David, commercial enterprises
Egbert, Donald, 132

Fead, Louis, 115, 120
Ferris, Governor William, 99, 180 n.27
Finlayson, John, 12
Fleming family, 166
Foley, Reverend Thomas Philip, 11, 15
Fortney, Augusta and Lena (sisters), 95,
  97

Gibsonville Altruistic Community, 50
Giles, Mildred, 83–84
Grabianka, Count Tadeusz, 6
Group marriages: of 1910, 91–94; of
  1914, 97–99; of 1917, 102; of 1919, 104;
  of 1923, 109

Halhead, Nathaniel B., 10, 13
Hannaford, William, 89
Hansel, Esther Johnson, 98, 117–18
Hansel, John, 104–6; suit against colony,
  106–7, 108–10

193

Hiawatha Valley Association, 50
High Island (Lake Michigan), 97, 98, 107, 125
Hinds, William, 130
Hoffman, Reverend Elisha A., 81–82
Hoskins family, 169–70
House of David: baseball team, 121–24; buildings, 75; charter, 56, 70–72, 177 n.34; commercial enterprises, 77–78, 79, 87, 125; legal entanglements, 72–74, 80–84, 104–10, 115–20; missionaries of, 78; organizational structure, 70–71; and Social Security system, 125–26
House of David colonists: American, 55–57; application process, 56–57; clothing, 76; confessions of, 66; devotion to Purnell, 68–69; 96–97, 98–99; diet, 76; education, 76–77; from England, 63–64, 177 n.40; expulsion of, 78–79 (*see also* scorpions); military service of, 101–2; rules governing, 78; and stages to immortality, 54; Wroeite group from Australia, 58–62
Humphreys family, 57, 64

The Israelite House of David, the New Eve, the Body of Christ. *See* House of David

James family, 168
Jezreel, Clarissa Rogers ("Queen Esther"), 33, 36
Jezreel, James Jershom (James White), 32–33; missionary activities of, 33–35; and "The New and Latter House of Israel," 32; posthumous charges against, 36; tower of, 35–36; writings, 32, 33
Johnson family, 165–66
Jones, James Warren, 142

Kanter, Rosabeth, 134
Klienknecht family, 171
Koreshan Unity colony, 138–39
Kraft, Helen, 72–74

Lane family, 170
Lead, Jane, 5
Leith, Jane, 62–63

McDermott, Mary, 55, 165
Markham family, 166

Matthews, Ronald, 11
Meldrim, Edith, 92, 109, 165
Meldrim family, 164–65
Meyers family, 168–69
Michigan, communal societies in, 49–51. *See also individual societies*
Middlekauf, Reverend B., 50
Miller, William, 28, 29
Mills, Michael Keyfor, 37, 175 n.17; charges against, 38–40; "God House" of, 37; as "Prince Michael," 37, 40
Mills, Mrs. Michael, 39
Mills, Walter Thomas, 50
Milton, Daniel (Daniel Trickey), 28–30; controversy with John Bishop, 30; conversion of, 28, 29; marriage of, 29; and prophetic tradition, 30–31
Mooney, Cora (Mrs. Silas), 46–47, 55, 109
Mooney, Silas, 46, 55

Nayler, James, 4
Nazirites, 23
Nichols, George, 115, 117, 177 n.32
Nordhoff, Charles, 130
Noyes, John H., 96, 129–30, 136–38

Oneida Community, 136–38
Osborne, Governor Chase, 94

Pate family, 167
Pelton, John, 46
Persons, Stow, 132
Philadelphians, 5
Pomeroy, James, 14
Pritchard, Irene, 92
Pritchard, Isabella, 64–67, 68, 104
Pullen, Charles, 111
Purnell, Benjamin, 42–43; arrest and trial, 113–20; death of, 120; and death of daughter, 47; descriptions of, 42, 61–62; flights from authorities, 91, 101, 108, 111; in Fostoria, Ohio, 46–47; millennial message of, 51–53; at the Mills colony, 43–45; move to Michigan, 47–49; political influence of, 94; and prophetic tradition, 102–4; relationship with Mary, 42, 43, 119, 179 n.97, 179 n.1; sexual advances of, 73–75, 83–84, 85, 95–97, 100
Purnell, Coy, 67, 111
Purnell, Heather, 47

Purnell, Mary (nee Stollard): arranges group marriages, 91, 92, 98; asserts leadership, 112–13; and City of David, 113, 121, 127; description of, 42, 62, 76; and Frances Thorpe, 75, 85, 88, 119; interview with Gov. William Ferris, 99, 180 n.27; relationship with Benjamin, 42, 43, 88–89, 117, 179 n.97, 179 n.1; suit against colony, 120–21

Race suicide, 60
Riasanovsky, Nicholas, 133
Ribeau, George, 11
Riford, I. W., 82
Robins, John, 3
Rogers, Clarissa. *See* Jezreel, Clarissa
Ryan family, 169

Sater, Judge William, 109–10
Schetterly, Dr. Henry B., 50
Scorpions, 78–79, 100
Sharp, William, 10–11, 15, 35, 173 n.36
Shaw, Albert, 131
Shaw, William, 23
Shiloh: Benjamin Purnell as, 51; and Joanna Southcott, 17, 19–20
Shoemaker, George, 56, 179 n.100
Sibley, Samuel, 20
Smith family, 171
Smith, Irving, 92–93, 100
Social compact approach, 133–34
Southcott, Joanna, 13–14; creed, 15; death of, 18–20; hysterical pregnancy, 17–18; prophesies of, 14–15; and pro-
phetic tradition, 19; sealing campaign, 16–17
Stewart, Allan, 24–25
Stollard, Dr. James, 88–89
Stollard, Mary. *See* Purnell, Mary
Stritch family, 166
Sunrise Community, 50
Swandt, Emory, 91
Sweepers, 66, 71, 78

Tany, Thomas, 3–4
Teed, Cyrus, 138–39
Thomas, Keith, 2, 5
Thorpe, Frances, 75, 85, 88, 98, 109, 119, 179 n.97
Trickey, Daniel. *See* Milton, Daniel
Turner, George, 11, 15, 20–21

Vaughan family, 165
Veen family, 167–68
Veysey, Laurence, 133
Virgin law, 53, 89

Wade, Ruth, 92–93, 100
Ward, John "Zion," 22–23
White, Charles E. 81
White, James. *See* Jezreel, James Jershom
Widders family, 167
Winfrey family, 170
Winnstanley, Gerard, 3
Wroe, John, 23–24; in Australia, 24, 26, 58; sexual excesses of, 24
Wroeites, 23–26, 58–60

Robert S. Fogarty is Professor of History at Antioch College and editor of *The Antioch Review*. He is author of *Dictionary of Communal and Utopian History* and editor of *American Utopianism* and of the series *The American Utopian Tradition*.